Communication and the Transformation of Economics

Also by Robert E. Babe

Cable Television and Telecommunications in Canada: An Economic Analysis, 1975
Canadian Television Broadcasting Structure, Performance, and Regulation, 1979
Broadcasting Policy and Copyright Law: An Analysis of a Cable Rediffusion Right (co-authored), 1983
Telecommunications in Canada: Technology, Industry, and Government, 1990
Information and Communication in Economics (edited), 1994

Critical Studies in Communication
and in the Cultural Industries

Herbert I. Schiller, *Series Editor*

Communication and the Transformation of Economics

Essays in Information, Public Policy, and Political Economy

Robert E. Babe

University of Ottawa

WestviewPress

A Division of HarperCollins*Publishers*

Critical Studies in Communication and in the Cultural Industries

Copyright © 1995 by Westview Press, Inc., A Division of HarperCollins Publishers, Inc.

Published in 1995 in the United States of America by Westview Press, Inc., 5500 Central Avenue, Boulder, Colorado 80301-2877, and in the United Kingdom by Westview Press, 12 Hid's Copse Road, Cumnor Hill, Oxford OX2 9JJ

A CIP catalog record for this book is available from the Library of Congress.
ISBN 0-8133-2672-9—ISBN 0-8133-2671-0 (pbk.)

The paper used in this publication meets the requirements of the American National Standard for Permanence of Paper for Printed Library Materials Z39.48-1984.

10   9   8   7   6   5   4   3   2   1

*To Warren J. Samuels
and
to CRITICAL: Students for Socially
Responsible Communication*

We human beings are being led to a dead end—all too literally. We are living by an ideology of death and accordingly we are destroying our humanity and killing the planet.

—*Herman E. Daly and John B. Cobb Jr. (1989)*

Contents

**12 "Life Is Information": Canadian Communication and
    the Legacy of Graham Spry**   211

Conclusion   221

Acknowledgments

Gratitude is expressed to Professor Herbert I. Schiller for his interest in including this volume in his Westview Press series on Critical Communication. I am indeed pleased and honored to contribute to this series.

Thanks are expressed also to those who originally commissioned or suggested work appearing here: Hank Intven, Warren J. Samuels, Vincent Mosco, Kosta Gouliamos, Gertrude Robinson, Rowland Lorimer, Barri Cohen, and Jean McNulty.

Appreciation is extended as well to those who read and commented on at least portions of the manuscript: Ian Parker, Kerry Pither, Frank Müller, Irene Spry, Kosta Gouliamos, Heather Menzies, Thomas Guback, Fred Bigham, Gary Hauch, and Kathryn Fredericks.

I continue to benefit from, and to be inspired by the teaching of my mentors, Warren J. Samuels and Walter Adams, even though nearly twenty-five years have passed since I left economics at Michigan State University. Warren initiated me into the joys of intellectual history, to the classical theory of economic policy, and to institutional economics. Walter introduced me to power in economics (political economy), suggested that I become familiar with the works of Kenneth E. Boulding, and like Professor Samuels, encouraged me to explore the limitations of economic orthodoxy and not to disdain unconventional wisdom.

I have learned much from my students over the years. Indeed, several of them are cited above, in the notes, and in the bibliography. Students in the Department of Communication who formed the association *CRITICAL: Students for Socially Responsible Communication Study* inspired a good deal of what appears here. Among my fondest memories of the Department of Communication at University of Ottawa will be the integrity, idealism, activism, and perseverance of these students in the face of concerted opposition.

I would also like to thank the Faculty of Arts, University of Ottawa, for providing a grant in aid of publication, and extending me a six month leave during which portions of the present manuscript were prepared.

Finally, the loving support of Jane, David, Mary, Michael, and Daniel was vital to the successful completion of this project. Thank you.

Robert E. Babe
University of Ottawa

Introduction

This book is written in the conviction that mainstream (or neoclassical) economics is leading us to a dead-end. In the words of Herman Daly and John Cobb, economic orthodoxy is "an ideology of death," destroying our planet and debasing our humanity.

Fortunately, neoclassical economics is not immutable truth; it does not depict with exacting precision and nuanced insight inexorable economic laws or ineluctable economic processes. Neoclassicism, rather, is mere social construction. It is a product of the human mind, or rather a product of the thinking of a small community of humans known as neoclassical economists, whose doctrines have spread into the very corridors of political and economic power. Today's mainstream or neoclassical economics consists largely of deductive reasoning based on a set of restrictive and (in the words of neoclassicist Milton Friedman) "descriptively false" assumptions. Useful undoubtedly to some, particularly the rich and powerful, as a schema or paradigm for interpreting economic life, mainstream economics remains nonetheless social construction.

Usefulness for certain segments of society does not in and of itself constitute a criterion of truth, philosophical pragmatism notwithstanding. To the contrary, if it be the case, as is contended in this book, that policy prescriptions flowing from economic orthodoxy cause immiserization of masses of people, environmental degradation, and breakdowns in human community, then even on the terms set by philosophical pragmatism, economic orthodoxy is fundamentally untrue. Neoclassicism is a false doctrine, promulgated for self-serving purposes by a small but inordinately influential élite.

By promulgating notions such as the efficacy of unmitigated market forces, competition, individualism, economic efficiency (narrowly construed), pursuit of profit, monetarization and commoditization of social life, mainstream economics has become a doctrine serving the worldly interests of the rich and powerful, but to the disadvantage of the poor and the oppressed. Neoclassicism indeed "justifies" the marginalization of millions.

Nor is economic orthodoxy a mode of thought consistent with a long term, sustainable development. It is, rather, a short run (take-the-money-and-run-or-tomorrow-we-may-die) type of ideology. These characteristics and limitations of standard economics, this book contends, hinge upon and stem from neoclassicism's reductionist and indeed ludicrously inadequate conceptualization and treatment of information and of communication.

In contrast, infusing mainline economics with more expansive and realistic conceptions of information/communication utterly transforms static neoclassicism into evolutionary political economy, and results in modes of analysis that, when applied through policy, can lead to a more just, more democratic, more humane, and more sustainable future. Such is the essential theme and proposal of this book.

Communication and the Transformation of Economics intersects two scholarly disciplines—economics and communication studies. Marshall McLuhan used to claim that "action" is to be found in the "gaps." He had several types of gaps in mind, for example those between figure and ground, and as well those between perception through eye vs. perception by ear. In this book the gap to be explored is located between the academic solitudes of economics and communication studies, a gap of vital importance for our present era. On the one hand, due to perfunctory and ill-conceived conceptions of information and communication, mainstream economics promotes and "justifies" policies (summarized in this book as "the neoconservative policy agenda") that increase disparities between rich and poor, that erode human community, and that poison the environment to such an extent that the survivability of our species is for some now in question. On the other hand, the discipline of communication studies, while perhaps on occasion influential in helping formulate policies respecting mass media, has been largely silent in matters of broader policy import. However, inasmuch as "life is information" (a favourite aphorism incidentally of Graham Spry, as noted in Chapter 12), communication studies and the methodologically collectivist discourse the subject matter implies, should be of acute relevance regarding a wide range of policy matters extending far beyond media industries narrowly construed. A rapprochement between the disciplines of economics and communication studies, then, should help not only to extend the domain of communication analyses, but as well to render economics more socially responsible.

Dedicated to helping fill the gaps between economics and communication studies, *Communication and the Transformation of Economics* at various points utilizes the language and modes of analysis of first one and then the other of the disciplines. Compare, for example, Chapters 1 and 3; focusing largely on the same topic (treatments of information by mainstream economics), the chapters differ markedly in approach, the first adopting communication studies' modes of analysis, the second analytical modes characteristic of economics. To fill gaps, one must tread upon separate shores. Readers more familiar with one or other of these scholarly disciplines are likely in turn to be more closely attuned initially to one or other of the chapters.

Eight of the twelve essays forming this volume were published previously, although all eight have been revised for republication here. Revisions do not alter in significant ways the meanings of the original papers. Revisions, rather, are intended to redress some inelegances in style, to correct an occasional error, and to provide greater continuity. Chapters 6 through 9 were written specifically for this volume.

The opening essay, "Information Industries and Economic Analysis: Policy-Makers Beware," was the first of the essays in this collection to be written and represents the author's initial foray into public exploration of the book's theme. The chapter addresses from the perspective of communication studies some of the major assumptions and modes of analysis of traditional microeconomic theory, concluding that economic orthodoxy is of but limited usefulness for analyzing or prescribing policies respecting media industries. Foremost among the deficiencies of neoclassicism in this regard is its inadequate conception of what information is. Information as factor of production, for example, is quite unlike the other, more traditional, factors (land, labor, capital) since it does not merely substitute for these factors, but in fact permeates and transforms them. It also transforms production processes. Likewise, as final output information defies mainstream treatments since information utterly transforms preference functions underlying consumer demand. Information, in other words, causes both costs (supply) and demand to be evanescent, rendering quite useless such basic neoclassical constructs as efficiency, optimality, optimization, equilibrium, and marginal analysis.

Chapter 2, "Commodities as Signs," extends the analysis of Chapter 1 to treat as informational and communicatory all commodity production and exchange, not merely the activities and products of "information industries" narrowly construed. Commodities in this chapter are viewed as "texts" or signs to be "read," and this treatment poses a formidable challenge to established modes of economic analysis.

Chapter 3, "The Place of Information in Economics," is the final chapter of this first part on mainstream economics' treatment of information/communication. The first half of the chapter is the most economically formal of the three. The chapter first reviews, then critiques three mainstream economics' treatments of information/communication: the information economy or macro-sector treatment, the information industry studies approach, and theoretical neoclassicism, known also as "information economics." Despite differences it is noted that all three approaches are alike in attempting to treat information as a commodity, and therefore positing information as being subject to supply, demand, and to valuations through market exchanges. The chapter next addresses the impossibility of the "information commodity" on account of the non-quantifiable nature of information. Commoditization pertains only to artifacts that contain information, not to information itself. The chapter then draws out implications for neoclassicism of the impossibility of an information commodity: In summary, neoclassicism's vaunted theoretical structure collapses. The final section of the chapter addresses what information is (form to which meanings are ascribed), with commentary on both the political economy of economics' insistence that information be commodity-alone, and on possibilities and advantages of treating information and communication as gift instead of commodity.

Part 2, on interrelations between economic and communicatory processes, also consists of three chapters. Chapter 4 compares and contrasts the disciplines of economics and communication studies, noting that both these scholarly areas, considered broadly, contain a heterodox or "political economy" component wherein expansive conceptions of information/communication prevail. The chapter first compares orthodox economics' market with mainstream (or administrative) communication studies' communicating system, particularly with regard to circular flow, autonomy vs. interdependence of agents, presence or absence of power relations, and notions of harmony/disharmony of interests. The chapter next focuses on heterodox economics' treatments of information and, comparing these with critical communications' (political economy) treatments, notes that it is through expansive treatments afforded information that economics and communication studies are conjoined as political economy.

Chapter 5 continues the analysis of political economy begun in Chapter 4 by demythologizing hegemonic doctrines of Market, Technology, and Evolution, particularly as expounded by formulators Adam Smith, Francis Bacon, and Herbert Spencer. In this analysis three streams of Political Economy—Liberal, Marxist, and Institutionalist—are compared. The final section, "Beyond Political Economy," argues that political economy itself needs to be reintegrated with moral philosophy, as it was 230 years ago when Smith wrote *The Theory of Moral Sentiments*, prior to penning *The Wealth of Nations*.

Chapter 6 privileges information in order to explore interrelations among economic, ecological, and communicatory processes. Referencing the works particularly of Kenneth Boulding, Nicholas Georgescu-Roegen, and Herman Daly, the chapter defines information as negentropy, meaning that all economic production is foundationally informational, and that all economic distribution and consumption are foundationally communicatory. Economics, ecology, and communication interrelate in several other ways as well: first, information, along with matter and energy, constitutes a basic factor of production; second, the pervasive practice of commoditizing information, which is then traded domestically and internationally for energy, resources, and labor, conjoins economic, ecological, and communicatory processes; third, the propagation of consumptionist ideology and mindset impinges alike on economic and ecological processes; and finally information processing constitutes the basis of all material production. The overriding conclusion is that by decommoditizing information and thereby giving greater emphasis to gift relations and to economies centered on persons-in-community, a more ecologically sound and sustainable future is possible.

The next three chapters review treatments of information/communication in heterodox (evolutionary) economic thought. Chapter 7 focuses on the origin of evolutionary economics in the writings of Thomas Robert Malthus. Malthus's Population Principle inspired both an economics of the right (Social Darwinism) that is fundamentally bereft of informational and communicatory insight, and an organic, evolutionary economics of the left, in which informational and communicatory considerations receive much further sway. An early and prolific expositor of a truly communicatory/evolutionary economics was Thorstein Veblen, whose communication theory is explored in Chapter 8. Veblen described and analyzed social-economic-political systems in flux, systems at once dynamic and comprised of components engaged in communicatory interaction. For Veblen systems (or "institutions"), more importantly than individuals, are "selected" for survival by suprasystems for which they are but components. Through his discourse, then, Veblen countervailed his era's prevailing Social Darwinism, recasting his readers' attention from biogenetically inherited characteristics of the individual onto the collectivized traits and knowledge/informational structures of institutions, helping thereby to restore ameliorative social policy to intellectual respectability. Chapter 9 reviews the communication thought of Kenneth E. Boulding. Boulding, more than any other economist, has infused economic analysis with expansive and realistic conceptions of information/communication. Boulding is therefore seminal in providing models of communitarian or gift economies, models which must be developed and given greater emphasis if a peaceable, more just, and ecologically sustainable economy is to be put in place.

The final three chapters apply an economics infused with informational/communicatory considerations to selected policy issues. Chapter 10 compares the emergence and development in Canada of the telegraph, telephone, and broadcasting industries, their industrial structuring, their underlying "technologies," and related government policies. This historical analysis helps dispel myths of technological dependence, particularly doctrines of the technological imperative and of technological determinism. Political economy modes of analysis as utilized in this chapter address directly power relations as they impact upon industry structuring and restructuring. Chapter 11 provides a political economy rendering of the prospective Canadian Information Highway, concluding that the Information Highway is primarily, albeit implicitly, a proposal to reapportion communicatory power: from domestic business to transnational enterprise, from labor to capital, from government to international corporations, and from providers and users of public services to providers and users of private commodities. As such, the Information Highway is part and parcel of the ideology of death referred to at the beginning of this Introduction.

Finally, Chapter 12 is an essay in the first instance honoring the memory of Canadian communication activist and scholar Graham Spry. It is also a comparison, however, of neoconservative ideology with communitarian thought. As well, the chapter endeavors to highlight the close interconnectedness of the New World Order, neoclassical economics, neoconservativism, and trends in communication media. Spry's conclusion, that "there is nothing here for tears, nothing to moan; what the situation demands is will, will, will," is a fitting conclusion for the book.

A transformation of mainstream economics, by infusing the discipline with communicatory insight, is vital for the late twentieth and early twenty-first centuries. Many countries are currently pursuing with relentless vigor a neoconservative policy agenda of globalization, privatization, deregulation, reduction in social programs, and down-sizing of the public sector. Countries are forming into giant "free trade" blocs. Increasingly they lack the will and desire to resist encroachments by world "superculture." Moreover, they continue to encourage heightened commoditization of information and knowledge, for instance through stiffer intellectual property laws and through "Information Highway" initiatives. The analytical underpinning and ideological justification for this neoconservative policy agenda is neoclassical economics.

Focusing on the centrality of information/communication to economic and ecological processes, this book shows the neoclassical paradigm to be logically unsound. Continuing to accept neoclassicism's false conception of information/communication for policy purposes is to disfigure perceptions of reality in ways that cause heightened environmental degradation, increased break-down of community, widening gaps between rich and poor, weakening of the relative influence of labor and of domestic business, increased concentration of transnational corporate power, and diminished importance of nation states. The present work, therefore, proposes amplification and operationalization of an economics centered on communicatory interaction, an economics infused with informational/communicatory considerations, in order to help reverse these deadly trends, recover lost ground, and progress toward a more sustainable, more just, more humane and democratic economic/communicatory order.

PART ONE

Information and Communication
in Mainstream Economics

1

Information Industries and Economic Analysis: Policy-Makers Beware

It is pretty clear that an economist, like a poet, uses metaphors. They are called "models."

—Donald M. McCloskey (1990)

The Information Age and Economic Analysis

Studies indicate that both the stock and the flow of information are increasing exponentially each year (Bell, [1977] 1980, pp. 54-57; also, Dordick and Wang, 1993). "Information workers" now account for about 50 percent of the U.S. labor force, up from 25 percent in 1940 (Porat, 1976, p. 189). Technological change in industries associated with the creation and movement of information has been extensive and rapid over the past several decades.

Consequently, many believe that western societies have entered a new era, variously termed Post-industrial Society (Bell, 1973), The Information Age or The Information Economy (Porat, 1976), The Global Village (McLuhan, 1964), The Age of Discontinuity (Drucker, 1968), The Third Wave (Toffler, 1980), and Post-modernism. Characterizing this new era is unprecedented activity in the production and distribution of commoditized information, that is of information produced for and sold in markets. Accompanying the growing economic significance of commoditized information has been heightened attention paid thereto by economists.

Patents, copyright, trademarks, and industrial designs; newspapers, book and periodical publishing; broadcasting and cable television; video on demand; telecommunications and computer networking; the economics of knowledge production and education—these are but some of the

9

industries, practices, and activities receiving increased attention from economists. This chapter addresses some of the major assumptions and modes of analysis of mainstream (neoclassical) economics, concluding that mainstream economics is of but limited value for forming policies to be applied to industries and processes producing or creating knowledge and information.

While the term, "information industries," is correctly applied to all industries engaged in the creation or production, processing, distribution, and/or storage of information, the analysis and critique in this chapter is confined to economic treatments afforded the creation or production of information, as opposed to information distribution and processing. Therefore, telephones, telegraphs, and other common carriers are not treated in this chapter. (See, however, Chapters 6, 10, and 11 of this volume).

Foremost among the deficiencies of microeconomics, as applied to information creation, is an inadequate conception of what information is. Information, as we shall see, is one universal concept, binding together many diverse phenomena. A second universal concept is money.

Money happens to be the measure employed by economists to analyze and compare otherwise diverse economic situations.[1] Money is a medium of exchange, a measure of value, and a store of value. Money therefore can be viewed also as a carrier of information. In this sense, money both measures certain economic situations (i.e., markets), and carries or transmits through its circulation these measurements to those concerned.

The question addressed in this chapter may be put as follows: Can money, the economists' measuring rod of value, and the carrier of information concerning value, itself measure the value of information, or carry information concerning the value of information?

There are two conceivable situations in which money could either measure information and/or carry information concerning the value of information; neither situation, however, generally holds. First, conceivably, money could itself *be* information and information could *be* money, in the way that matter and energy are but different states of the same concept. Indeed, as discussed more fully in Chapters 3 and 6, a basic premise of neoclassical economics is that prices *are* condensed information. Furthermore, neoclassicism presumes that the price system is a mode, indeed the most significant mode, of communication, informing participants of relative values (prices). As well, neoclassicism presumes that prices, as condensed information, can themselves be commoditized and exchanged for money in markets (Stigler, [1961] 1968). If these neoclassical suppositions are correct, then money could conceivably "map" information, or be precisely convertible into information, and vice versa, in the same way that energy and matter are mutually convertible through Einstein's formula, $E = mc^2$. If not, however, any attempt at direct conversion would be an error, analogous to measuring length by units of mass or to measuring mass (for all substances) by money. (See Leshan and Margenau, 1982, pp. 55-60).

Alternatively, while not necessarily *being* information (in the way for instance that matter *is* energy), money nonetheless conceivably could measure the *value* of information, as it purportedly measures the value of other items exchanged in markets. This too, as we will see, is a basic premise of neoclassicism. For this second basic premise to hold true, however, it is required that one be able to specify *units* of information. If units of information cannot be specified (a principal line of argument developed below), then basic neoclassical concepts and modes of analysis (including supply and demand curves, cost curves, utility functions, production functions, and so forth) will be inapplicable for situations involving the production, exchange, or transmittal of information.

Information

Information has been defined as an increment to knowledge (Machlup, 1980, p. 8; von Weizsäcker, 1980, p. 279). This definition raises questions concerning the definition of knowledge, a topic that need not be pursued here apart from noting that knowledge is variable from one person to another, and hence what constitutes an increment to knowledge is also variable from one person to another.

Information has also been defined as disconnected and apparently random events, data, impressions, stimuli, and so forth which, if and when connected systematically by means of perceived similarity/dissimilarity, contiguity, theory, story, history, model or otherwise, come to constitute knowledge or meaning (Machlup, 1980, p. 8). Information in this sense is the raw, unprocessed data from which knowledge is constructed, and by which knowledge is subsequently tested (Boulding [1956] 1961). In the absence of such connections, information is either invisible (that is, unperceived) or constitutes noise (i.e., is uncomprehended).[2]

Information has also been defined as what provokes a response in, or in some manner affects or transforms, the recipient (Thayer, 1970; Wiener, 1950, p. 27). In this view, if a receiver remains untouched by stimuli, he or she has not been "in-formed."

Finally, but not necessarily exhaustively, information has been viewed as a limitation of, or selection from, possibilities, a "closing of entropy" (Klapp, 1978, p. 10). As such, information is the formation of, or ordering from, conceivable chaos or randomness. For example, a word is a selection of a specific sound (or arrangement of written symbols) from an infinite variety of conceivable sounds (or scribbles). Accordingly, in this view, information is a measure of the improbable, and indeed the "less probable an event is, the more information it furnishes" (von Weizsäcker, 1980,

p. 278; see also Darnell, 1972, pp. 156-161). Information provides the recipient with an awareness of the unexpected, the unusual, the improbable. On the other hand, events with complete certainty of occurrence provide no information. They are not news. (These notions, incidentally, constitute the cornerstone of Shannon and Weaver's "mathematical theory of communication," addressed in Chapter 3).

The foregoing conceptions of information, however diverse they may at first appear, do entail some common features. First, information does not inhere objectively in the originator or source alone, although information emanates or proceeds from its source. Rather, information entails an interaction between source and recipient, whereby emanations from the former are assimilated by the latter (Wood, 1978). Communication, then, entails the *formation* within the recipient of characteristics of the originator. It may entail more than this, of course, as information is processed or interpreted by its recipient, but nonetheless communication always entails in the first instance an *in-forming* of aspects of the source by the receiver, since information proceeds from its source and is assimilated by its receiver.

Second, information comprises symbols or signs that represent or point to something else, a basic premise of semiology. Information does not stand alone but is inevitably in reference to something else. Light waves reflected from an object and perceived by a viewer transmit the surface characteristics of the object, but the light waves do not constitute the object. Likewise, the word "chair" signifies an object or a class of objects but is not itself that object or class of objects.

Inasmuch as information represents or signifies something other than itself, and always entails an interaction between its source and its recipient, we arrive at a third characteristic of information: its immateriality. Information is immaterial in destination, often in origin, and always in transmission. The following paragraphs justify this claim.

Signs point to things, but what they point to (their meanings or significations) are products of custom, learning, sensory perception and interpretation. For example, the words "house" and "la maison," while quite dissimilar in sound and in written appearance, signify the same thing, albeit to different language groups (differences in custom and in learning). Similarly, a very high profit rate may signify one meaning to a businessperson (excellent performance) and a completely different meaning to an antitrust economist (monopoly).

Information, in other words, is inevitably processed by the mind, and only in being processed is meaning or significance constructed. As far as we can conceive, there is an immaterial (or non-physical) dimension to the mind. This is because every materialist theory of the mind is unable to answer adequately the question: How can we know anything? Materialist theories are always falsified in self-reference. Behaviorism, for example, in taking the position that all human actions and "thoughts" are the determined outcome of physical stimuli, negates its own validity in self-reference: the writings of behavioral psychologists, while claiming to be universally true, must (by the logic of behaviorism), be the outcome of the investigator's own unique conditioning, quite destroying the general applicability of the theory. Similar remarks apply to sociobiology, a materialist theory of cognition and behavior claiming that thoughts and actions are chemically (genetically) determined.

Much information originates in one mind and is transmitted to other minds, and therefore much, if not most, information is immaterial in origin as well as in destination.

Not only is information often immaterial in source, and always in destination, it is also immaterial in transmission. To say this is not to deny that information must be transmitted through physical or material means (otherwise, we would be entering the realm of parapsychology). It is simply to point out that the means whereby information is encoded is not the information itself. Light waves, paper, air, and so forth are media that can be encoded (formed shaped, impressed) so as to be capable of imparting significations to a recipient.

Two illustrations may help clarify the point. Microelectronics has made possible the storage in a relatively tiny space (a few floppy disks) of information previously requiring libraries (Evans, 1979, p. 106). Obviously, the information stored is something other than the physical means of storage. Likewise, a five symbol equation ($E=mc^2$), or a well-turned sentence ("In the beginning was the Word ... and the Word was God") can speak worlds of meaning more than the collected works of a pulp novelist, or even a learned dissertation on the properties of linear, homogeneous production functions. Quantification—adding up the number of symbols— conveys no indication respecting the informational content of the symbols when conjoined.[3] (This, incidentally, as developed in Chapter 3 below, constitutes the principal critique concerning applications of Shannon and Weaver's "mathematical theory of communication" to economics).

There is, then, no definite, fixed, one-to-one relationship between the means of transmitting or storing information and the information transmitted or stored. Information, therefore, while dependent upon matter or energy for transmission and storage, is not itself matter or energy. Information, then, is epiphenomenal to matter/energy, and is in that sense immaterial.

Information and Economic Analysis

General Economic Modeling

Purporting to describe and explain economic phenomena (namely, the production and exchange of goods and services, mainstream (neoclassical) economics has become highly mathematized and complex, if not indeed arcane, even though in its essentials it is quite straightforward. The economic process is viewed as one of commodity exchange, whereby goods and services possessed by one are traded for goods and services held by another. An exchange will occur when both parties benefit due to differences in valuations of the articles in question. Money mediates the exchange process by valuating goods and services. According to the theory, the valuation process is a result of the interaction of demand (the valuation placed on the good or service by those without), and supply (the valuation by those who possess the good or service prior to exchange). Underlying demand is the added "utility" or the usefulness of the item in satisfying wants or needs; underlying supply is the cost (or foregone utility) in losing the item through sale. Money is the measure of both anticipated utility from purchase and of foregone utility from sale.

Production is frequently undertaken for purpose of sale. In such cases, the producer must purchase factor inputs (land, labor, capital, energy), and such purchases represent the decline in utility to the firm (i.e., its costs). Production will be undertaken only if it is anticipated that costs can be recouped through the sale of outputs over the long term.

Economic analysis is frequently employed to reach policy recommendations as to how the production process can be improved. In this regard, the criterion most frequently employed is that of "economic efficiency."

There are actually several dimensions to the economic conception of efficiency. First, given firm size, the good or service should be produced at the lowest attainable cost per unit for all possible levels of production (i.e., the firm should utilize the least-cost combination of factor inputs to produce at one of the costs depicted by the "short run average cost curve"). Second, the "optimal" *level* of output should be produced. Technically, the output level chosen should be at the lowest point on the average cost curve where price equals average cost equals the marginal cost of production.[4] Third, in recognition that over time firms may expand or contract production in response to secular demand shifts, output levels should create equality between price and long run marginal (or incremental) costs.[5] Fundamental to the foregoing are the notions that costs of production should be as low as possible and at the margin money costs should equal the monetary expression of benefits.

Economists take the demand "curve"[6] (a temporally fixed relation between quantities demanded and prices, all other relevant factors constant) as the measure of marginal benefits to the user (purchaser). Price paid is viewed as the monetary expression of the benefits received (or anticipated) from the last unit purchased. Consequently, the demand curve, depicting the unique relationship between possible prices and varying quantities, also depicts incremental benefits inhering in the various quantities.

Within the foregoing conceptual framework or model, economists analyze information industries and make recommendations that, it is
claimed, improve economic efficiency. In this regard, depending upon the
particular situation being analyzed, information can be viewed either as a
factor of production or as a final commodity. As a factor of production,
information is an input in the process of producing outputs, and in this
case economists compare the costs of attaining information with the
reduction in costs attributable to its use. At the margin, the cost saving
from applying information should equal its acquisition cost. As a final
commodity, the quantity of information produced or made available for
sale should be such that, at the margin, the price paid equals its cost of
production and distribution (Stigler, [1961] 1968; Demsetz, 1969).

Limitations to Economic Analysis of Information

Information as Economic Input. Information is not merely an input or
factor of production substitutable for other factors of production like
land, labor, or capital. Information, rather, defines, permeates, and transforms other inputs and indeed entire production processes. Technically,
information changes the production function, and consequently the cost
curves. In this respect, it is totally unlike traditional factor inputs.

Information, then, is a term that touches upon and perhaps encom-
passes notions of education, skill, and technological change. As soon as
information is admitted into economic analysis as a productive input,
static analysis on the cost side (given cost curves, given production functions) gives way (or at least should give way) to economic dynamics (that
is, changing cost curves, changing production functions).

But efficiency is an ambiguous and dubious notion in the world of
economic dynamics, for efficiency implies that output levels should be
chosen such that "the" marginal cost of production equals "the" marginal
benefits derived from use. Information, as a factor of production, however, inherently means that production processes are continually
changing, with the result that marginal cost is evanescent.

Moreover, information is embodied within the other factors of production, making them inseparable from the information they embody. As
information changes, knowledge possessed by labor changes, fundamentally changing the nature (qualities) of labor. Likewise, technological
change subverts the notion of quantifying capital.

Information as Economic Output or Commodity. For purposes of neoclassical economic analysis, information, when viewed as output, is
treated as a commodity not dissimilar from other commodities. Its
purported function is to satisfy consumer wants or preferences, and
consumers are assumed to procure information in quantities such that
price equals marginal utility. Information, however, possesses characteristics that weaken its status as commodity. For one thing, it is intangible.

While information to be exchanged must be either materially encapsulated (print, film, videotape, for instance), or encoded in energy flows (gesture, music, speech, Morse code), such encapsulations and encodings are epi-phenomenal to matter and energy. The disembodied or incorporeal character of information presents difficulties for economic analysis. First is the problem of quantifying information.

Economic analysis is concerned with prices of outputs and costs of inputs. The whole theory of supply and demand depends on the premise that units of an output bear a cost and a price. Consequently, in treating information as an economic commodity, there is an essential need to measure information in order to ascribe a price or cost per unit to it. In practice the measures employed pertain to the material or physical means of encapsulating information—number of pages, number of words, bits, hours of television program transmission, feet of film and so forth—rather than to the information itself. We saw previously that there is no one-to-one correspondence between the capacity of a medium to contain symbols or signs and the "amount" of information stored or transmitted.

A second factor weakening the status of information as a commodity is the absence of any final consumption. Rather than final consumption, there is only accumulation, dissipation or transformation. Any "piece" of information created by one and imparted to another transforms ("informs") the second person, affecting his or her thinking processes and actions (i.e., his or her behavior, perceptions, tastes and preferences, or outputs). Information continues to spiral down through the ages in dissipated and/or transformed forms, being altered to varying degrees through each transmission process.[7] This total connectivity through time weakens the capacity of economists to analyze information industries, since economists try to isolate an interval of time within which all final effects are resolved, an impossibility for information. From these remarks, it can be seen that information exemplifies the economist's notion of externalities (i.e., spillover or third party effects) which have always proven troublesome for empirical work (Chase, 1968).

A third characteristic of information, again detracting from its status as commodity, is its public good nature. Public goods comprise those outputs (1) for which it is difficult or costly to exclude from benefiting those who choose not to pay, and/or (2) for which the use or consumption by one does not subtract from, and may even add to, the use or consumption by others (Musgrave, 1959; Ferguson, 1972, p. 498). Information bears both of these characteristics insofar as (1) the disembodied qualities of information can be trapped and encapsulated on or in material form at low cost through reprography or otherwise, or even intercepted in transmission in the absence of material encapsulation;[8] and (2) use of information by one does not detract from use or possession by another; indeed, information tends still to reside with the producer after sale. Economic theory, virtually all economists admit, offers no guidelines as to efficient pricing or production in such circumstances (Besen et al., 1978; Samuelson, 1964).

Information as "Essence" [9]

Information is never a final output, consumed and thereby annihilated. Rather, it is ingested by the receiver *and the receiver is thereby altered.*

Nor is information mere input to the production process. We have seen that it permeates and transforms production processes.

Moreover, information permeates and transforms societies (Berger and Luckman, 1966). For example, the process of modernization of economies and cultures is viewed by some as being highly dependent upon, and interrelated with, the flow in high volume of communication which extols and facilitates market transactions (Lerner, 1958). Moreover, information patterns can unify a nation, fragment a nation, or lead to cultural dependency. It has been the position of many Third World countries that restrictions on the flow of information from outside their borders must be imposed in order to permit national sovereignty and induce economic development; this has been the call for the New World Information and Communication Order (UNESCO, 1980; Righter, 1978; Smith, 1980).

By approaching information from the standpoint of power, and of essence, as opposed to commodity, one begins to evaluate information by its intrinsic qualitative aspects and by its anticipated effects upon recipients, rather than by price alone. Commodity gives orientation to the quantitative, while essence gives orientation to the qualitative. Commodity gives orientation to the static (satisfying existing demands) while essence emphasizes the dynamic, transformative effect of information with respect to whatever it comes into contact. Information as commodity seems to be precise and objective, whereas, as reality transformer or essence information is qualitative and subjective; when viewed as essence, emphasis is on the interaction of the receiver with the information, and consequently judgements depend upon how the information is processed, in addition to intrinsic characteristics of the signs used to encode the information. This means that information as essence is more ambiguous, less amenable to objective, "scientific" analysis. Nonetheless, this conclusion in no way minimizes the extreme importance of the notion of information as essence.

For the information industries, qualitative factors are most significant. Virtually every manifestation of humankind's presence on the planet has had origins in the immaterial realm of the mind, and in exchanges of that ethereal essence known as information, from one mind to another. These impalpable foundations of society have led both to humanity's most glorious achievements, and to its most ignoble atrocities. Witness John Milton:

> The mind is its own place, and in itself can make a heav'n of hell, a hell of heav'n (Milton, 1674).

To ignore, or assume away as unimportant, the qualitative aspects of information, to "commoditize" information and value it only in accordance with price, is at best simplistic and partial.

Conclusions

Economic analysis, while in its basics is fairly simple, in its extensions and applications can be highly complex, and this complexity may cause some to miss neoclassicism's underlying confusions, ambiguities, inconsistencies, and reductionist assumptions. Policy-makers are advised to be quite circumspect in reviewing analyses of information industries prepared by neoclassical economists who view information only, or primarily, as commodity and who take "economic efficiency" as the sole or main criterion in their analysis.

The notion of information as commodity has an added danger. It means that the suppliers and producers of information need value the same only in terms of market price, outside of any ethical or moral framework; the "eyes of the heart" become blinded by price and the quest for power. Scholars such as Daniel Boorstin ([1961] 1978), Jacques Ellul ([1965] 1973), Walter Lippmann (1955), Combs and Nimmo (1993), for instance, have noted and decried the descent of much of public discourse into the realm of mere suasion and propaganda. Conscientious attempts to articulate truth, according to these scholars, have been largely superseded by efforts at being merely "credible."

Continued research into the information industries is of vital importance in our era, which has been termed the "Information Age." But, in the course of these investigations, we would do well to bear in mind the caution sounded by Theodore Roszak:

> What science can measure is only a portion of what man can know. Our knowing reaches out to embrace the sacred; what bars its way, though it promise us dominion, condemns us to be prisoners of the empirical lie (Roszak, 1973, p. 67).

Notes

Reprinted, with slight revisions, from *Proceedings from the Tenth Annual Telecommunications Policy Research Conference*, edited by Oscar H. Gandy Jr., Paul

Espinosa, and Janusz Ordover (New York: Ablex Publishing Corporation, 1983, pp. 123–135). Reprinted by permission of Ablex Publishing Corporation.

1. Alfred Marshall, father of modern (neoclassical) microeconomic theory, wrote: "Economists deal with facts which can be observed, and quantities which can be measured. ... The problems which can be grouped as economic, because they relate specially to man's conduct under the influence of motives that are measurable by a money price, are found to make a fairly homogeneous group" (*Principles of Economics*, p. 27, quoted in Mitchell, 1969, p. 141).

2. One can argue, however, that paradigms or theories develop first, and that information (facts, data) is inevitably perceived and selected in a manner so as to support or justify the model (Kuhn, 1970). In reality, there is undoubtedly an interactive process between information and knowledge whereby information supports or refutes models while, at the same time, the model tends to limit or suppress perceptions of information hostile to it. See Chapter 9 below.

3. While any given medium may possess a theoretical maximum to its capacity to transmit or store "bits" (quantity of symbols), this bandwidth or memory capacity provides no indication as to the amount of information (which depends *inter alia* upon the synergy conjoining bits) so transmitted or stored.

4. The "short run" is the current period when firms have in place fixed productive factors, and hence output can be expanded (beyond "capacity") only with difficulty. Marginal cost is the increment in cost attributable to production of the last unit.

5. The "long run" comprises the time period over which all costs become variable and the firm can adapt to new demand levels. The firm always operates in the short run, while looking at the long run. Economists have never been able to deal adequately with the question of which marginal cost schedule should pertain for efficient operations—short run marginal costs or long run marginal costs, or one of the infinite number of marginal cost schedules between the two extremes. Economic analysis, it can be seen, is much less rigorous than is often supposed.

6. Quotation marks about the word "curve" signify the general logical inconsistency in the notion of a demand curve. Demand curves are held to depict various prices and quantities, other relevant factors constant. But movement from one price to another on the "curve" will inevitably have repercussions on the "exogenous variables." For example, the prices and quantities of substitutes, by definition, will change in response to the movement down the demand "curve;" but this change in the price and quantity of substitutes annihilates the demand curve, since it was drawn under the assumption that all such related factors are constant.

7. Note the insights of Northrop Frye: "Just as a new scientific discovery manifests something that was already in the order of nature, and at the same time is logically related to the total structure of the existing science, so the new poem manifests something that was already latent in the order of words. ... Poetry can only be made out of other poems; novels out of other novels" (Frye, 1957, p. 97).

8. And hence the problematic nature of copyright in the age of electronic diffusion. See, *inter alia*, Hamilton and Ploman, 1980.

9. *Essence*: "That which makes something what it is; an existent being, especially an immaterial being or spirit." *Standard College Dictionary*, Canadian Edition.

2

Commodities as Signs

All institutions may be said to be in some measure economic institutions. ... [Nor does] the economic interest ... act in isolation.

—Thorstein Veblen ([1919] 1990)

It is highly significant that the publisher of R. S. Perinbanayagam's book, *Discursive Acts* (Hawthorne, New York: Aldine De Gruyter, 1991) requested a review in the annual publication, *History of Economic Thought and Methodology*. It is equally remarkable that the editor, Warren J. Samuels, undertook to provide one. For Perinbanayagam's book, which analyzes the dynamics of human conversations from the perspectives of rhetoric, semiology, psycho linguistics, and hermeneutics, does not address directly what many would consider to be "economic" phenomena at all. Economists, after all, are inclined to limit their professional attention to those human interactions or exchanges mediated by money, barter being a notable but minor exception. *Discursive Acts*, in contrast, focuses on non-monetarized, verbal, symbolic interactions, thereby calling attention to a bifurcation of the field of human interaction—into the realms of the "economic" and the "non economic" (or what I will term here the "purely communicatory").

This bifurcation may make sense, or at least be harmless if, as Gary Becker contended, all human relationships are essentially commodity exchange relationships (Becker, 1976), or alternatively if these two systems or modes of interaction are essentially independent of one another. On the other hand, if economic relations tend to encroach upon and transform otherwise non-commoditized or purely communicatory interactions—a process that economic historian and communication theorist Harold Innis termed "the penetrative powers of the price system" (Innis [1938] 1956)—or if the non-commoditized sector affects in complex ways the economic, then interrelations between economic and purely communicatory processes need to be explored more fully than has been the case hitherto. Preliminary to such exploration, however, is a re-appraisal of the economists' conception of information.

Certainly over the thirty-five years since George Stigler lamented information's occupancy of "a slum dwelling in the town of economics" (Stigler, [1960] 1968), information has moved up-scale, so to speak. Today, a still-burgeoning "Information Economics" literature is in place, focusing primarily on theoretical implications for economic behavior of "imperfect information" in capital, labor or product markets (Stiglitz, 1985; Lamberton, 1984, 1990; Spence, 1974; Jonscher, 1982). Moreover, information's new-found prosperity is underscored by pointing to a less voluminous, but nonetheless highly influential, "Information Economy" literature, proposing the predominance for the macro-economy of information production, processing, storage, and distribution (Machlup, 1961; Porat, 1977; Hepworth, 1990; Serafini and Andrieu, 1981; Dordick and Wang, 1993; Lamberton, 1994).

But, to extend Stigler's metaphor a bit, this heightened attention afforded information (of a certain type) distracts attention from the discrimination now being practised in the town of economics. "Information Economists" recognize and honor but one type of information. In the words of Kenneth Arrow, a seminal figure in the field: "The meaning of information is precisely a reduction in uncertainty" (Arrow, 1979, p. 306).

Such an impoverished conceptualization of what information is results in, at best, a superficial and inadequate comprehension of communication. To mainstream (neoclassical) economists, human relations are monetarized exchange relations, wherein sellers dispose of items or of labor power in order to attain products or labor services that they value more highly. In this paradigm, human interaction is a means to an end, namely the disposal and acquisition of products or services to attain higher satisfaction. "Information," (i.e. reduction in uncertainty) facilities such exchanges by helping buyers and sellers to locate one another, and also by making them more aware of the properties (value) of the commodities bought and sold. It is a major virtue of R. S. Perinbanayagam's book that it implicitly challenges economists to explore more deeply than hitherto the complexities and profundities of information and communication, and to reconsider the adequacy of current treatments.

Before enlarging on the challenges posed to mainstream economics by a fuller understanding of information/communication, I attempt first to synthesize the theoretical first half of Perinbanayagam's book, and also to summarize briefly the book's second half, which illustrates its preceding theories through analyses of recorded conversations.

It is Perinbanayagam's contention that "conversations lead to the emergence of selves, and selves in turn create conversations" (p. xi). Likewise, communication both produces, and is a product of, human relationships. For adequate understanding, then, symbolic exchanges need to be studied in the context of on-going and developing relationships.

Perinbanayagam declares that "meaningful interactions are not just an exchange of meaning with the help of symbols, [but] should rather be viewed as selves participating in encounters" (p. 7). In discourse, the initiator, upon articulation, surrenders control of the meaning of the message to the respondent whose job becomes one of "working upon" the message, reconstructing it, interpreting it—prior to framing a response. Such reconstructions and interpretations, however, Perinbanayagam writes, can be as much "full of a self as the articulations of the initiator" (p. 66), making the interpretive chain "replete with uncertainty" (p. 68). By engaging in communication, therefore, "a person enters a life with others, opening himself or herself up to responsive acts" (p. 114).

Following semiologist C. S. Peirce, Perinbanayagam contends that "in acts of discourse the initiator and the respondent practise mutual semiosis," semiosis being defined as "an action or influence which is, or involves, a co-operation of three subjects, such as a sign, its object, and its interpretant, this tri-relative influence not being resolvable into action between two pairs" (p. 31). Tri-relative influence implies that initiator and respondent may have quite different interpretations ("interpretants") for a given message or "sign," if and when their experiences of the external world ("object") differ. In summary, discursive acts "elicit active and responsive interpretations that to some extent are dependent on the original acts and their constituent features" (p. 86).

The last half of Perinbanayagam's book applies these observations and theories of human interaction to recorded conversations of various categories: first, to different forms of discourse (such as requests, instructions, compliments, insults, retorts, commands, jokes, scoldings, rebuttals, etc.); next, to different emotions in discourse (anger, frustration, catharsis, love, jealousy, joy, shame, malice); and finally, following Kenneth Burke, to drama in discourse (act, scene, agent, agency, purpose, attitude, mimesis, play, and display of self).

Perinbanayagam, it may be concluded, paints a much different picture of information and of human communication than do "Information Economists." This is because Perinbanayagam views people as "selves" experientially constituted through discursive interaction and engaged in on-going discursive acts. For that author, freedom characterizes conversation due to ambiguities and uncertainties in interpretations and responses, calling for creativity and adaptive strategies. How different is this view of human interaction from that of mainstream economists who routinely insist that people are behavioral units, mechanically maximizing utility (subject to income constraint) by buying and selling in depersonalized markets (Scitovsky, 1976). Whereas economists define information precisely as a "reduction in uncertainty," Perinbanayagam insists that symbolic exchange creates uncertainty, launching dialogic partners onto paths that take unforeseeable twists and turns. Far from viewing personal interaction as taking place solely between autonomous others intent on satisfying pre-existing wants through commodity transfer, Perinbanayagam insists that we all live in, and hence share, a semiological field ("a signifying culture") wherein symbolic interactions create self-identities, as well as "interpersonal presence and interactional resonance and engagement" (p. 4). Communication, that is symbolic interaction, affects others, and all are affected.

Furthermore, as Perinbanayagam notes, the "tri-level" nature of communication means not only that the "interpretant" of a sign can vary in accordance with one's experience with the sign's "object," but conversely that signs (or texts, or discourse) can in turn modify experiences with objects. An example provided in the book concerns food: One feels hunger and eats not just food

> but various natural substances that have been turned into hamburger or steak, pasta or pudding. In semiotic terms, a sign selected for an object is replaced by another one before it is presented for the elicitation of an interpretant. ... In this method of transformation, human experiences are perceived, defined, and represented in such a way that their significance is essentially altered. These experiences are typically carried in linguistic forms (p. 56).

Or, to coin another example, economic theory does not merely stand for or describe an external reality (its "object," namely economic processes), but also transforms perceptions of, or experiences with this "object." Recognition of this "active" role of economic theory and analysis has spawned an emerging literature on "Economics as Discourse" (Samuels, 1990; Klamer et al, 1988), from which it is but a small next step to view mainstream economics as ideology, as persuasion, as means of control, leading to a political economy approach to comprehending economic "knowledge" (Schiller, 1994).

Moreover, Perinbanayagam's analysis implicitly invites us to explore the implications for economic theory of comprehending artifacts or commodities as "signs" or as texts to be "read" or interpreted, rather than merely as "objects." Thorstein Veblen, influenced by Peirce, well understood that commodities are simultaneously "objects" and "signs" (Veblen, [1897] 1953), but his insights have been largely ignored by modern economic theorists. If, however, commodities are demanded not solely for their utilitarian properties, but also (often more so), for the messages they impart to the buyer and to others, then "users" of such commodities are not merely those who own or display them, but also those who "read" them as messages. Our on-going conversations, then, are not merely verbal (the focus of Perinbanayagam's book), but also artifactual. If selves exist and develop, as Perinbanayagam contends, in symbolic interactions, then commodities owned, used, and displayed contribute to such existence and development. Moreover, if symbolic interaction is to be studied in the context of on-going and developing relationships, as Perinbanayagam insists, then so too should the signifying properties of commodities. Commodities, the theories of discourse imply, are symbols or signs in flux. The meanings that people ascribe to artifacts, of course, derive in part from how these artifacts are circulated and used, and upon the meanings (i.e., "interpretants") that vendors (or advertisers) attempt to attach to them, as well as personal histories with things (Miller, 1987; Csikszentimihalyi and Rochberg-Halton, 1981; Appadurai, 1986; McCracken, 1988).

The implications for the economic theory of consumer behavior of viewing commodities as signs, then, may be quite startling and revolutionary. If each commodity is a sign in a semiological system that a "self" uses to "compose" statements concerning self-identity and relations with others, then all goods become "complementary goods," modifying one another syntagmatically. Indeed, Perinbanayagam views the self as a "maxisign," that is a "system of symbols and meanings" (p. 10). People can think only with signs, the author contends, and every conception people have, including that of self, is "cognizable," that is "signable" (p. 9).

Among the universe of signs used to constitute a particular self are commodities. Quoting G. H. Meade, Perinbanayagam notes: "The self as an object ... is dependent upon the presence of other objects with which the individual can identify himself" (p. 13). As the self changes through continued discourse, so too will the meanings of the commodities selected, and also the selection of commodities.

A further implication of treating objects as signs, potentially devastating for neoclassical theory, is that all economic transactions become replete with "externalities": all live in communicating, signifying systems in which objects are means of communication. No person is an island in his/her use of goods.

Commodities-as-signs challenges also the efficacy of static economic analysis. For in conversation, participants enter into relationship with unforeseen eventualities, and commodities-as-signs means that commodities participate in these uncertain and evolving relationships. As Perinbanayagam expresses it (p. 4), "Like Shahrazade's stories, all discourses are embedded in other discourses, which are embedded in other discourses, through which we make ourselves and our worlds." Commodities-as-signs, that is, commodities-as-discourse, imply that the foregoing statement can be applied to economic goods as well.

Perinbanayagam's analysis of dialogic interaction, for this reviewer/ economist, certainly crowds out the more specialized and reductionist conception of human symbolic interaction countenanced by neoclassical theory and by "Information Economics." Far from economics being "the imperial science" (Stigler, 1988, pp. 191–205), the mainstream discipline should be seen as giving inadequate rendering even to commoditized human interactions.

R. S. Perinbanayagam's informative and lucid book, *Discursive Acts*, is but one of many possible entry points whereby a fuller and deeper comprehension of information/communication bursts neoclassicism apart at the seams. A fuller rendering of symbolic interaction challenges many core neoclassical "truths": methodological individualism, static analysis, equilibrium, harmony, optimality, efficiency, and commodity exchange.

Of course, neoclassicists will continue to attempt to bar the door, maintaining that "the meaning of information is precisely a reduction in uncertainty." But their insistence in this regard has more to do with the political economy of discourse than with the search for truth. As Perinbanayagam remarks:

> Theories should not be treated as commodities demanding fetishistic loyalties or as religions but as incomplete programs forever demanding critique and development (p. xii).

Note

This chapter first appeared as a review article of R. S. Perinbanayagam, *Discursive Acts*," in *Research in the History of Economic Thought and Methodology*, edited by Warren J. Samuels, 1995. The article is reprinted here, with slight revisions, by permission of JAI Press Inc.

3

The Place of Information in Economics

There is no more important prerequisite to clear thinking in regard to economics itself than is recognition of its limited place among human interests at large.

—Frank Knight (1951)[1]

The very concept of a knowledge industry contains enough dynamite to blast traditional economics into orbit.

—Kenneth E. Boulding (1963)

Introduction

In recent decades theorists such as George Stigler, Gary Becker, and Richard Posner have endeavored to extend the applications of neoclassical theory into areas as diverse as family planning, racial discrimination, crime, marriage, divorce, drug addiction, politics, suicide. Indeed, for such "economic imperialists," (Stigler, 1988, pp. 191-205), *"all* behavior involving scarce resources" can be illuminated by neoclassical price theory (Adams and Brock, 1991, p. 6).

This chapter takes exception to that proposition. Focusing on information/communication, the chapter proposes instead that neoclassical economics be taken captive, contending that neoclassicists' notions of "market," "price," "value," "commodity," "demand," "supply," and "exchange" are but specialized and reductionist renderings of broader communicatory phenomena. Recognition and acceptance of this proposition have far-reaching implications for such basic economic constructs as efficiency, comparative advantage, optimality, equilibrium, and as well for such standard neoclassical policy prescriptions as deregulation, privatization, free trade, and down-sizing the public sector. Information/

communication poses severe challenges indeed for the neoclassical paradigm.

Four main parts follow this Introduction. The first addresses treatments of information/communication by three principal approaches within the mainstream discipline: the macroeconomic or sectoral approach; the applied microeconomic or industry studies approach, known also as industrial organization; and the theoretical microeconomic approach, often called "information economics." While differences in treatment afforded information/communication among these approaches are readily evident, of far greater importance are the similarities. In particular, they are of one accord in treating, or in endeavoring to treat, information as commodity.

The main thrust of the argument of the ensuing section of this chapter is as follows: Mainstream economics, premised as it is on the ubiquity of commodity exchange, needs to treat information as commodity in order to account for information within the mainstream or orthodox paradigm. Information, however, does not fulfill the definitional and conceptual requirements of commodity, thereby placing the discipline in a crisis concerning its own internal validity. Moreover, insisting that information is commodity obscures not only many essential properties of information, but as well consequences of informational exchange, creating thereby also a crisis of external validity.

The penultimate section reverses the Becker/Stigler/Posner proposal and explores possibilities for "economic colonization," contending that economics' crises can be resolved only if the discipline is viewed more modestly, as but one way to investigate communicatory interaction. The concluding section touches on political economy aspects of the "information commodity."

Despite internal inconsistencies and incongruity with external phenomena caused by conceiving information as commodity, mainstream economics retains this analytical mode and itself remains remarkably influential. To understand the source of this unwarranted influence requires acknowledgment of the broader political economy which shapes mainstream analysis. There is wealth, status, and other emoluments to be had from "proper" economics, since economics as discourse confers advantages to some. Put more positively, recognition of the limitations of mainstream economics, and positioning it within a broader communicatory context, offer the prospect of a more sustainable and equitable future.

Information and Communication in Mainstream Economics

Information Economy Treatment

Fritz Machlup's 1962 book, *The Production and Distribution of Knowledge in the United States*, was seminal in conceiving information and/or knowledge production, processing, and distribution as important economic activities. Prior to publication of Machlup's work, macroeconomic or aggregate analyses typically countenanced but a three-fold division for the economy, delineating agricultural, manufacturing, and service sectors. By calculating, however, that nearly 29 percent of U.S. output and 32 percent of the U.S. employment in 1958 were accounted for by "knowledge industries" whose annual growth averaged between 8 and nearly 11 percent, Machlup justified constituting a fourth sector, one based on informational and communicatory activities and products.

Subsequently Marc Porat (1977) took up and extended Machlup's work, pronouncing that the United States had become by 1967 an "Information Economy." Porat estimated that the information sector, in that year, accounted for about 46 percent of U.S. GNP.

In principle, macroeconomic or sectoral studies such as Machlup's and Porat's, by proposing a distinct informational sector, would seem to indicate that "economic activities associated with processing information have unique attributes, and deserve to be studied separately from other activities in the national economy" (Rubin, 1983, p. 1). To a limited extent some mainstream economists have pursued this line of thought, contending with Machlup, Porat, and Rubin for instance, that information/communication will continue to outpace manufacturing and agricultural sectors in the most developed economies, a perception that led the U.S. in particular to adopt aggressive "free trade" stances respecting informational products and services, both in GATT (Braman, 1990) and in bilateral negotiations (Parker, 1988).

Nonetheless it also remains true, in a broader sense, that aggregate or sectoral analyses proposing a distinct, even predominant, informational sector imply that informational/communicatory activities are equivalent to other transactional activity, and can with equanimity be studied in money terms. This is to say that these analyses imply that informational/communicatory processes can and should be treated as subsets of broader processes of economic (commodity) exchange.

There are problems with this approach, however, as hinted at by Marc Porat himself when he declared: "Information is by nature, a heterogeneous commodity... ." (Porat [1977] 1983, p. 16); and: "There is no single definition of information that embraces all aspects of the primary sector" ([1977] 1983, p. 16); and further: "Information cannot be collapsed into one sector—like mining—but rather the production, processing, and distribution of information goods and services should be thought of as an *activity*" ([1977] 1983, p. 18; emphasis in original).[2]

In a similar vein economist Beth Allen (1990, p. 269) wrote:

The preceding argument that various types of information may be available
in the economy suggests immediately that we should treat information as a
differentiated commodity (emphasis added).

The very notion of commodity requires, however, that units of the
good in question be "physically identical," even though available "in different places and at different times" (Ingrao and Israel, 1990, p. 5). Such
standardization permits counting. Indeed *measurement* according to
Abraham Kaplan (1964, pp. 173, 182), "in a word, is a device for
standardization, by which we are assured equivalencies among objects of
diverse origin. ... When we count, we are always determining how many
things there are of a certain *kind*" (emphasis in original). This is precisely
what Porat and Allen declare that informational commodities lack—a
standard with which to measure and compare.

Porat tried to resolve, or rather avoid, the measurement problem
respecting information by turning *from* "heterogeneous" informational
commodities *to* information *markets* and information *activities*, measuring
such markets and activities in two ways: by employment, and by value
added. Defining a "primary information market" as one which is
established when a technology of information production and
distribution is organized by firms, and an exchange price is established,"
Porat combined such diverse "markets" and "activities" as education,
banking, office furniture, mass media, telecommunications, advertising,
insurance, finance, and the post office.

Labor content or labor intensity does not, of course distinguish informational activities and commodities from other activities and commodities. Indeed there are huge disparities in "labor-intensity" within
Porat's information sector. While some informational activities may be
highly labor-intensive (live theatre, ballet, and authorship, for instance),
others are highly capital-intensive: much of the information "generated
and transmitted through the global telenet is processed and analyzed by
machines, not people" (Pelton, 1983, p. 59).

Note also that Machlup/Porat-type sectoral analyses restrict communicatory activities to those "organized by firms" and for which "an
exchange price is established" (Porat, [1977] 1983, p. 17). In other words,
much if not most of our communication is excluded from the sectoral
approach simply because it does not pass through markets and therefore
does not command a price or "value."[3]

The complex interrelationship between money, price, and informational "quantity" was addressed briefly in Chapter 1, and is pursued
again more fully later in this chapter. Briefly, money price states how
much exchange value an informational commodity "contains," but is
silent regarding the quantity of information that the commodity encap-
sulates.

Information Industry Studies Approach

The area within mainstream economics known as "applied microeconomics" or "industrial organization" investigates the structure and behavior of industries in an economy (Stigler, 1968, p. 1). William Shepherd (1975, p. 11) has remarked on characteristics of mainstream economic industry studies in general: (1) "Each market is regarded as a distinct entity, in line with Marshallian partial analysis." (2) "The context of the market is considered to be extraneous... ."(3) "Behavior is normally perceived primarily as matters of pricing and interfirm strategies." (4) "Performance criteria are matters of minimizing costs and prices; there is usually little attention to content or equity."

Whatever the implications of these aspects of mainstream economic analyses may be for "normal" industries, they are particularly disconcerting for economic studies of information industries, for the following reasons :

(1) Information pervades economies, and among other things helps co-ordinate through prices activities of disparate economic agents (see the section on "information economics" below). Therefore, it may well be unduly partial to apply "Marshallian partial analysis" to information industries.

(2) Since information is cumulative, or is at least dependent upon existing knowledge, and since symbols need to be comprehended in order for them to constitute information, it is a great and possibly improper simplification to consider the context of an information market as being "extraneous." Information "markets" both derive from the cultural/economic setting, and in turn impinge upon it.

(3) Behavior in information industries entails more than mere pricing since informational artifacts are unique creations which may, however, have many copies. For informational commodities, "product differentiation," then, is a primary consideration.

(4) Content and equity, many would argue, are of the essence for informational activity. For purposes of analysis economists, and others, however, tend to ignore content and depict output in terms of the "hardware," or "containers." "Containers" include: paper, videotape, compact discs, column inches, feature films as generic artifacts, books as generic artifacts, minutes of television broadcasting, and so on. Increasingly firms charge per call, per view, per bit, and per screenful of information (Mosco, 1989, p. 27). In *this* sense there is indeed an increasing commoditization of symbolic artifacts, but none of the quantitative measures used by economists touch directly upon the informational content; all relate rather to capacity for storing or transmitting symbols. Ignoring the informational content is a serious omission since it is the content that gives the

"hardware" most of its value. The hardware would be useless without the potential for encoding information, and indeed it is the specific encoded information that gives a particular item of hardware its particular market value.

The conclusion from these observations is that most mainstream economic analyses of information industries are fundamentally flawed.

Information Economics Treatment

Information and the Price System. For years microeconomic theorists paid scant attention to information. On the one hand, enraptured by the purely competitive model which assumes perfect knowledge, and on the other convinced that price theory provides abundant insight into real world phenomena, neoclassicists by and large rested content in the assumption that the price system generates and processes automatically information sufficient to ensure economic efficiency. Economies, neoclassicists assumed, are constrained by limited capacities for obtaining and processing materials, not by similar limitations concerning the information needed to organize and coordinate production and distribution (Jonscher, 1982, pp. 62-3).

The great Marshall, for example, introduced his classic treatise extolling money as the means whereby even inward "desires, aspirations and other affections of human nature" become measurable once expressed outwardly in market activity (Marshall [1890] 1934, pp. 14, 15). Marshall declared economics as being the most exact of the social sciences on account of the market's capacity to quantify.

Hayek too lauded the informational properties of the price system, viewing prices as "quantitative indices (or 'values')" (Hayek, 1945, p. 525). Each index or price, Hayek contended, should be understood as *concentrated information* reflecting the significance of any particular scarce resource relative to all others. The index or price borne by each commodity, Hayek enthused, permits autonomous economic agents to adjust their strategies "without having to solve the whole puzzle [input-output matrix] *ab initio*."

Prices, then, for Hayek, as for modern information economists, *are* information. Note, for instance, Arrow's more recent formulation of the idea:

> The competitive system can be viewed as an information and decision structure. Initially, each agent in the economy has a very limited perspective. The household knows only its initial holdings of goods (including labor power) and the satisfactions it could derive from different combinations of goods acquired and consumed. The firm knows only the technological alternatives for transforming inputs into outputs. The "communication" takes the form of prices. If the correct (equilibrium) prices are announced, then the individual agents can determine their purchases and

sales so as to maximize profits or satisfactions. The prices are then, according to the pure theory, the only communication that needs to be made in addition to the information held initially by the agents. This makes the market system appear to be very efficient indeed; not only does it achieve as good an allocation as an omniscient planner could, but it clearly minimizes the amount of communication needed (Arrow, 1979, pp. 313-4).

One begins to see, in this context, the reasoning behind Kenneth Boulding's remarks quoted at the start of this chapter, for as extracts from Marshall, Hayek, and Arrow indicate, "informational considerations [are] in fact, central to the analysis of a wide variety of phenomena," constituting as Joseph Stiglitz noted, "a central part of the Foundations of Economic Analysis" (Stiglitz, 1985, p. 21). But with up to 50 percent of the labor force engaged in informational activities, questions arise regarding the presumed capacity of markets spontaneously to generate information sufficient to ensure economic efficiency.[4] Indeed, long before Machlup published his seminal work, intimations of doubt were being expressed in the mainstream economics literature.

Precursors of Information Economics. One influential pioneer was Ronald Coase (1937) who defined the firm as an organization purposefully bypassing or suppressing the price mechanism. Firms, according to Coase, consciously or deliberatively administer internal flows of resources, instead of relying on markets to accomplish this. Coase then questioned why firms, or "islands of conscious power" as he called them, arise at all, given the purported efficacy of the price system. His response: "There is cost of using the price mechanism." He continued:

> The most obvious cost of "organizing" production through the price mechanism is that of *discovering what the relevant prices* are. This cost may be reduced but it can never be eliminated by the emergence of specialists *who will sell this information*. The costs of negotiating and concluding a separate contract for each exchange transaction which takes place in a market must also be taken into account (Hayek, 1937, p. 326; emphasis added).

A second notable precursor was Frank Knight ([1921] 1946) who constructed a theory of risk, uncertainty, and profit. True profit, Knight wrote, stems from uncertainty, since with perfect knowledge and zero transaction costs markets discount future shortages, obviating the possibility of economic profit. Profit he defined as the reward over and above a "normal" return. Profit, for Knight then, is a measure of market imperfection attributable to imperfect knowledge (that is, to uncertainty). Profit for Knight is the entrepreneur's reward for engaging in activities whose outcomes are uncertain even in the probabilistic or actuarial sense, making them uninsurable.

Knight has had his critics. Ben Seligman (1962, pp. 663–4) claimed his concept of profit, bereft of monopoly considerations, was a "panegyric to the entrepreneurs." Nonetheless, as was true with Coase, Knight addressed relationships among imperfect knowledge, information, and money, anticipating thereby today's "information economists" who define information as reduction in uncertainty and perceive it as commodity. According to Kenneth Arrow (1979, p. 307), for instance, "The meaning of information is precisely a reduction in uncertainty."[5] Likewise, information economist Charles Jonscher wrote:

> Demand for information arises because of the presence of uncertainty; without uncertainty there is no need for information (Jonscher, 1982, p. 63).

"Information economists" undoubtedly adopt a much narrower conception of information than do either the macroeconomic analysts (Machlup/Porat), or the information industries analysts. By defining "information" as "reduction in uncertainty," information economists endeavor to resolve the definitional problem besetting the other mainstream approaches. While their conception initially appears to be more precise (no talk here of information being a "heterogeneous" or "differentiated" commodity, for instance), in fact information still remains ill-defined, as we will see shortly. Moreover, for information to be incorporated as a commodity (as opposed to a residual) into the neoclassical model, information must itself be quantified and treated on "a par with ... a 'regular' (noninformation) economic commodity, such as iron ore" (Jonscher, 1982, pp. 67–67). This has proved impossible. While individual "packets" of information can command a price, there is no means of quantifying "information" as such; that is there is no means of measuring the amount of information that these "packets" contain.

We turn now to how neoclassicists have struggled with this conundrum.

The Modern Era. Despite implied or muted warnings by Coase, Knight, and others, analyses of information and implications for economic theory of imperfect knowledge languished in mainstream economics through the 1950s,[6] causing George Stigler in 1961 to remark: "[Information] occupies a slum dwelling in the town of economics" (Stigler, {1961} 1968, p. 171).

Proposing to begin rectifying this neglect, Stigler applied "standard economic theory of utility-maximizing behavior" (Stigler, 1983, p. 539) to one important problem of information—the ascertainment of market price" (Stigler, [1961] 1968, p. 171). Since prices are continually in flux, Stigler advised, there must exist at any given time and place ignorance as to what prices are. Buyers confronted with an array of prices for even homogeneous goods must "search" in order to find the lowest price. A search will entail a cost, but also will produce a benefit. The "value of information" in the face of this uncertainty, Stigler wrote, is "the amount by which the information reduces the expected cost to the buyer of his [*sic*] purchases" (Stigler, [1961] 1968, pp. 183–4). Stigler concluded that the "optimal amount of search" would transpire "if the cost of search is equated to its expected marginal return" (Stigler, [1961] 1968, p. 175).

More generally, given each economic agent's "subjective probability distributions over the possible states of the world," the value of information can be defined as "the increase in the expected value of the outcome resulting from a choice made after, as compared with before, the information becomes available" (Jonscher, 1982, p. 66).

It is to be noted that the approach suggested by Stigler and amplified by Jonscher seems to preserve the purported automaticity and effectiveness of the price mechanism, by turning prices ("information") into commodities. Ascertainment of knowledge respecting prices itself commands a price. The implication is that information required for markets to function effectively will be generated automatically in optimal quantities through the price system.

But Stigler's "solution" to the problem of uncertainty was more apparent than real, since he was unable to arrive at a general measure whereby information could be quantified, a requirement for supply and demand schedules to exist. Stigler assumed "the cost of search for a consumer may be taken as approximately proportional to the number of (identified) sellers approached" (Stigler, [1961] 1968, p. 175). Each "approach" then yields one seller's price.

But not all prices are equally informative: being apprised of one price is more informative if only one seller exists than if there are ten. As an aside it may be noted that some information economists conclude that markets with few sellers are more "competitive" than those with many: the higher information content of each price in markets with few sellers induces purchasers in these markets to search prices more extensively than they would in markets with many sellers, thereby increasing (relatively) price elasticity of demand (Dasah, 1992).

Returning to the main point, Stigler himself remarked in somewhat the same vein: "The expected saving from given search will be greater, the greater the dispersion of prices" (Stigler [1961] 1968, p. 175). What this statement essentially means is that the informational content of each ascertained price varies according to the dispersion in prices. If all prices are (known to be) the same, no information results from inquiring into the price of any additional seller; if prices are (known to be) almost the same, little information is attained from inquiry. But if the dispersion is large, each price ascertained can be highly informative. Rothschild (1974) demonstrated that price searches can inform searchers of the probability distribution of prices in addition to the price charged by individual sellers.

Stated more generally, information does not exist objectively in and of itself so as to be countable. It exists only in particular contexts; changing contexts changes (the "quantity" of) the information conveyed by a given sign or combination of signs. These arguments and observations indicate, then, that there is no one-to-one relationship between the commodity acquired (here a price), and its information content.

Shortly after completing his seminal article on uncertainty concerning commodity prices, Stigler prepared a second, addressing uncertainty over wages in the labor market ([1962] 1968). Stigler's work has proven to be influential, stimulating an evolving literature on the theory of price search (see *inter alia* Nelson, 1970; Telser, 1973; Rothschild, 1974; Diamond, 1978).

Meanwhile, others such as Debreu ([1959] 1989), and Radner ([1968] 1989) endeavored to incorporate uncertainty within general equilibrium models, attempts that have not been entirely successful (Grossman and Stiglitz 1980; Akerlof, 1970; Rothchild and Stiglitz 1976; and Pauly, 1974). Surveying the literature, Spence (1974) for instance, concluded that "in general the recent work reported here demonstrates that informational problems cause market failures of various kinds" (p. 57), while Stiglitz remarked:

> We have learned that much of what we believed before is of only limited validity; that the traditional competitive equilibrium analysis, though having the superficial appearance of generality—in terms of superscripts and subscripts—is indeed not very general; the theory is not robust to slight alteration in the informational assumptions. It is but a special—and not very plausible—'example' among the possible set of informational assumptions which can be employed to characterize an economy (Stiglitz, 1985, p. 21).

Why do some commentators feel that information and uncertainty undermine the neoclassical edifice? Why are they unconvinced by the Stigler/Jonscher approach, whereby commoditized information is seen to resuscitate neoclassicism? One answer relates to information's problematic status as commodity.

Critique Of Mainstream Treatments

Impossibility of the Information "Commodity"

To be sure, information economists have noted that the "information commodity" possesses some unique characteristics: Allen (1990, pp. 269, 270) for instance, remarked that "satiation occurs at one unit of information of *any given type* [since] identical copies of the same information [the normal requirement for "commodity"] are worthless unless the duplicates can be sold."

Stiglitz has pointed to another peculiarity of the information "commodity." How, he asked, is an individual to resolve the infinite regress of whether it is worthwhile to obtain information concerning whether it is worthwhile to obtain information ...?" (Stiglitz, 1985, p. 23). Arrow posed a different formulation of the same dilemma in 1962: "[Information's] value for the purchaser is not known until he [*sic*] has the information, but then he has, in effect, acquired it without cost" (Arrow, [1962] 1971, p. 148).

Other problems with information as commodity have been identified as well. For example, information is "indivisible," which means that partial information can be useless. Either one is informed of a price, or one is not informed (Allen, 1990, p. 270). Moreover, according to Arrow, since information can be reproduced at little or no cost while "the cost of transmitting a given body of information is frequently very low" (Arrow, [1962] 1971, p. 147), information can be difficult to appropriate; but capacity to be appropriated is a condition for commoditization. Market exchange entails, after all, the transmittance of property rights.

Difficulties of appropriation aside, it is not clear that ownership would be desirable in any event. Information is a "public good" in the sense that many can "possess" the same information at the same time, and possession by one does not detract from the ability of others to be apprised. To restrict access to those able and willing to pay is "inefficient," even in neoclassicists' terms, since there is no additional cost entailed in allowing greater access to information already produced. While some argue that markets for information are needed to induce production (Ploman and Hamilton, 1980), by neoclassical criteria the case for intellectual or symbolic artifacts being afforded commodity status is certainly not clear-cut.

Apart from the foregoing, however, the main problem, as far as "information economics" is concerned, is the absence of a measuring standard. Spence alluded briefly to this in writing:

> Economic agents have different "amounts" of information. Speaking about amounts of information suggests that we have an economically relevant measure of the quantity or value of information. This is not in fact the case.

Unfortunately, Spence quickly drew away from pursuing the implications of his insight by remarking:

> However, in the special case in which one person knows everything that another knows and more, we can say the former has more information. That suffices for my discussions of asymmetrically located information (Spence, 1974, p. 58).

Mention should perhaps be made of the one means thus far devised to quantify "information." Ascribed to Claude Shannon and Warren Weaver (1949) this "mathematical theory of communication" has been immensely influential in fields as diverse as engineering, physics, biology and cybernetics (Ritchie, 1991, pp. 7–8; Rifkin, 1989, pp. 208–218). Shannon and Weaver defined information in the context of selecting choices from an array of predetermined and known possibilities, lending at first blush a correspondence to information economists' definition of information as uncertainty reduction (Jenner, [1966] 1971).

According to Shannon and Weaver, the quantity of information in the simplest cases is the logarithm to base 2 of the number of available choices. If there are only two choices, a sender can inform a receiver of the selection of one of them with a single burst of signal (or "bit")—an "on" or a "one" instead of an "off" or a "zero," presuming the receiver knows the options from which the selection is made and is cognizant of the code used to designate that choice. Likewise, if there exist 16 alternatives, four "bits" (or binary digits) are sufficient to signal any given selection ($16 = 2^4$; i.e., $\log_2 16 = 4$). For this latter instance Shannon and Weaver denoted the "quantity" of information as 4 units or 4 bits since every one of the 16 choices could be uniquely identified by a sequence of four binary digits.

Unfortunately for "information economics," Shannon and Weaver's method quantifies something other than what is meant by "information" in the economists' sense. As Weaver explained, "information must not be confused with meaning" (Shannon and Weaver, 1949, p. 8).[7]

To understand the divergence between Shannon and Weaver's definition and method of measuring "information," and the neoclassicists' use of the term, it is useful momentarily to conflate these two systems. According to Shannon and Weaver's approach, a buyer confronting two possible and equally probable prices for a commodity receives one unit of information when apprised of a seller's actual price, whereas in facing 16 possible and equally probable prices receives 4 units of information. According to information economics, however, the "amount" of information imparted depends not at all on how many options from which a single seller has to select, but rather on the number of sellers and the dispersion in *their* prices. For information economics, each price denotes one unit of information, even though (as we have seen) a buyer in being apprised of one price receives more information in confronting two sellers than in confronting sixteen, and as well attains more information when prices are highly varied than when the variation in their distribution is low.

Implications

The Problem of Internal Validity. Frustration is evident in the ranks of information economists. Upon reviewing the uncertainty literature,

Spence sighed, "There is no sweeping conclusion to be drawn from this survey..." (Spence, 1974, p. 58). In like manner Stiglitz remarked: "There seems to be a myriad of special cases and few general principles" (Stiglitz, 1985, p. 21).

One reason for these lamentations is the fact that economists have not quantified and cannot quantify information. Each case becomes then a 'special case', since "information" means something different in each instance. "Information" in information economics is akin to an error term or residual that restores tautologies: If uncertainty exists over prices, then a unique parcel of "information" with "value" may restore equilibrium, but its "value" cannot be disassembled into price and quantity components (or alternatively, quantity is always equal to one for each unique informational "packet"). Information is, as Arrow suggested, "indivisible." The inability to devise a measure for information means, ultimately, that information stands outside of neoclassical modeling.

Since information on the one hand constitutes "a central part of the foundations of economic analysis," yet on the other stands outside neoclassical modeling, a fundamental inconsistency becomes apparent, giving rise to a crisis concerning neoclassicism's internal validity. A more promising approach would be to stop "force-fitting" information into the commodity mode and indeed to reverse the process, treating information no longer as commodity, but rather addressing "commodities" as being informational and communicatory. (See Chapter 2, above). Market exchange then would be viewed as an aspect of broader communicatory interaction. The concluding part to this chapter pursues facets of this approach.

The Problem of External Validity. In defining information as commodity, and indeed in the case of "information economics" confining it to uncertainty reduction, neoclassicists have rendered invisible many important consequences of informational interchange and transfer. To illustrate by but one of a veritably infinite number of possible examples:

On 30 October 1938, Orson Welles's science fiction broadcast, *War of the Worlds*, was heard by at least six million radio listeners. Of those, at least one million panicked or were seriously frightened, believing that Martians had indeed landed. According to Lowery and de Fleur (1988, pp. 61–2): "Terrified people all over America prayed and tried frantically in one way or another to escape death from the Martians. ... Hundreds of people fled their homes. Bus terminals were crowded. ... [In Pittsburgh] a man came home in the middle of the broadcast and found his wife in the bathroom with a bottle of poison in her hand and screaming, 'I'd rather die this way than that'... ."

Looking beyond the pale of information-as-commodity and information-as-reduction-in-uncertainty, new analytical possibilities open up. Consider the following:

First, the capacity to communicate, to package and diffuse information, means power. It is not simply the case, as mainstream economists contend, that buyers survey an array of informational commodities and purchase the one or ones that seem most in tune with the buyers' needs, given prices and income constraints. Albeit unintentionally, Orson Welles drove hundreds, perhaps thousands, from their homes. He affected, however briefly, the thoughts and emotions of six million or more people, many of whom took action based on these mental states. More generally, mass media give editors, writers, programmers, and other content providers, including advertisers, politicians, the military, public relations firms, news agencies, and entertainers, "access to the thoughts and emotions of people in the audience" (Vogel, 1989, pp. 155–6). Communication *means* influence, and a capacity to exert influence over perhaps millions means power. Power, however, is not a primary concern for most mainstream economists (Adams and Brock, 1986, Chapter 2), certainly not for neoclassicists; and commodity-alone/reduction-in-uncertainty treatments afforded information indeed enable mainstream analysts to skirt considerations of power. Stated another way, less restrictive conceptions of information restore considerations of power to economic analysis and so entail the replacement or succession of mere "economics" by "political economy." (See Chapter 5).

Second, Welles's broadcast shows that information is not enveloped or contained in a single place, as are "normal" commodities, but rather that information permeates both time and space (Innis, [1950] 1972). Moreover, information generates or spawns more information, as *inter alia* press reports on Welles's broadcast, an ensuing study by the Office of Radio Research of Princeton University, policy statements from the Federal Communications Commission, Lowery and de Fleur's chapter, and indeed this very page, indicate. Societal evolution, as Veblen (1909) and more recently Boulding (1978; 1981) have understood, is in the first instance informational.

Third, information constitutes a shared "space," a symbolic environment, a communications ecology (Nevitt, 1982), in which people live. Our physical environment is experienced or perceived in large part symbolically, and our symbolic constructs in turn influence action upon the material environment. I return to this at the close of the chapter.

Economics as Communication

Two Models

To infuse economics with internal and external validity, this section suggests that economic processes come to be viewed as special instances of more general communicatory processes.

At the outset it is to be noted that a superficial similarity exists between the economists' "market" and the communicologists' "communication system." (For a more in-depth treatment, see Chapter 4). Briefly, both processes entail circular flows. In the former instance, a seller transmits property rights in and perhaps physical possession of a "commodity" to a buyer and in return receives money, the amount being determined "impersonally" through supply and demand. In the latter, a sender transmits a message (heretofore termed "information") by means of some medium of transmission (visible light, air, paper, radio, etc.), to a receiver, who decodes or interprets it and responds in some way ("feedback"). The similarities, however, mask profound differences. In the economics model buyer and seller exert no influence on one another. They are assumed to be autonomous "others," rationally engaging in activities to maximize their individual welfare. By contrast, the communication system as a minimum posits influence by the sender on the receiver, and more often posits communicators as engaging in dialogic interaction, interpenetrating and transforming one another through "mutual semiosis"[8] (Perinbanyagam, 1991, p. 31).

Which of these two models—the market or the communication system—is most apt for any given analysis hinges on whether it is a "commodity" or "information" that is being exchanged. If what is exchanged is "inert," exerting no effect or influence upon the perceptions, values, or cognitive patterns of the receiver, and if monetary payment is made in compensation, then truly the economists' "market" is operative. It was argued in Chapter 2, however, that all artifacts are informational, and that therefore all exchanges or transmissions of artifacts are communicatory. Communication scholars, in other words, question whether it is possible to participate in any exchange and remain unchanged.

What Then Is Information?

Physicist Carl Friedrich von Weizsäcker affirmed "information" to be rooted in "form," or "pattern," or "structure." He wrote:

> This 'form' can refer to the form of all kinds of objects or events perceptible to the senses and capable of being shaped by man: the form of the printer's ink or ink on paper, of chalk on the blackboard, of sound waves in air, of current flow in a wire, etc. (von Weizsäcker, 1980, pp. 38-9).

Matter and form, von Weizsäcker continued, are conceptual complements: "In the realm of the concrete, no form exists without matter; nor can there be matter without form." He continued:

> A cupboard, a tree are made of wood. Wood is their "matter". ... But the
> cupboard isn't simply wood, it is a wooden cupboard. "Cupboard" is what
> it is intrinsically; cupboard is its *eidos*, its essence, its form. But a cupboard
> must be made of something; a cupboard without matter is a mere thought
> abstracted from reality (von Weizsäcker, 1980, p. 274).

Energy too, as with the telegraph, can be ordered or formed or
organized so as to be capable of being understood.

Information, then, may be termed *epiphenomenal* in the sense that "it
derives from the *organization* of the material world on which it is wholly
dependent for its existence"[9] (Beniger, 1986, p. 9). It is this epiphenomenal
quality of information, (what I termed its "immateriality" in Chapter 1),
that makes information so difficult to appropriate. Different substances,
and even human memories, can easily be shaped or formed to convey or
hold the "same" information.

The mere existence of form, however, is not sufficient to constitute
information; it is also required that meaning be conveyed. In addition to
matter/energy and form there must also be language, that is a code or
codes assigning pre-arranged meanings to these "forms." As well, the
receiver must be cognizant of the code that assigns meaning to the forms
(or "signs") (von Weizsäcker, 1980, p. 39).

In this conception, information defies measurement, and for a number
of reasons. First, as noted, information is immaterial; information relates
to the form matter takes, but is not the matter itself.

Second, forms have no meaning, or rather as symbols have no
meaning, in and of themselves,[10] but rather take on meaning because a
code or language exists which imputes or ascribes meaning to them. This
is probably what Lee Thayer meant in writing: "To be human is to be
denied life in a world of things; it is to be given life in a world of the *meaning* of things" (Thayer, 1987, p. x; emphasis in original). In this view,
meaning (information) does not exist objectively so as to be countable,
but exists only in subjectivity, that is in interpretation. For example, different languages or codes may ascribe different meanings to the "same"
form, and different message receivers or "readers," therefore, bringing
different codes to the "same" forms, may derive or impute markedly different meanings. According to Gregory Bateson, "nothing has meaning
except it be seen in some context" (Bateson, 1979, p. 14). Here, the context
is the code or language brought by the reader, but equally any given form
or component of a message exists only in the context of the whole
message where components modify one another syntagmatically. The
whole message thereby takes on much greater meaning than can be
ascribed to individual components considered separately. Likewise, the
meaning imputed to each form depends also on the "paradigm" from
which it was selected, and indeed the reader's knowledge of the elements

of the paradigm (Webster, 1980, pp. 166–204; Solomon, 1988; Bonney and Wilson, 1990).

It is evident that we have ventured into the field of semiotics, which aspires to answer how forms (signs) take on meaning. Without dwelling here, there is an added point that deserves emphasis. Languages, or codes, that enable us to decode or impute meanings relate to and are derived from cultures and subcultures (Fiske, 1982; Hall, 1982). We learn languages and codes from our communities. To quote Thayer once more, "To be human is to be *in* communication in *some* human culture and to be in some human culture is to see and know the world—to communicate—in a way which daily recreates that particular culture" (Thayer, 1987, p. 45). James Carey likewise defined communication as "a symbolic process whereby reality is produced, maintained, repaired and transformed" (Carey, 1989, p. 23). (See also Berger and Luckman, 1966; and Kuhn, 1970).

It follows, therefore, that information and communication should engage the analyst in a social or methodologically collectivist discourse (as opposed to the methodologically individualist discourse of the economist), for at least two reasons: First, messages frequently radiate into and permeate many minds, often simultaneously, producing, maintaining, and transforming societies and the individuals comprising them. Second, any individual's interpretation of forms (signs, text, or information) comes not only from his/her unique life experiences, but also (and more importantly) from the shared languages or codes of the culture(s) and subculture(s). As expressed by Mikhail Bakhtin, "Language enters life through concrete utterances (which manifest language) and life enters language through concrete utterances as well" (quoted in Perinbanayagam, 1991, front page).

The Political Economy of the Information Commodity

It may seem that we have strayed far from mainstream economics, but not as far as might at first appear. Following James Carey we can interpret mainstream economics, and particularly neoclassicism, as but a particular symbolic or "informational" system *producing, maintaining, repairing and transforming* economic reality. Even the physical sciences, as Boulding noted, do not merely investigate the world, but as well create the world they are investigating (Boulding [1969] 1971, p. 451). If that is true of the physical sciences (which, for example, have created new basic elements), how much more must this be the case for social sciences such as economics?

It was indeed in full realization that the economics discipline acts upon and transforms the economic world, that the "economics as discourse" and "economics as rhetoric" literatures arose (Samuels, 1990; Klamer, McCloskey and Solow, 1988), from whence it is but a short further step to the political economy of mainstream economics, that is to the study of the power, money, and control lying behind and motivating mainstream economic analyses (Schiller, 1994). Money is to be made from heightened commodity treatment of social interactions, and parties standing to gain therefrom benefit from the promulgation of the neoclassical paradigm.

Heightened commodity treatment of social life carries with it, however, enormous costs. Three of these are now addressed briefly: injustice in international communication; break-down of community; and ecosystem destruction. The implication of the analysis of this closing section is recognition of a pressing need for an alternative economics, a transformed economics, one that can help bring about a more sustainable and just future.

International Communication

By insisting within GATT (recently renamed the World Trade Organization) and in bilateral trade treaties that information be treated solely or primarily as commodity instead of as gift or public resource, and that there be a dismantling of informational trade barriers and beefed-up copyright, the United States, which domiciles the world's largest information companies, positions itself to increase exports of informational products in exchange for energy, resources, foreign currencies, and labor-intensive manufactured goods. The United States and corporations headquartered principally in the U.S.A., hold a competitive advantage in the mass production of informational "commodities."

Virtually all of the mainstream economics literature—from the sectoral analyses of Machlup/Porat, to the information industries studies, to the field of "information economics"—is supportive of information's commodity status, despite critical problems concerning economics' own internal and external validity arising from this commodity-only treatment.

If information/communication, on the other hand, were defined as, say, the mutual engagement of dialogic partners (Perinbanayagam, 1991), or as a basic human right, as was attempted in UNESCO's call for a New International Information and Communication Order (Preston, Herman, and Schiller, 1989), then America's trading partners could rightly insist on a free and *balanced* flow of information: international "communication" would no longer be a "one-way street."

But, dialogic interaction interferes with the commodity status of information, since receivers are no longer perceived and treated as mere "consumers." And communication as a basic human right is much less beneficial to the export trade of transnational communication industries.

Commodity treatment of information perpetuates and exacerbates international inequalities and Third World dependencies. Third World countries must concentrate on primary production (food production and resource extraction) for exports to pay for information and knowledge that the First World has commoditized through intellectual property laws (copyright, trademarks, patents, and industrial designs). In the "exchange," however, the First World retains the knowledge it sells due to the public good character of informational commodities, an injustice that has been noted by many (UNESCO, 1980).

Community

One of Kenneth Boulding's many remarkable achievements was to analyze the gift (or "grants") economy, and to compare that with the economy of commodity exchange. For Boulding, organizations (including economic organizations like markets) consist of role structures united by flows of information. The information flowing through economies and other organizations can be of three basic types: threat information, exchange information, and love (or gift) information. For Boulding, "all social organizations without exception are built by processes that can be classified into these three general types... ." (Boulding, 1970, p. 27).

He further advised that a too heavy reliance upon exchange as the mode of communication can lead to social and economic break-down. It is worth quoting him at length on this :

> The instability of capitalism may arise partly out of certain technical defects of an elaborate exchange system that results in unemployment and depression; it also results, however, from certain delegitimations of exchange, which may well arise because of strong preferences for integrative relationships, which are, after all, personally much more satisfying than exchange. To do things for love always seems to be more moral and progressive than to do things for money.

So, he continued,

> ... capitalism undermines itself, as Schumpeter pointed out, despite its success, because of the failure of exchange institutions, such as finance, banking, corporations, and so on, to develop an integrative matrix that will legitimate them (Boulding, 1973, p. 110).

By contrast, the gift economy integrates rather than alienates. The integrative system, or gift economy, is based on status, on love and affection, and on one-way rather than two-way transfers. It comprises processes whereby "culture is transmitted from one generation to another ..., whereby persons and institutions acquire dignity, respect [and] legitimacy" (Boulding, 1970, p. 26).

In the 1990's, North Americans are being increasingly enmeshed in processes that heighten the commodity treatment of social relations: continental and hemispheric "free trade" agreements; higher education offered increasingly on the basis of user-pay and cost recovery; downsizing social programs such as unemployment insurance, medicare, old age security; introduction of technical devices and systems falling under the rubric of "Information Highway" that expand manifold pay-per, transactional modes of human interaction. This movement toward heightened commodity treatment of human relations, in other words increased commoditization of informational/communicatory processes, Boulding would say, both reflects and contributes to a diminished sense of human community. Couple that with widening gaps between rich and poor (also an ineluctable concomitant of the market system) and societal breakdown through class warfare or massive individual alienation becomes a real possibility.

The Ecosystem

The transition to sustainable development, as recommended by the World Commission on Environment and Development (WCED, 1987),[11] entails rectifying a huge problem in symbolization. It means rejecting current practices of naming or symbolizing the ecosystem and portions thereof in money terms as commodity, and instead knowing it as gift. Conceiving nature instrumentally as mere commodity emphasizes humanity's apartness or otherness vis à vis the environment, despite the reality that in ecological terms we are all a part of the earth and it of us. Reconceiving the environment as gift, whether from God or from our ancestors, by contrast, would mean that we would again come to view ourselves as but temporary custodians or stewards of our environment, that we would again come to realize that we ought to act responsibly, with care, toward it in order that we can pass it along in love to future generations (cf. Dyer, 1989).

Treating nature as commodity, as our present economic system does, is in the words of Herman Daly and John Cobb, "an ideology of death," and we can indeed see the working out of this deadly ideology all about us, from species' extinction, to water contamination, to ozone thinning, to desertification, to acid rain. Treating the ecosystem as gift, by contrast, is an ideology of life, a mode of being, of perceiving, and of interacting with nature that humankind must revive if it is to have a future. This topic is taken up in much greater detail in Chapter 6.

The challenge of re-naming the ecosystem as gift rather than as commodity[12] is quite probably the most important communication/economic problem humankind faces. Indeed, "It's a matter of survival" (Gordon and Suzuki, 1990).

Notes

This chapter is a revised version of "The Place of Information in Economics," which appeared originally in *Information and Communication in Economics*, edited by Robert E. Babe (Kluwer Academic Publishers, 1994, pp. 41–67). Reprinted by permission of Kluwer Academic Publishers.

1. As quoted in Lutz and Lux (1988, p. 179).

2. Porat continues: "An information market enables the consumer to know something that was not known beforehand: to exchange a symbolic experience; to learn or relearn something; to change perception or cognition; to reduce uncertainty; to expand one's range of options; to exercise rational choice; to evaluate decisions; to control a process; to communicate an idea, a fact, or an opinion. An information market may sell topical knowledge with a very short, useful life; it may exchange long-lasting knowledge. It may involve a completely specialized or unique configuration of knowledge, useful only to one person in one situation, or it may be public knowledge available to all simultaneously" (Porat [1977] 1983, p. 16).

3. Below distinctions will be made among "value-in-exchange" (the only "value" recognized by mainstream economics), "value-in-use," and "intrinsic value."

4. Moreover informational activity challenges the static analysis characteristic of so much of the mainstream method. Information implies change—in wants and preferences, in production techniques, in produced commodities, in markets. In such a dynamic world, basic economic concepts, like efficiency, optimality, and equilibrium are in danger of being rendered meaningless. See particularly Chapters 7 to 9 below.

5. For the contrasting view of heterodox scholars, see Chapters 8 and 9. Veblen, for instance, remarked that information and knowledge *create* uncertainty, far from reducing it. Indeed, he mused, "it is something of a homiletical commonplace to say that the outcome of any serious research can only be to make two questions grow where one question grew before" (Veblen, [1908] 1990, p. 33).

6. In *History of Economic Analysis* Joseph Schumpeter declared that theoretical work on uncertainty peaked with Dobb and Knight in the 1920's, thereafter to "peter out," while "factual work in this field ... did not get beyond beginnings" (Schumpeter, 1954, pp. 894–5).

7. Weaver continued: "Two messages, one of which is heavily loaded with meaning and the other of which is pure nonsense, can be exactly equivalent, from the present point of view, as regards information. ... Information is a measure of one's freedom of choice when one selects a message. ... The two messages between which one must choose, in such a selection, can be anything one likes. One might be the text of the King James Version of the Bible, and the other might be 'Yes'" (Shannon and Weaver, 1949, pp. 8-9).

8. Following semiologist C. S. Peirce, Perinbanayagam (1991, p. 31) defined semiosis as "an action or influence which is, or involves, a co-operation of *three* subjects, such as a sign, its object, and its interpretant, this tri-relative influence not being resolvable into action between two pairs". Tri-relative influence implies that initiator and respondent may have quite different interpretations ("interpretants") for a given message or "sign," if and when their experiences with the external world ("object") differ. Symbolic exchange can *create* uncertainty, launching dialogic partners onto paths that take unforeseeable twists and turns.

9. But then, equally, the material world can be deemed "epiphenomenal" inasmuch as matter cannot exist without assuming form, while forms can "exist" without matter as pure thought.

10. The word choice is extremely important here, bearing on the question of whether forms (or objects, or subjects) have or can have meaning (value) in and of themselves (intrinsic meaning or value), or whether meaning/value exists only in relation to other objects. Communication studies and economics appear to be alike in contending that forms or objects have meaning/value only in relation to other forms or objects. Communication studies terms the relationship "symbolic meaning," whereas economics calls it "exchange value."

11. For critique and extension of WCED's proposals for sustainable development, see Goodland, Daly, and Serafy (1992).

12. For an extended comparison of gift and commodity, see also Hyde (1979), and Schumacher (1974, chapter 13).

Interrelations Between Economics and Communication Studies

PART TWO

Interrelations Between Economies
and Communities

4

Communication: Blindspot of Western Economics

There comes a time ... when the blind spots come from the edge of vision into the center.

—Walter Lippmann (1922)

Introduction

This chapter compares the disciplines of economics and communication studies. In their mainstream versions, known respectively as neoclassical economics and as administrative communication research,[1] these scholarly areas appear at first glance to be quite similar. The economist's *market*, after all, comprised of monetary and commodity flows between buyer and seller, has a seemingly close correlate in the communicologist's *communication system*, comprised of sender, receiver, medium, message, code, and feedback. Certainly it is interesting and important to compare and contrast these conceptual models that condition so much of what their mainstream practitioners have to say. Closer comparisons between these mainstream or dominant modes of analysis, however, reveal that their similarities are quite superficial and their antinomies deep-rooted.

In both the economics and communication studies disciplines, however, there is a subfield or specialty known as "political economy," whose thrust is to analyze the nature, sources, uses, and consequences of power, whether economic, political, communicatory, or otherwise—power being defined as "the possibility of imposing one's will upon the behavior of other persons" (Weber, 1954, p. 323). It is a principal contention of this chapter that scholarly treatment of the material (or "economic") and of the symbolic (or "communicatory") converge only with political economy, despite surface similarities between mainstream economics and orthodox communication research.

When scholars trained as economists practise political economy, they tend to emphasize either the legal system in its apportioning of rights, or they look to the social (class) structure, depending on whether they are respectively liberals/institutionalist (a distinction I draw out in the next Chapter), or Marxists. (See Figure 1.) When communication scholars practise political economy, they tend to concentrate on economic/institutional/legal factors constraining and shaping message production, viewing media products as concoctions fabricated by the established power system to preserve and extend itself. Despite these differences in emphasis, political economy, whether undertaken by those grounded in economics or by those schooled in communication studies, melds the material and the symbolic, economics and communication studies, a most vital enterprise (as I argue in the closing section) in a world facing environmental decay.

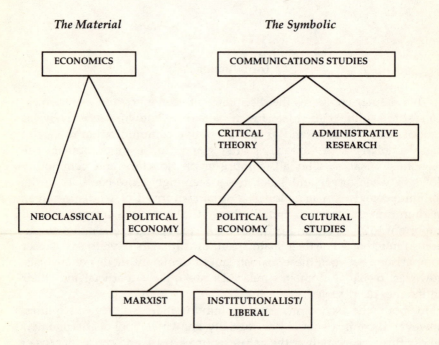

Figure 1. Typology of Economics and Communication Studies

To explore the foregoing themes more completely, the chapter is organized as follows. The next section describes and analyzes characteristics of mainstream economics, emphasizing particularly the unduly limited conception of communication countenanced by the orthodox version of this discipline. In the third section the chapter turns to administrative or mainline communication research, in order subsequently (in the fourth and fifth sections) to compare and contrast this field with neoclassical economics, particularly with regard to the treatment of communicatory processes. Neoclassical economics, it is argued, actually proffers a model of radical *non*-communication! Finally the chapter finds reconciliation between these two academic "solitudes" in political economy.

Mainstream Economics

Over the two centuries since publication of Adam Smith's *The Wealth of Nations* in 1776[2] mainstream economics has become theoretically refined, and can be formalistic, highly abstract, mathematized. It has also become predominantly an economics of incremental change, based on the maximization principle (setting dollar values equal at the margin). These characteristics help distinguish modern or neoclassical economics from its classical heritage.

In other respects, however, there is an historical continuity or sameness about the discipline. Three qualities in particular that characterized Adam Smith's formulation, and that continue with the neoclassical are: methodological individualism, reification of the market, and the assumption of harmonious interaction. I treat each of these aspects in turn.

Methodological Individualism

For Adam Smith the wealth of a nation was simply the summation of the wealth of its inhabitants. Whatever effectively promoted individual wealth necessarily promoted also wealth for the community. Smith argued that, since each individual knows best his or her own unique circumstances, national wealth is most effectively pursued by minimizing constraints on individual enterprise.

Methodological individualism in neoclassicism's reformulation of the economics of Adam Smith is apparent in its "theory of the firm," and in its "theory of consumer behavior," which, when combined, purport to explain, in the absence of historical context, relative prices and resource allocation. The firm in neoclassical price theory is an abstraction meant to represent any firm at any time and in any place. In the theory the firm is seen not as a collective or communal undertaking, but rather as an individual enterprise for the sole benefit of the owner. To neoclassicists, as noted by Horace Gray (1981, p. 105), the owner or "entrepreneur" conceives the project, procures the capital and raw materials, hires the workers, develops the market, and accepts the risks of failure. The consumer, too, is an abstraction meant to represent any consumer anywhere at any time. Buyers and sellers come together in markets where there results a circular flow, commodity traveling from seller to buyer and money flowing in the opposite direction. (See Figure 2). The economy is viewed as the aggregation of all such autonomous transactions.

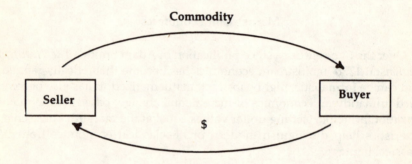

Figure 2. The "Market"

For neoclassical economists, human relations are, then, commodity exchange relations mediated by commodities and by money. In fact, the focus of attention of mainstream economists is not on human relations at all, but on things (commodities). The central questions are how much of a given commodity will be produced, and what will be its exchange value *vis-a-vis* other commodities.

In the wake of today's ecological crisis and the manifest heightening of environmental interdependence, methodological individualism (treating autonomous or quasi-autonomous individuals as the unit of analysis), must appear quaint, even pernicious (Daly and Cobb, 1989, pp. 85-96, 159-175). This methodological practice continues, however, as a mainstay of both contemporary mainstream economics and also (as we shall see) administrative communication research.

Reification of the Market

Adam Smith "reified"[3] the market. His "obvious and simple system of natural liberty" was said to arise spontaneously from the innate human "propensity to truck, barter and exchange," not at all from human design and the conscious exercise of the human will (Smith, 1776, Book 1, Chap. 2). Once generated, Smith reckoned, the Market functions automatically and is all-powerful; indeed, he likened it to an "invisible hand," channeling economic activity to an end, namely promoting the common weal, defined by Smith as the wealth of the nation, "which was no part of [the participants'] intention" (Smith, 1776, Book 4, Chap. 2).

While Smith understood that the Market could easily be subverted through monopoly power, particularly by the state bestowing exclusive privileges on its friends and supporters, modern day neoclassicists tend not to share this comprehension or conviction. According to George Stigler, for example:

> It is virtually impossible to eliminate competition from economic life. If a firm buys up all of its rivals, new rivals will appear. If a firm secures a lucrative patent on some desired good, large investments will be made by rivals to find alternative products or processes to share the profits of the firm (Stigler, 1988, p. 164).

While neoclassicists, deeming themselves to be neopositivists, substitute the model of pure competition for Adam Smith's "invisible hand" (Blaug, 1968, p. 59), the change is superficial at best, and certainly no less ethereal than the predecessor. *Given* consumer preferences, *given* the state of the industrial arts (technology), and *given* the initial distribution of wealth (endowments), all production and prices for neoclassicists are determined automatically by the Market and can be deduced logically by the principle of maximization. Provided that nothing "interferes" with the free flow of inputs, output and hence welfare will be maximized automatically, given the (Pareto) criterion that no one can be made better off without someone else becoming worse off (Himmelweit, 1977, p. 25).

For this chapter, the "givenness" in neoclassical theory of tastes and preferences is particularly important. "For the vast array of problems," neoclassicist George Stigler wrote, "including most of those we shall encounter, it is customary to treat tastes as fixed" (Stigler, 1966, p. 39). On those relatively rare occasions when tastes and preferences are allowed by neoclassical economists to vary, they are permitted to change only as a result of variations in "exogenous variables," that is, changes in factors residing outside the particular market being studied. Thus, for example, according to Stigler, "In a study of the long-term demand for housing, one naturally investigates changes in family size [while] in a study of the trend in employment in the medical professions one considers the age and sex structure of the population and its organization" (Stigler, 1966, p. 39). Seldom, if ever, in the neoclassicists' world, is it the case that promotional efforts of the producer (i.e. persuasion), or past consumption of the commodity (i.e., habituation or addiction), affect consumers' tastes and preferences.[4] As we will see shortly, this practice or assumption radically distinguishes mainstream economics not only from heterodox economics, but from mainstream communication studies as well.

Harmony

Adam Smith hypothesized "an obvious and simple system of natural liberty" premised on individual self-interest and the division of labor (i.e., labor specialization) that he alleged promotes harmony among participants: "It is not from the benevolence of the butcher, the brewer, or the baker that we expect our dinner," admonished Smith, but rather from their "self-love." He continued, "[We] never talk to them of our own necessities but of their advantages ... and show them that it is for their advantage to do for [us] what [we] require of them" (Smith, 1776, Book 2, Chap. 2).

Likewise today's neoclassicists emphasize the harmonious nature of economic interactions—if and when mediated by unregulated, impersonal markets. In the model of pure competition upon which so much of neoclassical perception is based, no seller is large enough to control price; in fact each seller is so small that he or she can sell everything produced at the established market price, eliminating all possibility of cut-throat competition. Nor do buyers or sellers possess coercive power over one another. When incipient conflict *is* considered, as when production inflicts damage on third parties (termed "externalities"), the ingenuity and brilliance of neoclassicists has been sufficient to demonstrate that under certain improbable conditions (namely, perfect competition, perfect knowledge, zero transaction costs), The Market will internalize the externality and resolve the conflict automatically, regardless of where legal liability resides (Coase, 1960; see also Chapter 6, below).

The more closely one adheres to the neoclassical model of pure competition and the neoclassical mode of marginal analysis, of course, the further removed one becomes from the every day world of power-plays, inequities, and injustices. It is to these latter dimensions of economic and communicatory life that political economy is addressed.

Mainstream (Administrative) Communication Research

The modern era of communication research is often held to have been inaugurated at the turn of the century by the writings of John Dewey and associates (Carey, 1981; Czitrom, 1982; Delia, 1987). Others, such as

Wilbur Schramm (1989), have argued that communication *as a behavioral science* did not really begin to take shape until the 1920s or 1930s. Be this as it may, there does seem to be a consensus that 1948 was an important year for communication research, as it was then that Harold Lasswell, by publicizing five questions as constituting the subject matter for the nascent discipline, did much to "structure the thinking of a whole generation of communication scholars and students" (Schramm & Roberts, 1971, p. 84). Lasswell's questions, of course, were: "Who, Says What, In Which Channel, To Whom, With What Effect?" (Lasswell, 1948, in Schramm & Roberts, 1971, pp. 84-99). Critical theorists have noted that Lasswell left out a sixth, and for them most important question, namely, "Why?" They also consider that he afforded too little attention to the context within which the communication takes place (Olson, 1989, p. 73).

In any event, Lasswell was highly influential, and in 1949 Claude Shannon and Warren Weaver synthesized and formalized his five questions by postulating a Communication System wherein encoded messages travel a unidirectional path from source (or sender) to transmitter (encoder), and via carrier or medium to decoder ("receiver" in Shannon and Weaver's terminology), and thence to ultimate destination (what we would usually term the receiver). (See Figure 3.) The model illustrated what, for Shannon and Weaver, was the quintessential communication problem: namely, reproduction at the destination, either exactly or approximately, of a message selected at another point by the source (Shannon & Weaver, 1949, p. 7). Communication, for them, was successful if "the meaning conveyed to the receiver leads to the desired conduct on his part" (Shannon & Weaver, 1949, p. 5). By merely incorporating feedback, or response from receiver to sender, Norbert Wiener (1954), Ludwig von Bertalanffy (1981), Kenneth Boulding, and others transformed Shannon and Weaver's linear model into a cybernetic system of mutual interdependence and interdeterminations. (See Figure 4.)

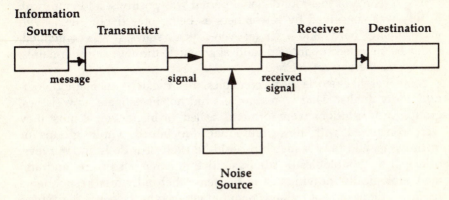

Figure 3. Shannon and Weaver's Linear Flow Model

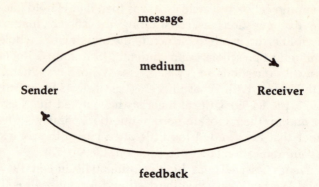

Figure 4. The Communication System

While it is safe to say that pioneering communication researchers seldom considered complete communicating systems in their studies, nonetheless attention was afforded selective interpenetrations, even in the early years. As noted by Daniel Czitrom (1982, pp. 123-127), during the 1940s and 1950s luminaries such as Frank Stanton (of CBS), Elmo Roper, George Gallup, Carl Hovland (working for the U.S. Army on the "laws of persuasion"), Harold Lasswell, and Paul Felix Lazarsfeld set boundaries for the emerging field by concentrating on five closely interrelated lines of research, namely propaganda studies, public opinion surveys and methods, market research, effects research, and interpersonal communication research.

The research of this foundational period was positivist and empirical. Reality was conceived by researchers as being objectively given, with events being "hard" and discrete; even psychic states, it was contended, could be detected, quantified, and aggregated through questionnaires, and norms thereby established.

Moreover, like neoclassical economics, this research was methodologically individualist. That is, researchers did not investigate how classes, groups, or institutions were formed, clashed, or interacted; at most they were concerned with how individuals functioned within groups or institutions, and how leadership could be exercised. Polls and surveys, principal methodologies of administrative research, also were (and are) methodologically individualist in the sense that individual respondents represent thousands or millions of autonomous others; society is deemed to comprise merely the summation of the individuals composing it (Ginsberg, 1986): unions, coalitions, communities, and advocacy groups tend to be disregarded. Laboratory experiments too, another principal research method of administrative communication research, were, and remain methodologically individualist, as it is the individual, not the class, group, or organization, that is the unit of analysis; the group, in other words, is represented by a small sample of autonomous individuals selected from the group.

A third characteristic of this research was its focus on behavioral or attitudinal change, a stance consistent with Shannon and Weaver's emphasis on how senders can influence receivers. Communication was presumed to result in overt effects that could be both measured and replicated. Sponsors of the research, intent on influencing more strongly the attitudes and behavior of message recipients, were desirous to uncover "the magic keys" of persuasion (Lowery & DeFleur, 1988, p. 137).

Similarities of the Orthodoxies

One feature common to neoclassical economics and mainstream communication studies, then, is the existence at the very heart of the disciplines of formal models upon which much else is constructed (Figures 2 and 4). Indeed, on the surface, these models appear almost identical. Both models lend themselves readily to a methodologically individualist paradigm of single seller and single buyer, or sender and receiver, interacting—obscuring the importance of groups, coalitions, and other power concentrations, as well as the various contexts within which the interactions take place. Significantly, both models abstract from the sources of potential asymmetries in power between seller and buyer or between sender and receiver.

Components of the two models bear striking surface similarities as well: The seller in the "market" seemingly corresponds to the message source or sender; the buyer and the message recipient appear analogous; the commodity flowing from buyer to seller appears to link the parties in a manner not unlike the way in which messages or information link sender and receiver. On this basis one might well ask whether communication studies is not then "really" but a special instance of the economist's market,[5] or conversely whether the economics model depicts but a special instance of an information flow, in which case commodities and money should more generally be viewed as messages or as information. (See Chapter 2).

Orthodoxies Contrasted: Blindspots Edge into Vision

Communication Interpretation of Market

The primordial model of a Communication System poses at least implicitly a number of profound questions concerning, for example: relationships between sender and message, between sender and medium, between codes and various other elements of the system, between medium and message (Innis's question), between medium and receiver (c.f., McLuhan), between message and receiver, between sender and receiver, and of course concerning how all these components interact in ongoing interdependence and mutual transformation. Mainstream communication researchers tend not to address all these questions, but they at least agree that the act of communication entails the exertion of influence, if not indeed control, by a sender over a recipient.[6]

To a communicologist, the economist's model of the market, for example, is but an instance of a communication system, and as such it depicts influence or control. Prices, of course, embody information to which buyers and sellers respond (and neoclassical economists would give assent to this). But, moreover, commodities are viewed by the communication scholar, even in the mainstream, as message carriers. Apparel, for instance, is analyzed by communicologists as language, with both "vocabulary" and "grammar." Its vocabulary includes hairstyles, accessories, jewelry, make-up, body decoration, and items of clothing. Like human speech, apparel comes in many languages where "dialects" and "accents" co-exist (Lurie, 1985, p. 4).

More generally, for communication scholars, consumer goods of all types carry and communicate meanings: "Clothing, transportation, food, housing exteriors and interiors, adornment, all serve as media for the expression of cultural meaning according to which our world has been constructed" (McCracken, 1988, pp. 71, 83). Very often commodities are purchased by buyers for the express purpose of communicating cultural meanings to third parties. In our economy sellers through advertising frequently attempt to attach meanings onto products as a ploy to stimulate sales, and it is often precisely these meanings that consumers hope will be transmitted to third parties in their "conspicuous consumption." Not infrequently commodities are symbolically endowed by their manufacturers with "magical" properties that will (it is implied but seldom stated directly) alleviate or resolve the most perplexing existential needs of users; through commercial imagery and incantations, manufacturers and advertisers communicate "healing" to buyers, dispensing brand-name soaps, soft drinks, and automobiles as potions or placebos (Williams, 1980, pp. 177-191).

A key area of administrative communication research investigates how advertising can be made more effective—that is, how sellers can more strongly influence tastes and buying behavior of message receivers. As far as administrative communication researchers are concerned, it is certainly not a question of denying influence or control, but rather one of discovering and deploying enhanced persuasive techniques.[7]

Economics and Communication in the Marketplace

Conceivably, the market model could induce neoclassical economists likewise to pose a broad array of questions concerning, for instance, the two-way interaction of seller and commodity, of seller and buyer; the ramifications for workers of being treated as mere commodity; indeed the consequences of mediating so many human interactions by money; the change in meaning for commodities of their being valuated solely in money terms; the range of impacts of different commodities on buyers, and so forth. While questions such as these are not avoided by political economists, neoclassicists either give perfunctory answers ("the value of a commodity *is* its money price"; "the commoditization of labor leads to efficiency in the flow of labor inputs"), or avoid such questions altogether. And for good reason!

If, to take just two examples, either the producer of the commodity or the commodity itself were deemed to affect tastes and preferences of buyers, then the harmonious and "simple system of natural liberty" proffered by Adam Smith would fall into disarray, and in its place would arise models comprising influence, powerplays, and disharmony.

Two renegade economists to have averred that producers and/or commodities indeed affect consumer tastes are John Kenneth Galbraith and Tibor Scitovsky. Galbraith's emphasis was on the manipulation by producers through advertising of consumers' tastes and preferences, contending caustically that the free market "protects not the individual's right to buy [but] the seller's right to manage the individual" (Galbraith, 1967, p. 217). Likewise Scitovsky noted that the use of products tends to habituate users, meaning that increased consumption will not necessarily increase welfare, but simply appease temporarily the pangs of addiction (Scitovsky, 1976, p. 136). Articulation of both positions poses formidable challenges to neoclassicism, decomposing its "psychic balm" (Samuels, 1990, p. xxvi).[8]

While at first glance, then, similarities abound between the two models—namely, the Market and the Communication System—closer inspection reveals that they are interpreted radically differently. Economists do not research "communication" at all. Indeed, in important respects, the economist's ideal is one of perfect *non*-communication! Communication *means* influence; communication *requires* that someone or something affect someone else or many others. These requirements are precisely what neoclassical economists decry as "imperfections" in the market—as instances of market power and hence of "market failure." In perfect competition (the ideal against which the economic 'real world' is measured or interpreted), no seller exerts any influence on any buyer or other seller. Rather, each is pushed and pulled by the "impersonal" forces that derive from aggregated, infinitesimally small influences of each participant.

Nor are commodities seen by neoclassical economists as having effects, that is, as constituting messages. Commodities, rather, are "inert," in the sense that buyers select them in accordance with price, incomes, and pre-established tastes and preferences. As the product wends its way from source to destination, buyer's attitudes toward the product and toward everything else remain unaffected, in the neoclassical model.

It is not merely consumer products in general that are for neoclassicists devoid of message-carrying properties. So too (implicitly) are books, film, TV and radio programs, news stories, and so forth. The commoditization of information (Mosco, 1989; Mosco & Wasko, 1988) means precisely that messages are produced as commodities for sale in the market, that buyers select messages in accordance with preexisting tastes and preferences (subject to budgetary constraints and relative prices), and that buyers' tastes and preferences remain uninfluenced by "consuming" the information. If these assumptions of minimal influence and control are not maintained, Smith's "simple system of natural liberty" gives way to political economy. No wonder Abraham Rotstein cautioned that "the pursuit of the economics of culture is not entirely an innocent endeavour that sheds light on dark corners; it carries with it some unexpected consequences" (Rotstein, 1988, p. 149).[9]

This is not to say that neoclassical economists are not cognizant of flows of information. They most assuredly are. The model of perfect competition, for example, assumes perfect information or perfect knowledge. For the economist relative prices, costs, and profits are pecuniary signals derived from aggregated economic activity, constituting an "invisible hand," directing flows of commodities and of factors of production. Anything that inhibits the generation of, or flows in such information makes for a less efficient allocation of resources (Stigler, 1968). But the price information circulating in markets, according to neoclassicists, is "objective," impersonal, and inconsequential as regards tastes, preferences, and attitudes. And, to repeat, it derives, not from the actions of single sellers or buyers alone, but from the aggregated activities of multitudinous sellers and buyers, each of whom on his or her own is inconsequential.

Recapitulation

It is to be concluded that it indeed makes a difference whether one is an economist or a communicologist, even in the mainstream. The former hypothesizes an impersonal, mechanistic world of individual autonomy and natural harmony; the latter envisages interdependence, influence, and control, even while providing analysis that furthers the capacity of those in power to maintain and extend the same. Communicologists would argue also that senders (sellers) necessarily alter psychic states of receivers inasmuch as messages are absorbed on account of novelty—otherwise no information has been imparted (Bates, 1989).

Political Economy

Not all economists are neoclassicists. Political economists, unlike their neoclassical siblings, place the question of power front and center. For them, as Frank Knight has written, "the central issue of economic policy is the distribution of power" (Knight, 1953, p. 282). Or, in the words of Galbraith, "Economics divorced from consideration of the exercise of power is without meaning and certainly without relevance" (Galbraith, 1983, p. xiii). Rather than reify markets, political economists look to a host of factors, particularly law and social relations, to explain market outcomes. The market for them is an artifact, a human institution. Like other institutions, it too can be modified to achieve different results. There is no spontaneity or automatism to the market, and to think this is to be blinded to the underlying framework of power, including the legal system, which conditions market forces (Samuels, 1971).

Moreover, political economists writing in or from an economics tradition, acknowledge the importance to economic affairs of the symbolic. Belief, knowledge, myth, "common sense," ideology—all contribute to the political economy framework within which goods are exchanged. Indeed, the very discipline of neoclassical economics can be interpreted and analyzed as a symbolic or rhetorical system, serving to condition the economic system that it purports to describe (Klamer et al., 1988; Samuels, 1990b; Daly & Cobb, 1989).

Institutional economist Clarence Ayres went even further when he advised that "all property rights derive from the *culture* which defines and honors them," making the task of the economist, in his view, one of comprehending "something of the nature and functioning of the ideology of our own society" (Ayres, 1989, pp. 29-30, emphasis added).

If not all economists are neoclassicists, neither are all communicologists administrative researchers. Non-administrative or "critical" communication scholars are of two persuasions: namely, cultural studies and political economy (Robins & Webster, 1987, pp. 71-89; Mosco, 1989, pp. 41-66). The former group, the cultural theorists, is concerned most with the "generation and circulation of meanings in industrial societies" (Fiske, 1987, p. 254). Political economists in the communication studies tradition, on the other hand, are less text centered, presuming rather matter-of-factly that hegemonic institutions will as a matter of course produce texts that maintain and extend their hegemony. Interest of these latter writers, therefore, is directed not only to the texts circulating in society, but as well to the "context" of cultural production—how the production of culture takes place; how it is organized, politically, economically, and institutionally; who produces it and why (Magder, 1989). Such scholars routinely question the justice of the current distribution of communicatory power, and analyze the consequences, broadly framed, of the deployment of the same.

It is with political economy, then, as stemming from both the economics and communication studies traditions, that the material and the symbolic, the economy and the culture, are conjoined. Political economy unites these two disciplines, which are only superficially similar in their mainstream forms.

In considering origins of political economy as melder or unifier of economics and communication studies it is instructive to turn to the early institutionalists, and in particular to Thorstein Veblen (1857-1929), an acknowledged founder of institutional and evolutionary economics (Ramstad, 1994; Samuels, 1987) and as such one who pioneered the integration, or perhaps more properly reintegration, of the symbolic and the material. Veblen's contributions to communication studies, however, while certainly more profound and extensive than those of John Dewey, for example, have been scarcely acknowledged.[10] In résumé, it may be noted that he placed institutions at the very center of his analysis, eschewing the methodological individualism of his economist colleagues. Institutions he defined as "widespread social habits" or as "habits of thought." For him "the gradual accumulation of small changes in man's habits of thought are responsible for all achievements of the race" (Mitchell, 1969, p. 605). It is important to study institutions, Veblen contended, because they alone explain societal change or evolution. Whereas generations of individuals differ little in terms of intellectual capacities or in instinctive propensities, institutions (ways of seeing or "habits of thought") undergo cumulative change, transforming culture, society and economy (Veblen, [1909] 1990).

Through his definition of institution, then, Veblen emphasized the importance of the symbolic and the communicatory for the study of economic affairs. Furthermore, in *The Theory of the Leisure Class*, Veblen pioneered an embryonic analysis of the symbolic or informational properties of consumer goods. He declared that commodities are demanded not merely for their utilitarian value, but also and primarily for their capacity to signal wealth and attract prestige. He argued,

In order to gain and hold the esteem of men it is not sufficient merely to possess wealth and power. The wealth or power must be put in evidence, for esteem is awarded only on evidence. ... Conspicuous consumption of valuable goods is a means of reputability to the gentlemen of leisure (Veblen, [1899] 1953, pp. 42, 64).

Third, Veblen contravened the neoclassicists' contention regarding the neutrality of money. Prices, for Veblen, are messages which affect (not merely reflect) the value placed on goods:

> Precious stones ... are more esteemed than they would be if they were more plentiful and cheaper. A wealthy person meets with more consideration and enjoys a larger measure of good repute than would fall to the share of the same person with the same record of good and evil deeds if he were poorer (Veblen, [1909] 1990, p. 246).

Like Chicago School contemporaries—John Dewey, Robert Park, Charles Cooley—but unlike modern-day administrative communication researchers, Veblen perceived communication as being more than the mere imparting of information or the exertion of influence on receivers. Communication for Veblen, as for John Dewey, was "the constitutive force in society;" communication was "the entire process whereby a culture is brought into existence, maintained in time and sedimented into institutions" (Carey, 1989, p. 144).

Parallels between Veblen and the Chicago theorists run deeper yet: Veblen, like Dewey, was under the thrall of Herbert Spencer's evolutionism and, as well, of his organic conception of society.

Dewey, Park, and Cooley have been singled out by several commentators as founders of the communication discipline (Czitrom, 1982; Carey, 1981; Delia, 1987; Robinson, 1984, 1986). In light of this all-too brief discussion, the omission of Thorstein Veblen's name from that honor roll is an incompleteness in need of rectification. Veblen's contributions to communication studies, therefore, are explored in greater depth below in Chapter 8.

Notes

This chapter first appeared in *Illuminating the Blindspots: Essays Honoring Dallas W. Smythe*, edited by Vincent Mosco, Janet Wasko, and Manjanuth Pendakur (Norwood, New Jersey: Ablex Publishing Corporation, 1993, pp. 15–39). This revised version is printed here by permission of Ablex Publishing Corporation.

1. The term administrative research was coined in 1941 by a leading (administrative) communication scholar of the day, Paul Felix Lazarsfeld, to denote research "carried through in the service of some kind of administrative agency of public or private character." He added that such research is intended generally to "solve little problems generally of a business character." As antimony to administrative research, Lazarsfeld posed "critical research," which he characterized as developing "a theory of the prevailing social trends of our times ... [and which implies] ideas of basic human values according to which all actual or desired effects [of media] should be appraised" (Lazarsfeld, 1941, pp. 158-160).

Critical scholar Dallas Smythe has located the differences between these two types of research in terms of *(a)* the types of problems selected, the former asking how an organization can do what it is doing more effectively, the latter questioning whether the organization should be doing this at all; *(b)* the research methods employed, the former being neopositivist, behaviorist, and individualist, the latter historical, materialist; and *(c)* treatment of results, the former ensuring they do not disturb the status quo, the latter inviting radical change. See Smythe & Van Dinh (1983).

2. As Wesley C. Mitchell has remarked, if economics starts with Adam Smith, it is "not because he represents the beginning of economic theory—he does not—but because his formulation was the earliest which exercised a potent influence upon the work of later times." Mitchell adds, "in large measure Adam Smith summed up and presented in superior form the contribution of his predecessors, and the people who have made constructive contributions to economic theory have in general not felt the need of going back earlier than *The Wealth of Nations* in their researches" (Mitchell, 1967, pp. 48-49).

3. In Georg Lukács's sense of the term, namely that the world of things appears to have "'a phantom objectivity', an autonomy that seems so strictly rational and all-embracing as to conceal every trace of its fundamental nature: the relation between people" (Lukács, 1971, p. 83).

4. See footnote 8 below and the associated discussion in the main body of the text.

5. Economics has in fact been termed the imperial science; its proponents claim applicability of neoclassical modes of analysis to an array of situations, including family planning, discrimination, marriage, divorce, suicide, addiction, and crime; see Becker (1976). For an appraisal of the dangers in such extensions see Rotstein (1988).

6. Shannon and Weaver, for example, defined communication as "all of the procedures by which one mind can affect another." Carl Hovland, likewise, stated that communication is "the process by which an individual (the communicator) transmits stimuli (usually verbal) to modify the behavior of other individuals (the audience)." Charles Morris defined communication as "making common of some property to a number of things. ...Whatever medium serves this purpose of making common is a means of communication (the air, a telegraph system, a language)." (See Forsdale, 1981, pp. 9-11; also Schramm & Roberts, 1971, pp. 1-53).

On the other hand, two groups of communicologists minimize the impact of senders' messages on receivers. On the administrative side the "law of minimal effects" has been around for nearly a half century, while among "radical" theorists the claim is sometimes made that subgroups of any culture are able to construct their own readings from any text, even those put out by hegemonic institutions. See, respectively, Katz and Lazarsfeld (1955), and Fiske (1987 and 1989). These theses of minimal effects are quite consistent with the Stigler/Becker thesis of note 9 below.

7. Here one of the central seeming paradoxes of administrative communication research comes to the fore. On the one hand, considerable attention of researchers has been focused on discovering means of making communication more "effective" (that is, persuasive). Likewise, billions of dollars are spent annually on advertising. Meanwhile, a public relations industry has been spawned that

thrives on the premise that attitudes, perceptions, and behavior of audiences can be manipulated to the advantage of message senders.

On the other hand, the "official" position of the communication discipline for years was one of "limited media effects." Indeed it was shortly after both the rise of Hitler, who employed loudspeaker and radio to mesmerize a nation, and broadcast of Orson Welles's *War of the Worlds* (Halloween 1938), sending millions into a panic, that Paul Felix Lazarsfeld developed the limited effects model of the media, which was then accepted uncritically by most administrative researchers for over 30 years (Chaffee & Hochheimer, 1985). The limited effects model, of course, helped deflect pressures from Hollywood studios and broadcast networks for increased media accountability by contending that media content was unimportant.

8. Note in this regard, George Stigler's seemingly desperate "reformulation" of the theory of consumer demand, illustrating well Thomas Kuhn's astute asseveration concerning the lengths to which "normal science" will go to buttress flagging theories under siege (Kuhn, 1970). In the current instance Stigler and colleague Gary Becker proposed that what consumers *really* demand are not "products" at all, but rather "commodities." Commodities they define as want-satisfying outputs *produced by the consumer,* using as inputs, not only products purchased in the market, but also the consumer's time, skill, training, other human capital, and other inputs. By thus reconstructing the theory of consumer demand the authors contended they had bypassed the dual problems of advertiser manipulation and product addiction. Changes in demand for products for Stigler and Becker are but surface phenomena since underlying tastes and preferences for commodities (they hypothesize) are unchanging and everlasting: "One does not argue over tastes for the same reason that one does not argue over the Rocky Mountains— both are there, will be there next year, too, and are the same to all men."

That the Stigler/Becker article fails, even on its own terms, can be seen by extracting from two juxtaposed paragraphs of its concluding section: "We claim, however, that no significant behavior has been illuminated by assumptions of differences in tastes. ... Needless to say, we would welcome explanations of why some people become addicted to alcohol and others to Mozart."

In the Stigler/Becker world "addiction" to Mozart vs. addiction to alcohol is of no "significant" difference; nor are the foregoing addictions "significantly different" from nonaddiction. See Stigler and Becker (1977, pp. 76, 89).

9. Some of the flavor of a neoclassical treatment of media can be gleaned from the following extract: "While the production of 'Hollywood-style' feature films or general interest magazines may suffer from a competitive disadvantage in Canada, it is unclear why such ventures should be promoted at the public expense, any more than Canadians should be expected to subsidize the growing of bananas in Canada" (Globerman, 1983, p. xxii).

10. Veblen, in American intellectual circles, was for years considered a *bête noire*, a "mad prophet." As noted by Horace Gray, "reactionary capitalistic interests, to protect their economic power, launched a vicious propaganda attack against Veblen; they elevated him to the godhead of all devils. ...Veblen was a wild man, a primitive, uncivilized creature, a libertine, an anarchist, a communist, a revolutionary conspirator. ... Some faculty men lost their posts for suspected Veblenism, others were denied appointments and promotions" (Gray, 1981,

pp. 104-107). One would hope that, in the 1990s, communication studies would have reached a level of maturity such that acknowledgment could now, if belatedly, be paid to one of the discipline's principal founders, however controversial he may have been.

5

On Political Economy

It is impossible to build true peace on abstractions.
                                        —Gabriel Marcel ([1952] 1978)

Neoclassicism and Political Economy

Political Economy, as a minimum, denotes the melding for comprehension and analysis of economy and polity, that is of business/financial affairs and legal/governmental processes. It is an important term to keep in mind in our day when mainstream (neoclassical) economists segregate for analytical purposes economy from power, and politics from business.

Intellectual fashion was not always thus. From publication of Adam Smith's *The Wealth of Nations* in 1776 until almost the beginning of the current century, economy and polity were united intellectually to form the classical discipline of political economy. Thomas Malthus, Jeremy Bentham, David Ricardo, John Stuart Mill, Karl Marx, as well as Adam Smith, were among the most renowned of the classical political economists.[1]

Bifurcation of economics and political science did indeed occur, however, around the turn of the century, giving rise to a circumscribed *neo*classical economics devoid of explicit political considerations, even though the market economy, "more than a system of resource allocation and income distribution, is a system of governance" (Bowes and Gintis, 1986, p. xi). Alfred Marshall's *Principles of Economics*, first published in 1890, probably went furthest in contributing to this fracture. Marshall had his marginalist precursors of course—notably Carl Menger, Stanley Jevons, and Léon Walras—but Marshall it was who turned what had been but an "esoteric" method making "little impression on the intelligent public or even upon most English economists" (Mitchell, 1969, p. 103), into mainstream doctrine. Neoclassicists since Marshall's time, enthralled by the seeming rigor of classical physics, have dedicated themselves to formulating and exploring purportedly timeless and universal economic laws (Daly and Cobb, 1989, pp. 25–8), leaving but little opportunity or incentive for acknowledging, let alone analyzing, human volition, human discretion, or asymmetries in the distribution and deployment of power.

Comparing Marshall's text with John Stuart Mill's earlier (1848) *Principles of Political Economy* Larry Wade, for example, remarked that Marshall's "is a book in which modern economic analysis predominates and is strikingly more consistent, rigorous and formal than Mill's" (Wade, 1983, p. 2). Marshall's formality was achieved through abstraction— abstraction, of course, from *singularities* in the phenomenal world; abstraction also, however, from *power* and *human volition*, considerations that would threaten the sought-after mechanicity, autonomy, and ubiquity of economic "laws;" and also abstraction from *change*, since the neoclassical enterprise is one dedicated to elaborating eternal verities.

Defenders of neoclassical modes of abstraction sometimes distinguish between the discipline of economics and economics as praxis; and as well between models and theories. *Models*, they assert, entail deductions from premises or axioms, and provided the logic is sound the models will necessarily be "absolutely true," at least in that limited sense (Bronfenbrenner, 1966, p. 9);[2] models may be taken as the domain of the economics *discipline* (Daly and Cobb, 1989, pp. 129-30). *Theories*, on the other hand, go a step further by claiming that given models are "reasonably applicable to a given set of situations" (Bronfen-brenner 1966, p. 9); when such claims are made, model builders engage in economics *praxis*. Milton Friedman, for example, ventured from discipline to praxis in declaring: "I have become increasingly impressed with how wide is the range of problems and industries for which it is appropriate to treat the economy *as if it were* competitive" (Friedman, 1962, p. 120; as quoted in Gramm, 1989, p. 289).

Dissidents to the neoclassical enterprise mount two principal critiques. First, they charge that in abstracting from change, from power, and from inequities in the distribution of wealth and income, neoclassicism becomes irrelevant. Adams and Brock have put it this way:

> [The modern economist's] primary concern seems to be not with the real problems of our times—poverty in the midst of affluence, the degeneration of our inner cities, the growing gap between rich lands and poor lands—but with esoteric model building. A prisoner of self-imposed categories of thought, the academic economist appears to dispense a conventional wisdom and recite an orthodox catechism. He seems to use the most sophisticated techniques to arrive at the most irrelevant conclusions (Adams and Brock, 1986, p. 12).

The second critique goes even further, dissidents warning that abstract, "descriptively false" (Friedman, 1953, p. 14) neoclassical models are lenses or filters distorting perceptions of reality: "If the only tool one has is a hammer," write Daly and Cobb, "then everything begins to look like a nail" (1989, p. 128). In less jocular manner neoclassicist Paul Samuelson made the same point: "When you adopt a new systemic model of economic principles, you comprehend reality in a new and different way" (Samuelson, 1967, p. 10, as quoted in Klamer, 1990, p. 136).

Viewing economic affairs through the neoclassical prism exaggerates the prevalence and efficacy of Market as Mechanism, and blinds spectators and analysts to problems of human suffering, and to the existence, use/misuse of economic power. Neoclassicist and Nobel laureate George Stigler stated as much in his acceptance speech: "Any preoccupation with fairness and justice is uncongenial to a science in which these concepts have no established meaning" (quoted in Lux, 1990, p. 161).

Dissidents to the neoclassical method of abstracting from power, change, and inequities may be called *political economists*. *Political economy*, as a minimum, seeks to reintegrate, for purposes of comprehension and analysis, the polity and the economy. By this minimalist definition, political economists address the impact of laws, regulation, political influence, and governmental processes on economic activity, and conversely the manner and degree whereby economic activity and financial matters impinge upon legislation and legislative processes. Political economy, then, as a minimum, denotes the study of power in economic affairs. It is indeed the study of the economy as a system of power.

Political economy, however, is often ascribed a broader meaning too. According to Clement and Williams (1989, p. 7) political economy entails the study of "processes whereby social change is located in the historical interaction of the economic, political, cultural, and ideological moments of social life, with the dynamic rooted in socio-economic conflict." Each of the key terms in the Clement/Williams definition serves to distinguish political economy radically from neoclassicism: "Social change," for example, contrasts with the neoclassical agenda of elaborating purportedly universal and timeless laws; "historical interaction" similarly contrasts with the purported timelessness, universality and ahistoricity of neoclassical analysis; "interaction" furthermore is the opposite of neoclassicists' penchant of hiving off the economy from political, cultural and ideological "moments of social life;" and finally "socio-economic conflict" contrasts with the neoclassical presumption of a harmony of interests.

In order to extend our depiction of political economy and to contrast it more fully with other modes of analysis, the following section describes three distinct schools or strands of political economy —liberal, Marxist, and institutionalist—concluding that all three bear the common characteristic of incorporating considerations of conflict, power, and dynamic change. Yet another common feature of these three political economies is their capacity to demythologize. Consequently the third section addresses three common mythologies of our day—Market, Technology, Evolution. These mythologies, as ideologies, are part and parcel of the current system of power, and hence political economy, as demystifier, challenges the established power system. The fourth section illustrates how political economy demythologizes, focusing particularly on these three myths. The final section, "Beyond Political Economy," hints at what else is needed, in addition to political economy, for harmony and justice in our world.

Increasingly political economists are turning to information and communication to analyze sources and dispositions of political/economic power. Communicatory power derives from and contributes to economic power as the foregoing remarks on mythology and ideology indicate. Those in control of the media of communication (including mainstream scholarship in universities) are among the most influential in the political economy; the messages they propagate help sustain and extend the pattern of dominance and economic control (Chomsky, 1989; Herman, 1989). The ensuing analysis is, therefore, of direct relevance to communication studies.

Three Strands of Political Economy

We can distinguish three distinct, yet related, "political economies": the liberal, the Marxist, and the institutionalist.[3] All three emphasize interrelations between legal and economic processes; all three, I will argue in a subsequent section, demythologize constructs whereby mainstream scholars skirt questions of equity and power in the phenomenal world; finally all three fit well with Clement's and William's more expansive definition of political economy, albeit in different ways. This section addresses these three streams of political economy in terms of founders, contemporary expositors, and main positions.

Liberal Political Economy

Liberal political economy, as a discipline distinct from moral philosophy, dates from 1776 and publication of Adam Smith's *The Wealth of Nations* (Lux, 1990, pp. 13-27; Mitchell, 1967, pp. 126-130). Smith's treatise on political economy is notable and perplexing inasmuch as, on the one hand, it heaped scorn on "self-love," particularly of business persons, and their propensity to exploit laborers and the poor (Gramm, 1989, pp. 297-8), while on the other it exalted "self-love" as agent or engine for prosperity for all. This paradox or tension in Smith's treatment of "self-love" redoubles when *The Wealth of Nations* is considered alongside Smith's *The Theory of Moral Sentiments* ([1759] 1966), a book of moral philosophy cele-brating beneficence or "sympathy" as the highest of human virtues.

Smith's immediate successors—classical political economists including Malthus, Ricardo, J. B. Say, and Nassau Senior—followed Smith's lead in lauding self-love's capacity to spur individual enterprise, but retreated from Smith's critical posture toward business persons and from his sympathy with the plight of workers. As Wesley Mitchell has remarked, to read Smith's classical successors today "is to become aware that the writers were far more keenly alive to the viewpoint of the employing class than to that of the mass of workers" (Mitchell, 1967, p. 506). Malthus, for example, opposed poor relief, social programs, alms giving, hospital care, and peace societies on grounds these contravened such natural checks to population growth as war, pestilence, famine, disease—checks, he perceived, a beneficent Providence had put in place to prevent over-population (Barzun, 1958, p. 63; also Chapter 7, below).

Today, humane liberal political economists faithful to the writings of Smith, and hence opposed to the class bias of many of his classical successors, advocate watchful and active anti-combines or antitrust policy to prevent and roll back agglomerations of business power. It was Smith's contention, assented to by modern liberal proponents of antitrust, that competitive markets are required to help turn private vices of greed and envy into the public virtue of economic prosperity for all—into a veritable "wealth of nations." Sensing each human heart to be afflicted to some degree at least by selfishness, contemporary humane liberal political economists remain apprehensive lest concentrated power put to self-serving ends inflict great injury. Far better, in the view of these analysts, to deconcentrate and decentralize economic decision-making in order to lessen the capacity of individuals to do harm, as well as to give greater play to the price system as impersonal allocator of goods and resources[4] (Adams, 1990, pp. 349-376).

Notwithstanding their advocacy of competitive markets as allocators of goods and resources in the economy, contemporary humane liberal political economists are cognizant also of the darker side of competition—that competition can mean elimination or subjugation of the weak by the strong in the struggle for survival. Humane liberal political economists hence are at pains to disassociate themselves from neo-conservative or neo-Darwinist positions, advocating rather both active government to preserve competition in the face of monopolistic pressures, and to enact social measures to redress economic and social inequities. Liberal political economy, then, whether of Adam Smith or of his humane contemporary interpreters, is a prescription for increased equality as well as for economic freedom (Adams and Brock, 1986).

Unfortunately, just as many of Smith's most articulate and influential classical followers lost sight of their master's sense of human dignity, so today neoconservatives may be characterized as selectively interpreting Adam Smith in ways that would further the capacity of the strong to oppress the weak. Far from viewing markets as devices to deconcentrate power and foster equality, neoconservatives put forth Market as neo-Darwinist Mechanism rewarding the strong, powerful, and efficient, and eliminating the weak, the disadvantaged, and inefficient, never mind the suffering and power concentrations that ensue. Elimination of the weak, to neoconservatives, ensures evolutionary progress, while concentration of power is for them a non-issue in the face of Market as omnipotent Mechanism (Stigler, 1988, p. 164).

Marxist Political Economy

For Karl Marx the humane liberal political economists' prescription of an active and ameliorative state ensuring competitive markets by opposing economic concentration would be sheer fantasy. In *Communist Manifesto* (1848) Marx with Engels declared, "the Executive of the modern state is but a committee for managing the common affairs of the whole bourgeoisie." In seeking to supply constantly expanding markets, Marx maintained, the capitalist class "agglomerates property, centralizes the means of production in large units and concentrates property in fewer and fewer hands," tendencies that require concomitant political centralization (Cole, 1967, p. 249). Moreover, under capitalism, labor is converted to mere commodity; in losing individuality, the worker becomes appendage to the machine, receiving a mere subsistence wage to ensure continued propagation of the species, a position assented to, incidentally, if not bemoaned by, classical liberal political economists including Malthus and Ricardo.

Rather than privileging the market as the *topos* or center of analysis, Marx proffered, even reified,[5] the process of production. Far from perceiving workers as being guided in freedom by an invisible hand to their workplace, Marx railed against the coercive power of the market system and particularly its capacity "to mobilize and allocate labor power for ends that are not those of the laborers themselves" (Heilbroner, 1990, p. 111). For Marx, exploitation would stop only when class relations based on private ownership of the means of production disappeared.

Contemporary Marxist and other radical analysts are less prone than was Marx to reify the mode of production. Theodor Adorno (1991), for example, did not claim that "conditions of production" *per se* determine people's thoughts and consciousness; rather, he turned to the "cultural industries" as means whereby hegemonic groups inculcate "useful" values and perceptions in the minds of the laboring populace. In modern

Marxism mass communication is seen as a system of indoctrination and propaganda. Indeed neoclassical economics is to be viewed as scholarly ideology in the service of hegemonic interests.

Institutionalist Political Economy

This third stream of political economy was born about 1900 through the work of Thorstein Veblen and John R. Commons and has been carried to the present by writers such as Harold Innis, Clarence Ayres, and John Kenneth Galbraith. In contradiction to neoclassicists, institutionalists deny "that scarce resources are allocated among alternative uses by the market" (Ayres, 1957, p. 26). For institutionalists, rather, "the real determinant of whatever allocation occurs in any society is the organizational structure of that society—in short, its institutions; at most, the market only gives effect to prevailing institutions" (Ayres, 1957, p. 26; quoted in Samuels, 1966, p. 248).

Cognizant that the economy is indeed occupied by large institutions and agglomerations of power, institutionalists deem neoclassical analysis unduly circumscribed, if not quite fantastic. Recognizing that institutions frequently conflict, institutionalists disparage neoclassicism for concentrating unduly on harmonious and mutually advantageous exchange relationships; equally, however, they upbraid Marxism for its (to them simplistic) class analysis. Finally, institutionalists view the economy as evolving, distinguishing them from neoclassicists who endeavor to elaborate universal, timeless laws; but dynamic change for institutionalists differs from Marxism too insofar as the former privilege non-class forms of conflict (that is conflict within as well as between classes) and evolving technology, while the latter posits dialectical materialism based on class conflict and inherent contradictions of capitalist production (Elliot, 1978; Gruchy, 1973).

If liberal political economists recommend deconcentration of economic power to allow for fuller play of competition, and if Marxists look forward to the overthrow of class relations by the elimination of private property, institutionalists have no such definite vision; institutionalists rather tend to be absorbed in the woof and warp of concrete reality of the present as it unfolds historically, and to view the economy/society as undergoing continual and cumulative change toward an undetermined future (Mitchell, 1969, pp. 657-8).

Mythologies

Mainline scholarship often mythologizes, either by deflecting attention from conflict and from the distribution and exercise of power by proposing an essential harmony of interests, or by justifying conflict and suppression of the disadvantaged by claiming such to be natural and unavoidable—the veritable Road to Progress, or the Order of Things. In this regard neoclassicists specialize in mythologizing Market, but they are not alone, as non-economists too evoke mythic concepts ultimately supportive of established power. Mythologizing as developed here is akin to idolatry in a religious context[6] and to reification[7] in a Marxist context. By invoking the Name, a *seeming* explanation is given, which *pari passu* cuts off further debate, averts the search for deeper explanation, and denies the efficacy of policy interventions.

Three "ultimate" explanations or mythologies are selected for discussion here: (1) Market; (2) Technology (*aka* Machine); (3) Evolution (*aka* 'March of Time'). Collectively these three mythologies may be referred to as *The Three M's.*[8] Each mythic doctrine has a famous progenitor—Adam Smith in the case of Market; Francis Bacon as regards Machine; and Herbert Spencer, extending the works of Darwin and Malthus, in the case of March of Time. Political economists, as we will see, characteristically "deconstruct" these myths to reaffirm the efficacy of human volition and discretion.

Market as Mythology

Despite Smith's status as political economist, elements of mythologizing can be detected in his magnum opus, *The Wealth of Nations*, particularly when considered apart from another of his major works, *The Theory of Moral Sentiments*. In *The Wealth of Nations* Smith proposed "an obvious and simple system of natural liberty," said to arise spontaneously from an innate human "propensity to truck, barter and exchange." Once generated, this system operates like an "invisible hand," channeling economic activity to a goal, namely promoting the wealth of nations, "which [is] no part the participant's intention." Indeed, to the contrary, "by pursuing his own interest [a person] frequently promotes that of society more effectually than when he really intends to promote it." On the basis of these brief but famous extracts it seems quite clear that Smith was prone to mythologizing.

But, as we have seen, Smith was a paradoxical writer. On the one hand, he was a moral philosopher, extolling benevolence and sympathy as the highest of human virtues and warning that even competitive markets need to be restrained by community and by shared values lest they undermine the social fabric. On the other, he was political economist, lauding greed and envy (in his words, "self-love"), as engines of economic prosperity.

It is in fact only in the paradoxes, the tensions, or in the dialectic, that Smith can be fully understood and appreciated. Appropriating or overemphasizing one side of Smith's paradox misconstrues Smith and leads to fundamentalist and ultimately bizarre positions. Since, however, Smith himself constructed a dialectic or tension between greed and empathy, he is ultimately absolved of mythologizing Market (See Gramm, 1989, pp. 285-289).

Not so today's neoclassicists. In discounting humanity's altruistic higher nature, and in celebrating only its greedy lower nature, neoclassicists mythologize Market. For in their abstractions, neoclassicists *assume* conditions ("perfect competition," perfect knowledge," zero transaction costs) under which selfish behavior evokes "perfect markets;" and from these initial premises, neoclassicists then demonstrate deductively that perfect markets indeed appear under the assumed conditions! This tautological strategy was referred to above as economic modeling. Neoclassicist Milton Friedman, for example, put forth the following as his model from which, in his opinion, "eternal verities" can be deduced:

> In its simplest form, such a society consists of a number of independent households—a collection of Robinson Crusoes, as it were. Each household uses the resources it controls to produce goods and services that it exchanges for goods and services produced by other households, on terms mutually acceptable to the two parties to the bargain (Friedman, 1962, p. 13; quoted in Lux, 1990, p. 162).

In Friedman's society, as noted by Lux (1990, p. 162), "no one can affect another except by that person's choice, and no one can impose unwanted costs on another. ... By conceiving of society as independent Robinson Crusoes, Friedman is able to avoid dealing with the moral and human dimensions of the unmoderated pursuit of self-interest."

Neoclassicists then mythologize Market: first by modeling imaginary worlds, populated by archetypically small firms and by calculating individuals, all with perfect knowledge, in which impersonal Market is all powerful (modeling); and secondly by proposing that said Market is operative and efficacious also in the phenomenal world (praxis).

Neoclassicists have proved highly influential, as governments privatize, deregulate, abandon antitrust, cut back social programs, and enter continental and indeed hemispheric "free trade" agreements. "Interventions," neoclassicists aver in Panglossian fashion, are unnecessary if not altogether undesirable; Market will allocate resources in the best of all possible ways.

Technology (Machine) as Mythology

With *Novum Organum* ([1620] 1952) and *New Atlantis* ([1617] 1952) Francis Bacon contributed substantially to an enduring Western proclivity to mythologize Science and Technology. "Access to the kingdom of man," wrote Bacon, "is founded on the sciences" (Bacon, [1620] 1952, p. 116).

From the premise that "Knowledge and human power are synonymous" (Bacon, [1620] 1952, p. 107), Bacon upheld the scientific way of knowing as the best means whereby nature could "more assuredly be subdued." Scientific knowing and the subduing of nature required, according to Bacon, relegation of the unique, the personal, and the intuitive to the private sphere, for true knowledge he opined is repeatable, objective, and observable.

The power gained from scientific knowledge ("technologies"), in Bacon's view, is "noble" and "wholesome," as compared to other outlets for humankind's innate proclivity to aggression: Politics he termed "vulgar" and "degenerate," whilst imperialism he deemed "covetous." Only scientific research culminates in power, not of some over others, but rather of "the human race itself over the universe" (Bacon, [1620] 1952, p. 135).[9]

In his inability or refusal to see that scientific knowledge and its technological outworkings can and do permit some to dominate others, Bacon fell into mythologizing. Scientific research, after all, is engaged in by the few, not the many, and generally through funding from powerful institutions that have their own agendas as to what is worth exploring and developing. Nor are the outworkings of scientific research—technologies and their infrastructures—controlled by humanity at large, but rather by the powerful few (Franklin, 1990). Power does not exist in Science or in Technology, but rather with those who control science and deploy technologies.

Not only did Bacon deem scientific pursuits to be more honorable than political and imperial ones, he also saw them as being of greater consequence. Three discoveries or innovations in particular—the printing press, gunpowder, and the magnet—Bacon wrote, "changed the whole face and state of things throughout the world ... insofar that no empire, no sect, no star seems to have exerted greater power and influence in human affairs than these mechanical discoveries" (Bacon, [1620] 1952, p. 135).

From the foregoing, certain commonalties between *The Wealth of Nations* and *Novum Organum* come to light. First, whereas Adam Smith proposed Market as an effective device for amassing wealth and riches, Bacon advanced Science and Technology.[10]

Second, just as Smith credited Market with transforming odious greed into public virtue, so did Bacon perceive scientific pursuits as turning innate will-to-power from ignoble political and imperial goals into honorable and wholesome ones.

Third, while Smith deemed Market to function as an invisible hand, impersonally and potently directing economic affairs, Bacon viewed the practical outworkings of scientific knowledge—Technologies—as most powerful influences, causing politics and religion to pale in comparison.

Finally, Smith's contention that Market creates a harmonious system of reciprocal aid is paralleled by Bacon's assertion that through scientific knowledge "the human race itself" exerts dominion over the universe.

Mystifications inaugurated by Bacon remain commonplace today. Surely it is the common connotation of media coverage of Science and Technology that humankind progresses lock-step with each scientific advance (Nelkin, 1987). Meanwhile for writers such as Leslie White (1949), Daniel Bell (1977), Marc Porat (1978), and Alvin Toffler (1981), Technology is *the* organizing principle, the self-propelling power, the *deus ex machina*, upon which all else depends. These writers mythologize Technology as they privilege It as Ultimate Explanation for the order of things, much as neoclassicists privilege Market (Babe, 1990, pp. 247-258).

Evolution (March of Time) as Mythology

Building on the work of Thomas Malthus, Charles Darwin proposed:

Thus, from the war of nature, from famine and death, the most exalted object of which we are capable of conceiving, namely the production of higher animals, directly follows. There is grandeur in this view of life (quoted in Barzun, 1958, p. 15).

Darwin maintained that Natural Selection, the elimination of the weak through death, motivates progress, i.e. the ascent of life forms. Natural Selection in the biosphere is then the analogue of Market in the economic sphere. While Darwin's "theory" of natural selection has been shown to be mere tautology, devoid of predictive power (Koestler, 1979, pp. 165-192; Macbeth, 1971; also Popper, 1963), nonetheless, it retains today great rhetorical power: the very words, Evolution and Natural Selection seem to embody Ultimate Explanation.[11]

In the hands of Herbert Spencer (1820-1903) Evolution and Natural Selection were extended well beyond the biological to the realms of ideas, psychology, society, ethics, and morals. Each perceivable object, wrote Spencer, has a past and will have a future—a coming into being and a passing from existence. The coming into being and the associated gain in coherence and complexity Spencer termed Evolution; the decline in complexity, dissipation of coherence and eventual passing away he termed Dissolution (the more modern word being "entropy"). All things that exist, he wrote, have histories and futures that embrace Evolution and Dissolution (Spencer, 1904).

Spencer, like Malthus before him, was spokesperson for what came to be known as Social Darwinism, the doctrine that progress in biological, economic, and social life is automatically assured through Natural Selection, whereby the strong and efficient persevere whilst the deficient are condemned to extinction. In this "Progress Principle" Spencer claimed to have discovered if not the ultimate organizing principle of reality, then at least the Penultimate One.[12]

Of powerful intellects influenced by Spencer, John Dewey is especially notable (Czitrom, 1982, pp. 91-121). While he and his associates (particularly Charles Cooley and Robert Park) accepted Spencer's organic, evolutionary conception of society, they were appalled by his version of Natural Selection, substituting in its place Instrumentalism as the dynamic force underlying social change. Instrumentalism is the belief that all forms of human activity are instruments to solve problems, whether individual or social. Since problems change continually, Dewey maintained, so must the instruments. Through instrumentalism, then, Dewey helped inspire a doctrine of inevitable progress through Technological Evolution, a belief now current and widespread (Weizenbaum, 1979; Winner, 1977).

Subsequent years have seen a corruption in the sophistication characterizing Dewey's analysis, pundits espousing reductionist, and essentially mythological versions of Technological Evolution (see Winner, 1979; also Chapters 10 and 11, this volume). The following from Arthur C. Clarke is perhaps the apotheosis of this corruption:

> Can the synthesis of men and machine ever be stable, or will the purely organic component become such a hindrance that it has to be discarded? If this eventually happens—and I have ... good reasons for thinking that it must—we have nothing to regret and certainly nothing to fear. The Tool we have invented is our successor. Biological evolution has given way to a far more rapid process—technological evolution. ... No individual exists forever; why should we expect our species to be immortal? Man, said Nietzsche, is a rope stretched across the abyss. That will be a noble purpose to have served (Clarke, 1964, pp. 212, quoted in Winner, 1977, p. 138).

Political Economy Critique

The Three M's—Market, Machine, and March of Time—constitute the base of today's neoconservativism. Each implies automaticity and inevitable betterment, if government would only leave things alone. Market to neoconservatives is the "invisible hand" that allocates resources in the most efficient way possible, rewarding the meritorious with financial success and growth while eliminating the inefficient. Likewise Technology, as the very embodiment of knowledge, is seen as conditioning human interaction—cultural as well as economic: If there are concentrations of power, Technology requires it; if a de-industrialization is taking place in North America, a Tide of "New Technologies" requires it. Humanity, neoconservatives contend, has departed the era of biological evolution and entered an era of Technological Evolution, the guiding force, or invisible hand of Natural Section bringing about ever higher states of being.

By positing abstract, omnipotent Mechanisms like Market, Technology, and Evolution as being in charge of human affairs, neoconservativism annihilates the pursuit of justice. It also constitutes a mystical apologia for inequity, environmental degradation, and imperialism. Neoconservativism is then an ideology comprised of mythologies that make appear as inevitable, and hence as good, the sacrifice of many for the benefit of the few.

Political economy, on the other hand, unmasks the Powers—whether Market, Machine, or March of Time—by recontextualizing powerplays, conflict, and domination through reaffirmations of free will and the efficacy of human intervention.

Market, for example, to political economists is not some ineluctable force that holds sway over human interaction. Markets, rather, for political economists, are artifacts. Market forces function only within the context of the legal system. "Property and law are born together and die together," noted classicist Jeremy Bentham. "Before laws [including common laws] were made, there was no property; take away laws, and property ceases" (Bentham, [1830] 1978, p. 52). Modern political economists affirm Bentham's insight.

This is not to suggest that political economists are necessarily in agreement as to what sort of markets should be constructed. Liberal political economists recommend competitive markets sustained by vigorous antitrust policy. Marxist political economists, maintaining that class relations devolve from property relations, recommend greater common as opposed to private property. Institutionalists probe beyond property rights to explore religious belief, educational systems, tradition, cultural systems, and so forth as conditioning markets, and tend to make policy recommendations on a case-by-case basis.

Despite differences, marked as they are, all three schools of political economy maintain that markets are contingent and hence subject to alteration through the exercise of human volition and discretion. If current market arrangements lead to environmental devastation, then, political economists affirm, new markets can be devised to permit a more sustainable development (Daly and Cobb, 1989). If current markets tolerate huge agglomerations of economic power, new markets can be constructed to promote equity (Adams and Brock). If current markets exploit the poor and sanction widespread poverty, unemployment, and hunger, then new ones can be fabricated which generate greater justice (Lux, 1990).

Likewise with regard to *Technology.* Political economists do not side with Francis Bacon, who maintained that scientific knowledge and its practical outworkings represent power possessed by humankind; nor do they propose, along with Arthur C. Clarke, an autonomous technological evolution leading to inevitable betterment. Rather, political economists of all three schools acknowledge scientific research and the development and deployment of technologies to be part and parcel of the struggle for power—not only of humanity over nature, but also of some people, firms, and nations over others.

This is not to say that the three schools of political economy treat technology in the same way. For liberal political economists, technological innovation is an outcome of rivalry among firms and industries; technological innovation for liberal economists is an effective way of breaking down monopolies reliant upon older means of production, provided governments do not sanction restrictive trade practices or enact protective measures (Irwin, 1984; Schumpeter, 1962). For Marxist and radical scholars, technological development consists in the displacement of skilled workers by automated processes as part of a continuing process of domination of labor by capital (Garson, 1988; Franklin, 1990); radicals also perceive that technologies can allow for greater control by hegemonic groups over the flows of information, and hence over consciousness, domestically and internationally (Schiller, 1989; Wilson, 1988). For institutionalists such as Harold Innis ([1950] 1972, [1951] 1971) technological change is induced by the quest for monopoly power, but gives rise to wide-ranging, unintended cultural, economic, and social effects; technological evolution is an outcome of the distribution of and struggle for power.

Beyond Political Economy

Political economy, then, de-illusions us: It highlights rather than obscures the reality of human volition. Nor does it sanction asymmetries in the distribution of power by invoking Abstract Powers. Rather it asks three basic questions: Who gains? Who loses? Who decides? Political economy's realism is then essential to informed policy.

But, even the realism of political economy does not suffice to lead us from our present darkness to a world of justice, peace, and sustainability. Political economy as such knows nothing of altruism, mercy, forgiveness, redemption, self-restraint, understanding, peace. While it views the world as a struggle for power and aligns itself with the underprivileged, it is unable to transcend that struggle in the present.

What is required, also, is a "public philosophy" (Lippmann, 1955) — a belief, a faith, a hope that transcends mere greed and will to power by recognizing the ultimate dignity and equality of all human beings

(Tinder, 1989, pp. 27–34). This recognition or belief flies in the face of observable differences in capacities, attainments, and circumstances. It flies in the face certainly of the three M's. It derives from a belief in destiny, in existence beyond the immediate, the material, and the observable. Political economy provides no ground for this belief, and indeed in its cruder materialist formulations can be quite inimical to such a belief.

According to Glen Tinder, for example, Marx's was an "illogical humanitarianism" (Tinder, 1989, p. 49). While certainly incensed by the squalor in which working people were forced to live, his thorough-going materialism provided no philosophical ground for treating *all* humans with dignity. Likewise, Veblen's materialism may have robbed him of even a sense of *self*-worth. (See Chapter 8, below).

Consider also Adam Smith. He at least knew that the greed ("self-love") he exalted in *Wealth of Nations* needed to be restrained, not only by competitive markets but also by—why by *Moral Sentiments*. Smith's *Wealth of Nations* and *Moral Sentiments* remain in dialectical tension to this day because political economy alone gives little indication as to how peace with justice, or justice with peace, can be achieved.

Clues as to what is needed are provided by Glenn Tinder in advising us to learn from the Jews as well as the Greeks. For the ancient Hebrews, the universe was personal. No abstract, changeless, impersonal laws or principles like Natural Selection or Market governed events for them. Rather Ultimate Reality was to be glimpsed as through a glass darkly in the uniqueness of the events themselves (Tinder, 1989, pp. 75, 68).

Whereas the Greeks and their successors—Bacon, Spencer, Darwin, Smith, Malthus, Marshall—were preoccupied with finding causal, time-less, and universal laws that determine all particulars, the Hebrews found it sufficient to "remember and tell what had happened," to embrace the unique, and to glimpse reality through the singularities of historical unfolding (Tinder, 1989, pp. 75, 68).

Only by exalting the particular in its uniqueness can political economy contribute to the pursuit of both justice *and* peace.

Notes

This chapter first appeared under the title, "Neoclassicism and Political Economy" in *Mediating Culture: The Politics of Representation*, edited by Kosta Gouliamos and William Anselmi. 1994, pp. 13–45. Republished, with revisions, by permission of Guernica Editions Inc.

1. Adam Smith defined political economy as "a branch of the science of a statesman or legislator [that] proposes two distinct objects: first, to provide a plentiful revenue or subsistence for the people, or more properly to enable them to

provide such a revenue or subsistence for themselves—and secondly, to supply the state or commonwealth with a revenue sufficient for the public services." Quoted in Mitchell (1967, p. 39).

2. Francis Bacon (1561-1626) whose scientism is discussed later in this chapter, critiqued such deductive systems, derisively calling them "idols of the theatre... so many plays brought out and performed, creating fictitious and theatrical worlds" (Bacon, 1952, p. 110).

3. Perhaps note should be made here of a fourth movement sometimes known as the "new political economy," which attempts to enfold legislative processes and policy within the assumptions, principles, modes of analysis, and indeed vocabulary of neoclassical economics (Staniland, 1985, pp. 1-9). The appellation "political economy" seems most unsuited for this endeavor, however, insofar as the "political science" being absorbed is necessarily abstracted from considerations of power and conflict.

4. To the question whether masses of people may not also *en masse* set in motion injurious trajectories, humane liberal political economists would be inclined to recite Lord Acton's dictum of *power* being the corrupting force. There is, then, perhaps a certain Rousseaunian romanticism to humane, liberal political economy.

5. In *Critique of Political Economy* (1859) Marx wrote: "The method of production in material life determines the general character of the social, political, and spiritual processes of life. ... It is not the consciousness of men that determines their being, but, on the contrary, their social being determines their consciousness." (Quoted in Barzun 1958, p. 133).

6. One is reminded here of Dostoevsky's dictum, "A man cannot live without worshipping something," to which Glenn Tinder adds, "Anyone who denies God must worship an idol—which is not necessarily a wooden or metal figure" (Tinder, 1989, p. 50).

7. Reification, according to Georg Lukács, occurs when "a relation between people takes on the character of a thing, and this acquires a 'phantom objectivity,' an autonomy that seems so strictly rational and all-embracing as to conceal every trace of its fundamental nature: the relation between people" (Lukács, 1971, p. 83).

8. The author thanks Dann Downes for suggesting the alternate alliterative appellations.

9. He wrote further: "The benefits derived from inventions may extend to mankind in general, but civil benefits to particular spots alone; the latter, moreover, last but for a time, the former forever. Civil reformation is carried on without violence and confusion, whilst inventions are a blessing and a benefit without injuring or afflicting any"(Bacon, [1620] 1952, p. 135).

Bacon obviously did not anticipate high-tech wars, assembly lines, environmental devastations, or mass media of propaganda.

10. "The real and legitimate goal of the sciences is the endowment of human life with new inventions [i.e. "technologies"] and riches" (Bacon, 1952, p. 120).

11. As with the following example where George Basalla applies the Darwinian theory of Natural Selection to historical considerations of technologies. Basalla declares: "In support of Darwin's theories, biologists have proceeded to identify and name more than 1.5 million species of flora and fauna and have *accounted for this diversity* by means of reproductive variability and natural selection. ... *A theory*

that explains the diversity of the organic realm can help us account for the variety of things made" (Basalla, 1988, pp. 1, 2; emphasis added).

12. "The Ultimate Cause cannot in any respect be conceived because it is in every respect greater than can be conceived. ... The reality existing behind all appearances is, and must ever be, unknown" (Spencer, 1966, pp. 81, 50).

6

Information, Economics, and Ecosystem

The world can, in effect, get along without natural resources.

—Robert M. Solow, Nobel laureate in economics (1974)

Overview of Themes

Integration of Economics and Ecology

In 1987 the United Nations' World Commission on Environment and Development (WCED), chaired by Gro Harlem Bruntland, published its report, *Our Common Future*, on environment, growth, and development, advising that "many of the development paths of the industrialized nations are clearly unsustainable." According to the WCED, "today we are close to many ... thresholds; we must be ever-mindful of the risk of endangering the survival of life on Earth" (WCED, 1987, pp. xii, 33).

Our Common Future reviewed yet again environmental strains with which we have become all too familiar: the greenhouse effect or threat of global warming, attributable primarily to the burning of fossil fuels and the cutting and burning of forests; depletion of stratospheric ozone, due principally to the release of chlorofluorocarbons (CFC's); the killing of trees and lakes through air pollutants (acid rain); desertification of arable land (each year 6 million hectares are degraded to desert-like conditions); the dumping or leaking of chemicals and other toxins into land and water, poisoning the food chain; and drastic reductions in genetic diversity (annually 11 million hectares of tropical forests are destroyed, utterly extinguishing plant and animal species).

For the authors of the report, poverty and wealth alike contribute, albeit in different ways, to environmental degradation. Extreme poverty forces people to eke out existence as best they can—for instance by over-cultivating arable land or by clear-cutting rain forests—irrespective of long term environmental damage. Conversely, wealth encourages people to over-consume and hence deplete resources, to use disproportionate amounts of energy, and thereby generate pollution per capita in quantities far exceeding average levels.[1]

Cognizant of the contributions of rich and poor alike to the environmental crisis, the WCED counseled that henceforth "economics and ecology must be completely integrated in decision-making and lawmaking processes." After all, the report noted, the economy and the ecosystem are completely "integrated in the workings of the real world" (WCED, 1987, pp. 37, 62).[2]

Information, Communication, and Environment

This chapter is written in the spirit of pursuing Bruntland's goal of integrating economics and ecology in decision-making. In this regard, the chapter proposes infusing standard economics with more expansive and realistic conceptions of information/communication. Information in the real world, as argued below, constitutes an essential link between the economy and the ecosystem.

However, since mainstream or neoclassical economics gives inadequate and reductionist treatments to information and communication, an unfortunate bifurcation between economics and ecology has resulted. Mainstream economics, in fact, is quite antithetical to ecological considerations on account of deficiencies in its conceptualization of information/communication. Neoclassicism routinely postulates that all information required for economic decision-making can be, in principle, encapsulated in market prices, and further that communication relevant for economic decision-making consists entirely of market transactions. Reducing information/communication to matters of price and commodity exchange, however, necessarily reduces as well Nature (in the economics literature termed "land") to mere commodity, masking the true, vital nature of human/ecosystem interactions.

As a general principle, a subsystem can never give adequate expression to, or embody, the complexities of the system of which it is mere component.[3] Since markets exist only within, and because of, the larger ecosystem, it follows that notions of price and commodity exchange, however satisfactory (or for that matter unsatisfactory) they may be for understanding economic processes narrowly construed, will fail utterly to capture the complexities of the larger system (here the ecological), and of system/subsystem interactions.

Put more positively, this chapter argues that conceptions of information/communication that are fuller and more realistic than those employed by neoclassicism lead to a fuller and more realistic understanding of the complexities of ecosystem/economy interactions, and hence make more likely policies consistent with "sustainable development."[4] As intimated elsewhere, however, introducing fuller conceptions of information/communication to neoclassicism necessarily transforms neoclassicism into political economy. (See particularly Chapter 4).

Broadening conceptions of information beyond mere price, and deepening notions of communication beyond mere commodity exchange, open new possibilities for comprehending economy/ecosystem interactions. Three of these ways, listed now, are addressed in the third section of this chapter. First, viewing information as negentropy (that is, as negative entropy) not only highlights production, distribution, and consumption as being foundationally informational and communicatory, but as well draws attention to ineluctable entropic consequences of all material production. Second, positing matter-energy-information as elemental factors of production, in place of the more traditional triad of land-labor-capital, makes abundantly evident the inseparability of economy and ecosystem. Third, treating information as perception of pattern and as power means that human symbolic systems establish cultural paradigms, for instance of value and of the good life, once more conjoining economy and ecology through informational/communicatory processes.

The fourth and final section, drawing on preceding analyses, provides rudiments of an eco-centered communication strategy, focusing on communication policies regarding mass media and telecommunications, and proposing that a communitarian economics be developed to supersede the neoclassical.

The overriding conclusions of this chapter are first, that neoclassical modes of analysis, which characteristically minimize or reduce considerations of information/communication, are inadequate for integrating economics and ecology in ways conducive to long term sustainability; second, that interrelations between economic and ecological processes constitute information/communication policy issues, since information/communication are of the essence in conjoining economy and ecosystem; and third, that by at least partially *decommoditizing* economic activity generally, and communicatory processes in particular, and in approaching more closely a gift or communitarian economy, an ecologically more sustainable future *is* possible.

The Environment and Communication in Neoclassicism

Forerunners: Marshall and Pigou

In *Principles of Economics* (first edition, 1890) Alfred Marshall opened a door for economists to consider economy-ecosystem interactions.

Marshall introduced the concept of *external economies*, that is, cost savings per unit of production accruing to a firm as a result of increases in industry-wide production (Marshall, [1890] 1947, p. 266; see also Mishan, 1971a, p. 1). Marshall maintained that individual firms could benefit from industry-wide growth by being able to access a more highly trained work force, through higher health standards, and on account of improved infrastructure.

Externalities, then, denote the notion that benefits (and costs) experienced by one firm or individual can depend *directly* on activities of others.[5] It needs to be noted at this point that, from an ecosystem perspective, Marshall's conception of externalities, seminal though it was, was deficient insofar as he posited only third party savings or benefits, omitting entirely consideration of third party costs or harms.

Subsequent to Marshall externalities remained unexplored within the mainstream economics literature until A. C. Pigou, a disciple of Marshall, reintroduced them in *The Economics of Welfare* (1920). There Pigou focused on discrepancies between individual economic interests and interests of the community, explaining that even in purely competitive economies private and social interests can diverge. Smoke from a factory for instance, Pigou elucidated, imposes costs on third parties in terms of "injury to buildings and vegetables, expenses for washing clothes and cleaning rooms, expenses for the provision of extra artificial light, and in many other ways" (Pigou, [1920] 1932, p. 184). In all such instances, Pigou suggested, welfare would be increased if governments took measures to narrow the gap between "marginal social net product" and "marginal private net product" (Pigou, [1920] 1932, pp. 131–135). Running through Pigou's analysis, then, was an appeal for an activist government; Pigou simply did not believe that market forces automatically produce optimal results.[6]

Neoclassical reaction to Pigou's environmentalism has been of two sorts. One group of neoclassicists, represented here by Ronald Coase, Milton Friedman, Harold J. Barnett & Chandler Morse, endeavored to depict, whether explicitly or implicitly, Pigou's work as being either faulty or trivial. A second, and now much larger group, known as "environmental economists," extended Pigouvian analysis to recommend various means of commoditizing or pricing environmental degradations in order to bring them within the ambit of market activity. Both approaches are treated critically in this section. For a world beset by environmental decay, the second approach, on the surface, may well seem more beneficent than the first but, it is argued, neither suffices; indeed, both are fundamentally flawed and dangerous. The approach recommended here, therefore, is that of an *ecological economics*, an economics that places ecological considerations at the very heart of the analysis. See, for example, Daly and Cobb (1989), and Daly (1991).

Neoclassical Denials

The Coase Theorem. Ronald Coase was the first to challenge the Pigouvian doctrine that factories belching smoke necessarily produce gaps between private and social interests. Moreover, Coase disputed Pigou's contention that governments should normally set about closing such gaps (in the event they indeed exist) by taxing pollution or polluters. At the heart of Coase's analysis, as will be developed below, is a reductionist conception of information/communication. Let us, then, explore Coase's argument in a bit more detail.

According to Coase, a polluter cannot inflict damages unless people are present to suffer injury, which is to say that, in his view, polluter and victim are *reciprocally responsible* for damages, the former by producing noxious emissions, the latter by virtue of mere propinquity. Therefore, Coase concluded, on the basis of simple justice, questions of economic efficiency aside, there need be no *a priori* presumption that the party *emitting* the pollution should bear legal liability for damages; rather, the principle of co-responsibility points to the victim also as being to blame.[7]

Satisfied, therefore, that considerations of justice provide no guidance on how to frame environmental legislation, Coase turned next to the criterion of economic efficiency, and from that perspective addressed two prototypical situations. The first comprised "perfectly functioning markets" (i.e., pure competition, perfect knowledge, zero transactions costs) for which, Coase opined, *all possibility* of externalities by definition are precluded. He provided a simple numerical example of wandering cattle destroying neighboring crops to prove his point, the essentials of his argument being as follows: If legal liability for damages is imposed upon the polluter (cattle rancher), free contracting will enable the polluter to bribe those harmed into agreeing to allow continuation of polluting activities, and the polluter will have incentive to proffer a bribe of such magnitude that the marginal benefit of being able to continue the noxious activity at any given level just equals the added costs experienced on account of having to pay additional money in a bribe. Likewise, those damaged by pollution will find it advantageous to accept a bribe of such magnitude that the last dollar received slightly more than compensates for damages wrought by incremental pollution. On the other hand, if the legal system does not impose on the polluter liability for damages, free contracting, Coase averred, will permit those being damaged to bribe the polluter into cutting back production; and, moreover, aggrieved parties will find it beneficial to offer bribes of such magnitude that the marginal benefit they attain from a further decrease in pollution just exceeds the cost of bribing the polluter with an extra dollar.

Next came Coase's *pièce de résistance*. By comparing the two instances—the first being the situation where liability resides with the polluter, the second envisaging no such liability—an obviously satisfied Coase concluded: "The ultimate result (which maximizes the value of production) is independent of the legal position if the pricing system is assumed to work without cost" (Coase, 1960, p. 8). For perfectly competitive markets—those with perfect competition, with perfect information, and with zero transactions costs—then, Coase (and neoclassicism) concluded, it does not matter whether or not the law ascribes liability for pollution since the market commoditizes pollution so as to ensure that only "optimal" amounts will be produced.

Coase's second situation concerned imperfectly competitive markets beset by transactions costs. In such circumstances, he agreed, private bargaining will not automatically bring about "optimal" results. Nonetheless, he cautioned, it could still be better for governments *not* to act than to impose liability on the polluter as recommended by Pigou. Imposing liability for pollution on the polluter, Coase remonstrated, redounds to third parties (employees, suppliers, and customers) as an "externality" (Coase, 1960, p. 42). Better, perhaps, that those experiencing the consequences of pollution continue to bear the full cost.

Coase of course can be critiqued. Objections can be raised, for instance, to his rather infantile conception of justice and to the blind eye he cast, perhaps unwittingly, toward the possibility, nay likelihood, of extortion. Second, even under the purely competitive conditions that he assumed, the Coasean system of bribery can *increase* pollution levels. As noted by Fisher and Peterson, "under plausible assumptions though the bribe does indeed reduce emissions *per* firm, it will tend to *increase* them at the industry level." New firms will find it profitable to enter an industry now enriched by bribes (Fisher and Peterson, 1976, p. 15, emphasis in original).

Third, the Coasean examples were all typically trivial. In addition to cattle trampling a neighbor's crops Coase explored, for instance, a case where damages were inflicted "by a person keeping an unusual and excessive collection of manure in which flies bred and which infested a neighbour's house," for which Coase pronounced that the economic problem centered on "ownership of the flies" (Coase, 1960, p. 37).[8] In the Coasean world, in other words, there are no Three Mile Islands, no Love Canals, no Persian Gulf Wars, no Chernobyls, no Exxon Valdezes, no Bophals. Coase's marginalist techniques confined him to weighing the merits of one less cow *vs.* one more cow; a slightly smaller or a slightly larger pile of manure.

Fourth, in typical neoclassical fashion, Coase assessed benefits and costs of alternative courses of action from the standpoint of individual, not social or collective human preferences. Nor did he incorporate in his analysis considerations of ecological balance. Indeed his illustrative benefit/cost analyses presumed perfect knowledge of outcomes flowing from alternative courses of action, a most inappropriate assumption for ecological matters. Finally, he presumed that all relevant information can be incorporated in market prices and that market transactions constitute sufficient means for communicating such information. None of these assumptions or modes of analysis is warranted, and fundamental criticisms of them are developed below.

George Stigler, a Nobel laureate, thought so highly of Coase's environmentalist contribution, however, that he afforded the so-called Coase Theorem (a neologism, incidentally, for which Stigler assumed credit) a chapter, suitably entitled "Eureka," in his slender autobiography. But even Stigler, like-minded though he was, granted that Coase's work possesses a certain air of the fantastic.[9] Indeed, it might very well be dismissed altogether as simply the musings of a crank were it not for the prominence it has been afforded within mainstream economics circles, as indicated by the awarding to Coase, largely on the basis of this "seminal" article, of the Nobel prize for economics.[10]

Friedman and the "Subversiveness" of Social Responsibility. For Milton Friedman, dean of neoclassicists and also a Nobel laureate, "there is one and only one social responsibility of business—to use its resources and engage in activities designed to increase its profits so long as it stays within the rules of the game, which is to say, engages in open and free competition without deception or fraud" (Friedman, [1970] 1985, p. 25).[11] For Friedman, a business manager unethically spends other people's money when he or she makes "expenditures on reducing pollution beyond the amount that is in the best interest of the corporation or that is required by law in order to contribute to the social objective of improving the environment." To recommend that business managers be "socially responsible" and *voluntarily* cutback noxious emissions, Friedman admonished, is to be "fundamentally subversive" (Friedman, [1970] 1985, p. 25). Far better, in his view, that stockholders, customers and workers voluntarily "spend their own money on the particular action if they [choose] to do so" (Friedman, [1970] 1985, p. 22).

Indeed, Friedman castigated the "doctrine of 'social responsibility'" as nothing less than "pure and unadulterated socialism" (Friedman, [1970] 1985, pp. 23, 21). For him, voluntary curtailment of pollution involves "acceptance of the socialist view that political mechanisms, not market mechanisms, are the appropriate way to determine the allocation of scarce resources to alternative uses" (Friedman, [1970] 1985, p. 23).

For Friedman and Coase alike, then, unalloyed individual maximizing behavior in markets leads to optimal resource flows, even in a world beset by pollution and resource depletion.[12]

Barnett, Morse, and Uniformity of Matter-Energy. An oft-cited 1963 book, *Scarcity and Growth: The Economics of Natural Resource Availability* by Harold J. Barnett and Chandler Morse, is a neoclassical mainstay on why one need not be concerned with regard to the economy's impact on the ecosystem. According to the authors the earth's resources, when considered in the context of human knowledge and evolving technology, are essentially infinite. Whereas in a preceding era resources may perhaps have been constrained on account of low levels of human knowledge and technology, such is no longer the case. Rather, they contend, human knowledge has transformed the earth's crust and broadened humanity's resource base to encompass "such ubiquitous materials as sea water, clays, rocks, sands, and air" (Barnett and Morse, 1963, p. 10). In brief, "advances in fundamental science make it possible to take advantage of *the uniformity of energy matter*," making it feasible, "without preassignable limit, to escape the quantitative constraints imposed by the character of the earth's crust" (Barnett and Morse, 1963, pp. 10, 11, emphasis added). Since for these authors the "natural resource building blocks [are now] to a large extent atoms and molecules,"[13] conservationist practices and the naturalist ethic of a previous era are rendered, in their view, anachronous and perverse.[14] They write:

> There is no need for a future-oriented principle to replace or supplement the economic calculations that lead modern man to accumulate primarily for the benefit of those now living. The reason, of course, is that the legacy of economically valuable assets which each generation passes on consists only in part of the natural environment. The more important components of the inheritance are knowledge, technology, capital instruments, economic institutions. These, far more than natural resources, are the determinants of real income per capita (Barnett and Morse, 1963, pp. 247–8).[15]

Barnett & Morse, and like-minded neoclassicists, then, are apostles of a new alchemy for a post-industrial or postmodern era. Content no longer to aspire merely to turning lead into gold, neoalchemists quest after nothing less than complete transformations of "uniform energy matter." On the one hand, evincing zero awareness of entropic processes inherent in all matter/energy transformations, and on the other blithely ignoring principles of biospheric balance, neoclassical neoalchemists exude confidence that supply and demand, coupled with individual short term maximizing behavior, will ensure welfare not only for present, but as well for future generations.[16]

Environmental Neoclassicism

"Neoclassical deniers" like Coase, Friedman, Barnett & Morse, in opposing Pigou, remain confident that market processes automatically produce optimal results, including "optimal" amounts of pollution. Other neoclassicists, however, have expressed concern about the economy's impact on the environment. These latter analysts are usually referred to as "environmental economists," although a more apt designation would be "environmental neoclassicists" since, after all, non-neoclassical economists too can be concerned about the environment.

Neoclassical environmentalists, unlike neoclassical deniers, affirm that unguided market forces perpetuate and exacerbate ecosystem crises. Following Pigou, these environmentally-concerned neoclassicists recommend, therefore, that activist governments implement measures to commoditize externalities (that is to place transferable property rights on pollution) and that governments ensure that pollution, or rights to pollute, are traded at "correct" prices. To that end, they have devised several means for commoditizing pollution, including: unit environmental taxes; unit subsidies; and auctions for marketable emission rights.[17] They have also proposed methods for setting "correct" prices, for example "contingent valuation methods,"[18] a variant of cost-benefit analysis.

Appropriate price adjustments accomplished, environmental neoclassicists aver, economic agents will modify their activities in socially desirable (ecologically healthy) ways. "Once pollution is priced, it becomes another commodity in our economic system, and will be exchanged efficiently if markets are perfectly competitive" (Olewiler, 1993, p. 1).

Moreover, many neoclassicists attest, the revised purchasing pattern will be the same regardless of whether or not economic agents have been apprised of the environmental reasons for the higher prices. In other words, environmental neoclassicists deem prices (albeit, in the case of externalities, adjusted prices) as being sufficient to signal all information required to cause economic agents to pursue individual maximizing activities in socially optimal ways. Hayek's classic statement setting forth this neoclassical doctrine is worth quoting:

> The price system [is ...] a mechanism for communicating information. ... The most significant fact about this system is the *economy of knowledge* with which it operates, or *how little the individual participant needs to know* in order to be able to take the right action. In abbreviated form, by a kind of symbol [i.e. a price], only the most essential information is passed on, and passed on only to those concerned. ... The marvel is that in a case like that of a scarcity of one raw material, without an order being issued, without more than perhaps a handful of people knowing the cause, tens of thousands of people whose identity could not be ascertained by months of investigation, are made to use the material or its products more sparingly, *i.e.*, they move in the right direction (Hayek, 1945, pp. 526–7, emphasis added).

Environmental neoclassicists and neoclassical deniers alike, then, conceive economy-ecosystem interactions solely in terms of neoclassical price theory—that is, in terms of commodity exchange, supply and demand, profit and utility maximization, price, marginal analysis, methodological individualism, and so forth. Furthermore both groups of neoclassicists apply an essentially static (or comparative static) mode of analysis to inherently dynamic and evolutionary processes. Like Coase, environmental neoclassicists too maintain that static economic efficiency can be attained if pollution is but commoditized and priced appropriately. They differ from Coase only in recommending that governments intervene specifically to help commoditize pollution and establish "appropriate" prices.

From a neoclassical perspective, pollution and resource depletion are then at worst problems in pricing, which is to say that they are problems in information/communication. Given "perfect and costless information ... bargaining by individuals or groups [will] internalize the activity" (Dewees, Everson and Sims, 1975, p. 4).

Critique of Neoclassical Environmentalism

Given the sway that neoclassical economists have had with policy makers over at least the past decade and a half,[19] and given also the dramatic increase in commodity relations that have arisen and continue to arise through globalization and its concomitants (e.g., Information Highway, New World Order, Free Trade, and so forth), and further given mounting ecosystem crises, it becomes urgent to inquire into the informational properties of prices (whether adjusted or unadjusted), and into the communicatory qualities of commodity exchange, in order to assess implications for the future of these trends and of neoclassical policy proposals. This third section describes and critiques in turn neoclassicism's two main informational/communicatory postulates: first, its contention that prices in principle summarize all information requisite for good economic decision-making, and second that the only communicatory activity relevant for economic analysis is the act of commodity exchange. If either of these postulates (interrelated as they are) is invalid, the neoclassical program of handling environmental stress solely through commoditization of pollution and price adjustments will be recognized as being, at best, inadequate or partial. In any event, even assuming for sake of argument the validity in principle of these two neoclassical postulates, estimating "correct" prices in practice, even on neoclassicism's own terms, is fraught with difficulty, as we see next.

Informational Properties of Prices

Setting the "Right" Price. While Hayek maintained that individual economic agents need not know, or even be concerned over, factors giving rise to changes in market prices, such insouciance certainly cannot be shared by governments responsible for making price "corrections." Governments, rather, require abundant information, including of course information not generated automatically in markets, if they are to carry out this task at all well.

However, as noted for instance by Baumol and Oates, social harms and benefits are usually extremely difficult to estimate quantitatively. These writers state, "Virtually every author points out that we do not know how to calculate the ideal Pigouvian tax or subsidy levels in practice" (Baumol and Oates, 1971, p. 53).[20] Many environmental harms, for instance, are not local, immediate, or readily observable—for example, acidification, climatic effects, ozone thinning, ground water contamination—making even rigorous *qualitative* specification of damages difficult (Hafkamp, 1991, p. 21). Ecosystem interactions are, if anything, complex, continuous, and cumulative.[21] Indeed it can in truth be said that knowledge of ecosystem interactions *in principle* will be forever partial,[22] and that consequently valuations of externalities in principle too will forever be incomplete.

Furthermore, the neoclassical agenda of pricing and commoditizing externalities to help preserve ecosystem vitality is fraught with problems since, in neoclassicism, all valuations, regardless of the degree and quality of scientific input, are ultimately premised entirely on subjective human preferences. In setting prices through cost-benefit analysis, governments therefore are urged to estimate what value the market would accord, say, survival of an insect species, were all market participants fully apprised of the situation, including ensuing repercussions of the species' disappearance. Difficulties, of course, abound in projecting consequences of any species' disappearance (for example in projecting the long terms costs of having foreclosed discovery of a new medicine on account of the extinction of a plant species), and as well in guessing the value people would apply to preservation of a species even if fully informed. Even given the finest possible procedures for making such estimates, the nagging doubt remains that the whole enterprise is quite misguided. Should the momentary, and easily-manipulated, subjective valuations of "consumers" (here, "consumers" of the preservation of an endangered species), constitute the basis upon which such ultimate (i.e., irreversible) questions are decided?

There is yet a further fundamental issue. Markets, of course, aggregate by weighting individual evaluations on the basis of income and expenditures; people that spend a lot and who have larger incomes count for more than the poor. So too, typically, are formal government-sponsored cost-benefit analyses tilted in favor of high-income earners. Components of the ecosystem more highly valued by the rich and powerful minority, therefore, consistently receive disproportionate weight per capita than do elements favored by the poorer majority. Weights apportioned according to income, however, need bear no necessary positive correspondence to the contributions of ecosystem elements to, say, sustaining a habitat conducive to improving prospects for human survival.[23] Therefore, although principles of Pigouvian tax and subsidy appear clear on the surface, in practice neoclassicism fails because attaining information required for appropriate price adjustments is highly problematic. Resolution of the environmental crisis through commoditization and simple price adjustments remains, therefore, illusive if not altogether illusory.

Prices and Infinite Substitutabilities. Difficulties of estimating "correct" prices aside, the more basic question is whether prices can even in principle connote sufficient and suitable information for individual decision-making in the context of ecosystem vitality. Following Daly and Cobb, the argument developed here is no. Prices as "names" for objects, processes, and relationships fundamentally transform social meaning, rendering components of the ecosystem mere commodity, effacing thereby qualities such as uniqueness, intrinsic value, and sacredness (Dyer, 1989).

Even for classical economists like David Ricardo, for example, nature ("land") was merely a factor of production whose price (rent) depended directly on its capacity to yield crops. Since Ricardo's time neoclassicism has deepened and extended commodity treatment of nature. According to neoclassical theorist Joseph Stiglitz, for instance, "natural resources are basically no different from other factors of production" (Stiglitz, 1979, p. 64). Indeed, nature in neoclassicism is but a *produced* commodity,[24] for analytical purposes generally subsumed into the category "capital." Even when given distinct title, as in neoclassical analyses of natural resources, land nonetheless is still held to be almost infinitely substitutable for capital and labor, and as being comprised of elements (namely, the panoply of natural resources) also almost infinitely substitutable one for another. From the premise of infinite substitutabilities the statement by Solow quoted at the start of this chapter (Solow, 1974, p. 10), and analyses such as those by Stiglitz, Ely & Hess (1937), and Barnett & Morse, ineluctably follow.

Neoclassicists fell into the error of infinite substitutabilities because they reduced all economic information to that of price and all economic communication to that of commodity exchange. Prices seem to turn guns into butter, butter back into guns, land into capital and capital back into land. Neoclassicists perceive humanity as being momentarily perched at one point or another along a "production possibilities curve," shifting first in one direction and then the other in response to the slightest fluctuation in relative prices. There is little or no recognition of "time's arrow," that is of history and the unidirectional flow of time. Money, rather, by ostensibly providing the common de-*nom*-inator (or common "name") for all things, creates an illusion of virtually limitless substitutabilities.

From an environmentalist and realist perspective, however, the neoclassical doctrine of infinite substitutabilities between, for example, natural resources and produced capital, is most troubling. The waste gene-rating properties of all production, including the production of "enhanced" land, leads to exponential increases in waste. In this context, natural resources need to be seen as *complements* for, rather than substi-tutes of, human-made capital. Indeed current ecosystem crises in large measure result from vast accumulations of human capital which now strain the regenerative capacity of natural cycles (Daly, 1992; Haavelmo and Stein, 1992, p. 39).

In other traditions, as Daly and Cobb have noted, life has been held to have intrinsic value: "Existence in general, and especially life, are to be affirmed in themselves" (Daly and Cobb, 1989, p. 104). Not so, however, for the price system and neoclassicism. Prices depict all value as relative; with price, value is expressed solely in terms of potential for trade, *this* being substitutable for (or transformable into) so much of *that*. Being worth something on its own merits (intrinsic value) is totally antithetical to the logic of the price system and to neoclassicism.

Neoclassicism and the price system, then, *as systems of information, knowledge, and communication*, utterly efface intimations of uniqueness, sacredness, and intrinsic value. The uniqueness of species (let alone uniqueness of individual members of a species), and the sacredness of life, are precluded by neoclassicism and the price system because, by neo-classicism's internal logic and mode of naming, uniqueness and sacred-ness are quite unthinkable and unimaginable. Uniqueness and sacredness alike imply incapacity for, or inappropriateness of, substitutions, which is to say they imply an absence or inappropriateness of price; but absence of price, by neoclassicism's logic, means an absence of value.

For neoclassicism, therefore, conservation of a pristine forest is sense-less since, *qua* forest, it has no commodity exchange value. On the other hand, viewed from the standpoint of being a supply of newsprint, the forest can be "valuable" indeed.

Furthermore, prices as deposits of economic information not merely obscure, but again make quite unthinkable, notions of ecological limits and thresholds. A threshold denotes a point of no return, a place where bi-directional substitutions are no longer possible. Events have finality once a threshold is passed. Likewise limits are not normally congruent with the logic of the price system since, at a limit, there is no option as to the direction in which to proceed. Ecologists, in contrast to neoclassical economists, posit the existence of both limits and thresholds: species become extinct, for example, and emissions from radioactive substances can never be reversed.

The very logic of markets and of neoclassicism, therefore, by preclud-ing vital concepts like uniqueness, sacredness, intrinsic value, thresholds and limits, is fundamentally at odds with sustainable development and, in consequence, with long term human survival. The price system as a mode of encoding information and communicating knowledge, stands at the very heart of the environmental crisis.

Communicatory Properties of Market Exchanges

Commodity exchange is one mode of communication, and as such has far-reaching consequences relevant to economy/ecosystem interaction. However, some of these effects are invisible to neoclassicism, since neoclassicism can envisage no other communicatory mode with which to compare.

Marx was one who envisaged other modes of communication. He is well known for, among other things, remonstrating how commodity relations alienate people one from another, that is, how markets inhibit and destroy fully textured communication. Less well-known, yet prophetic, was his analysis of how commodity relations alienate people also from nature. Under systems of private property and ubiquitous commodity exchange, Marx maintained, people relate to nature "in the mode of possession, of having and grasping" (Parsons, 1977, p. 18). People come to think of nature as dead and submissive to their whims and their demands.[25]

Economic historian Karl Polanyi deepened and extended Marx's analysis of alienation in showing how, by virtue of estranging people from their habitat, commodity treatment of land folds back to yet further estrange people from one another.[26] More recently, interrelations among commoditization, alienation from nature, and breakdown in human community have been afforded extended treatment by Daly and Cobb (1989, pp. 97–117).[27]

Communication through commodity exchange leaves parties to transactions untouched (Hyde, 1979). The whole point of commodity trade is to exchange equivalents. The focus is entirely on the items being exchanged, as opposed to relations among those doing the exchanging. Since parties to commodity exchange each have something the other party wants, and since each wants to retain as much as possible of what he/she already has, there is as well an element of conflict to all commodity exchange, further alienating parties participating in this mode of communication.

"Land," analogously, can be perceived and treated as being a "party" to commodity exchange. In return for fertilizer, water, pesticides, and other capital items, it "trades" crops that bear a cash value. According to utilitarian principles of individual maximization, the party "trading" with land will endeavor to minimize expenses (i.e. retain as much as possible of what he/she already has) consistent with exacting what the land has to offer, so as to maximize present values, given time constraints, discount rates, time horizons, and so forth. Affording land no intrinsic value means that qualities not passing through markets receive no attention from those engaging in market activity. Present benefits receive greater weight than future costs, so that over-cultivation leading to desertification may seem "rational" from a profit maximizing perspective. Instrumentalist or commodity-type treatment, moreover, displaces and obscures other modes of interaction whereby land "communicates" with humans—for instance by providing a sense of individual identity, and helping constitute human community.

This instrumental, commodity treatment of land—our island home—is deadly. Far from merely "communicating" with land, we literally *commune* with land, whether we are aware of it or not, and must forever do. Norbert Wiener some forty-five years ago expressed as elegantly and lucidly as anyone humanity's intimate relationship with land. He wrote:

> The pattern maintained by ... homeostasis ... is the touchstone of our personal identity. Our tissues change as we live: the food we eat and the air we breathe become flesh of our flesh and bone of our bone, and the momentary elements of our flesh and bone pass out of our body every day with our excreta. We are but whirlpools in a river of ever-flowing water. We are not stuff that abides, but patterns that perpetuate themselves (Wiener, {1950} 1967, p. 130).

How can we objectify and represent ecosystem elements solely by price, and reduce our interactions with ecosystem to the mode of commodity exchange, to the mode of "having and grasping," when it is "flesh of our flesh and bone of our bone," when we are part of it, and it of us?

From an eco-centered perspective, there are in nature no divisions; all things are inextricably interwoven, not so much as *substitutes* as neoclassicists contend, but rather as *interdependent and interacting components of larger systems*. We are all parts of something larger, and we are all in continuous *communion* with this larger entity, and thereby necessarily with one another as well. This communion neoclassicists refer to as "externalities," and this is what they strive to commoditize, internalize, and privatize.

Indeed, neoclassicism insists that *there would be no externalities in a world of perfect prices, costless transactions, and total commoditization!* If all interactions and interdependencies could only be commoditized, neoclassicists aver, there would be no "third party effects," and economic optima would result automatically! Hence, neoclassical environmental economists recommend commoditizing and pricing any and all "interactions" that currently transpire outside of markets.

However, environmental neoclassicism's project of transforming as many ecosystem interactions as possible into the *quid pro quo* mode of commodity exchange alienates. It causes us to lose sight of ineluctable interdependencies and interactions among components and between components and the larger ecosystem. Indeed, neoclassicism's methodological individualism means that the school of thought is quite oblivious to larger operating systems, such as ecosystems!

Few would question the need for, and desirability of, commoditization and commodity exchange—in moderation. A deep concern arises, however, with regard to neoclassicism's project of extending commoditization so far so as to encroach upon all of nature, and of viewing market transactions as typifying all of human communication, including human relations with the environment.

The continual "internalization" of "externalities," that is, the continual enclosure of more and more of nature into the commodity form, *is* the neoclassical response to the environmental crisis. This neoclassical response is not merely misguided; it gravely threatens our very survival.

Economy/Ecosystem Interaction as Informational and Communicatory

Information/communication join economy and ecosystem in ways at once more basic and profound than those recognized by neoclassicism. In this section, three of these ways are discussed.

Information as Negentropy

Thermodynamics is the "science of the conservation of the quantity and the change in quality of energy in a system" (Ruth, 1993, p. 48). Two basic laws of thermodynamics were formulated in 1865 by Clausius (Georgescu-Roegen, 1971, p. 129). The first, the Law of Conservation, maintains that matter-energy can be neither created nor destroyed, that in an *isolated system* matter-energy is conserved.[28] The second, the Law of Entropy, states that in an isolated system the amount of free energy (energy capable of doing mechanical work) decreases continually. Free energy is lost, for example, when heat moves unidirectionally from warmer to colder bodies, thereby increasing in equal amount the quantity of unavailable (or bound) energy. Maximum entropy occurs when "all energy is degraded to heat at a uniform temperature" (Ruth, 1993, p. 49).

The entropy law implies that in an isolated system, order (that is, structure, pattern, or differentiation) declines steadily until a completely random (or unordered, undifferentiated) state is reached. This so-called "Heat Death," or maximum entropy state, occurs when a system or subsystem so melds with its environment as to become indistinguishable from it.

Information is the opposite of entropy. Information is co-extensive with distinguishability, since pattern or form means perceptible differentiation of components one from another and from their environment.[29] For an entity to become completely entropic is for it to lose its distinct and distinguishable form, i.e., its information (Ruth, 1993, p. 114; also Chapters 1 and 3, *infra*).[30] Entropy, then, is related inversely to information.[31]

Nicholas Georgescu-Roegen was probably the first, and remains certainly one of the few, to place the notion of entropy, borrowed from thermodynamics, at the very heart of economic analysis. He has maintained that economic processes are governed by, and hence manifest, the first two laws of thermodynamics. For Georgescu-Roegen, production means the *net* conversion of low entropy inputs into high entropy outputs[32] since, in accordance with the second law, every local decrease in entropy (for example commodity manufacture, organic birth, metabolism, the creation of cities, roads, and so forth) is ineluctably accompanied by a more than commensurate increase elsewhere in entropy (i.e. loss in information or organization) (Georgescu-Roegen, {1971] 1993, pp. 77–9).

The first way in which information can be seen as uniting economic and ecological processes, therefore, is through thermodynamics and the concept of entropy. On the one hand, production means the manufacture of low entropic (high information) artifacts; on the other, production always transpires at the cost of producing even more than commensurate waste (net decrease in information). Had Solow, Stiglitz, or Barnett & Morse understood information in this way, they could not have made their gargantuan errors, proposing infinite substitutabilities of capital for nature.

Matter, Energy, Information as Basic Factors of Production

The second way whereby information unites economy and ecosystem is by information's status as a basic factor of production, as first proposed by Kenneth E. Boulding. For Boulding all production, "whether a chicken from an egg or a house from a blueprint," is a process whereby "some kind of *information* or knowledge structure directs *energy* toward the transportation, transformation, or rearrangement of *materials* into less probable structures than those existing at the start of the process" (Boulding, 1978, pp. 12, 34; emphasis added). According to Boulding, so universal is this process of production that economics' traditional triad of production factors—land-labor-capital—should be replaced by the alternative triad of energy-materials-information.[33] Boulding maintained that the elements of his proposed triad are far more "precise" than those of the traditional one.

Precision aside, for present purposes there are additional advantages to Boulding's formulation. First, as Boulding intimated, the revised triad encourages treating markets and the economy in thermodynamic terms, an essential step if Bruntland's prescription that economy and ecosystem be fully integrated in decision-making is to be realized. For production in *open systems* matter, energy, and information are *throughputs* that maintain existing structures and allow for the possibility of increasing complexity. For "production" in *isolated systems*, by contrast, there can be no throughputs, only decreases in complexity, i.e., increases in entropy. Finally, for *open systems* like our planet earth, energy and information are throughputs, while matter neither enters as an input nor is discharged as output (Boulding, [1966] 1970, pp. 276ff).

Second, and related to the first point, the triad of matter-energy-information bypasses the commodity-only treatment inhering in land-labor-capital. Not all energy, after all, is commoditized, or even commoditizable—solar energy, for example, upon which all life ultimately depends, is a "free gift of the sun" (Georgescu-Roegen, 1971, p. 21).[34] Likewise, much matter (air, for instance) is exceedingly difficult to fully commoditize. Of particular relevance to the topic at hand is the unsuitability of information for commodity treatment. (See particularly Chapters 1, 2, and 3, above). Nor does all production assume the commodity form, as Boulding's comparison of the chicken from an egg with the house from a blueprint well illustrates.

While of course significant, and indeed increasing, amounts of matter, energy, and information *are* indeed being made subject to market exchanges, nonetheless Boulding's triad is not, and never can be, comprised exclusively of productive factors that enter markets in processes of commodity exchange. His proposal, therefore, opens possibilities for recognizing that human economic activity takes place not only within the bounds of markets, but also within the frame of broader, non-market relations of which the ecosystem is the broadest in material (as opposed to spiritual) terms.

Boulding's position has been amplified most fully (albeit evidently independently)[35] by James R. Beniger (1986). Like Boulding, Beniger treated economy as organism rather than as mechanism, whose components function in integrated ways to achieve and sustain the vibrancy of the whole in the face of encroaching entropy.[36] Since parts or subsystems—for example individual firms, productive factors, consumers, or in the case of organisms particular bodily organs—must interact in coordinated fashion to achieve the synergy that we recognize as higher level operating systems, information/communication/control are to be seen as central to both the maintenance of systems (i.e., to "being") and to their evolution (to "becoming").

Matter and energy, Boulding noted, are subject to the Law of Conservation; they can be neither created nor destroyed, merely transformed into more or less entropic states. In combination the two laws of thermodynamics imply an inevitable, continuous build-up of waste, that is of more highly entropic forms, certainly in isolated systems but quite possibly in closed systems as well. Boulding remained generally buoyant, however, in the face of mounting pollution (Boulding, [1966] 1993). Information, he declared, being immaterial (that is deriving from the shape or form that matter or energy takes, and being therefore epiphenomenal to matter/energy) is not constrained as matter and energy are, making information/knowledge, in his eyes, "primal" to evolutionary processes. Knowledge alone, he pointed out, is what can really increase and change. As he explained:

> The through-put of information in an organization involves a "teaching" or structuring process which does not follow any strict law of conservation even though there may be limitations imposed upon it. When a teacher instructs a class, at the end of the hour presumably the students know more and the teacher does not know any less. In this sense the teaching process is utterly unlike the process of exchange which is the basis of the law of conservation. In exchange, what one gives up another acquires; what one gains another loses. In teaching this is not so. What the student gains the teacher does not lose. Indeed, in the teaching process, as every teacher knows, the teacher gains as well as the student. In this phenomenon we find the key to the mystery of life (Boulding, {1956] 1961, p. 35)

At this point, however, it seems advisable to qualify Boulding's optimism. Although epiphenomenal to matter and energy, information remains nonetheless dependent upon matter-energy which, as Boulding remarked, *is* subject to the two laws of thermodynamics. Indeed, entropy *is defined* as the inevitable lessening in differentiation (i.e. loss in information) of matter and energy. Information, therefore, is not as far removed from the laws of thermodynamics as Boulding in the foregoing extract seemed to indicate. While Boulding and his students assuredly departed from his lectures much enriched, all continued to produce entropy simply by living, learning, and eventually dying.

In isolation from the great body of Boulding's work, the paragraph quoted above could be invoked as supportive of the claims of Solow, Stiglitz, Ely, Barnett & Morse on the inevitability of progress through accretions in knowledge. One can accept Boulding's point that knowledge grows incrementally, unlike matter and energy, without however accepting a second proposition explicit in Solow, Stiglitz, Ely, and in Barnett & Morse, namely that knowledge is *infinitely substitutable*, or at least nearly so, for natural resources and for natural ecocycles. Certainly Boulding himself made no such monumental error (Boulding, [1966] 1993).

To recapitulate, broadening conceptions of information/communication from mere price and commodity exchange to encompass information as a basic factor of production again shows information/communication as linking economy and ecosystem in very fundamental ways, ways however that escape neoclassical modes of analysis.

Information and Mindset

According to both Boulding and Beniger, as we have just seen, information is a basic factor of production. Production (that is the conversion of inputs to outputs) occurs through the mediation of informational or knowledge structures (i.e., "programs," or in Boulding's terms, "know how"), that direct energy to reconfigure matter. "Know-how," or "programs," inhere in information processors. DNA, for instance, is an information processor, as are assembly lines and blueprints. Human brains are information processors *par excellence*, whose "programs" consist of learned values, ideologies, algorithms, ways of perceiving, paradigms in the Kuhnian sense, beliefs, experience, and so forth. As messages (sensory stimuli) enter the programs of the brain, decisions are taken to act upon these inputs, and outputs result.

Conversely, however, informational inputs can also impact upon programs, re-programming (or "mutating") them, causing them to make thereafter different selections of inputs, and to take different actions upon inputs once selected, producing thereby different arrays of outputs. For human minds, such reprogramming is called teaching, learning, and education, or more derisively conditioning, indoctrination, brainwashing, persuasive advertising, and propaganda.[37] In the context of continual and pervasive programming and reprogramming, it is instructive to delineate the neoclassical position, and indeed to position neoclassicism as itself a program or knowledge structure, and as an informational input that affects and transforms society's processes and procedures of converting inputs to outputs.

Neoclassicism's position with regard to the origins and development of knowledge structures and preference systems has been succinctly expressed by Stigler and Becker (1977) as "De Gustibus Non Est Disputandum." (See above Chapter 4, note 9). Economic etiquette, in other words, requires that matters of tastes and preferences simply "not be discussed." This means (to revert to previous terminology), that the "programs" or knowledge structures whereby commodities are selected and processed so as to yield satisfaction, and changes to these "programs," are beyond the pale of neoclassical analysis—quite an omission (and admission!) for an "imperial science." Indeed, it is upon the assumption of constant informational structures ("programs"), (or alternatively *exogenous* changes thereto), that neoclassicism's static and comparative static modes of analysis hinge.

By implication, a more thorough consideration of information/communication, as for example transpires in considering dynamic interrelations between informational flows and knowledge structures, opens up static neoclassicism to economic dynamics, surely an essential step for comprehending economy/ecosystem interaction. (See Chapters 7, 8, and 9).

Even more to the point, neoclassicism is itself a "program," or system of understanding, and as such constitutes a knowledge structure that influences the selection of (and modes of selecting) inputs and their conversion into outputs. Basic elements of this neoclassical "program" are: the notion of the efficacy of the market, the belief that each individual narrowly maximizing his or her own well-being is directed as if by an invisible hand to contribute to the betterment of all, the perception of society as merely the aggregation of the individuals comprising it, the idea that government is inherently wasteful and oppressive, the notions that communication consists entirely of commodity exchange, and that prices embody all relevant economic information.

Generally speaking, wide acceptance of *any* program or paradigm impacts on the way in which resources are processed. As Donella Meadows noted sagely:

Widely shared programs bring forth systems. The paradigm of the ancient Egyptians brought forth papyrus and pyramids; that of Hapsburg Vienna brought forth gilt cherubs, opera houses and Sacher torte; the modern industrial paradigm brings forth skyscrapers and acid rain, personal computers and global warming, heart transplants, oil spills, nuclear power, stock market booms and busts (Meadows, 1991, pp. 71–2).

The *neoclassical* paradigm, she might well have added, brings forth free trade zones, deregulation, and privatization; down-sizing social programs; erosion of national sovereignty and concomitant empowerment of transnational enterprise; neo-Darwinism; commoditization of information and nature; breakdown of community; and degradation of our habitat.

"Paradigms," Meadows continued, tell us "what systems to care about, what goals to set, what signals to monitor; *a change at the level of paradigm figuratively and then literally reconstructs the world*" (Meadows, 1991, p. 72; emphasis added). Neoclassicism, then, by virtue of being a dominant paradigm, is vitally important. To the extent that there is indeed an ecosystem crisis, and to the extent that it flows at least in part from having operationalized the neoclassical paradigm, the conclusion is inescapable that there needs to be a paradigm shift, a reconstruction of our world, first figuratively and then materially. We must change our dominant program—the manner in which we select our inputs, the operations we perform upon them, and hence the outputs that result. Moving toward sustainable development requires recognizing the neoclassical mindset for what it is, and abandoning it forthwith in favor of something quite different. It entails recognizing limits, and sufficiency, and improvement, rather than focusing steadily on growth. It means recognizing "that welfare is increased by *decreasing* options, by *limiting* production, and *guiding* technology ... that investment spending and increases in GDP can *reduce* welfare" (Hayden, 1993, p. 411, emphasis added).

Neoclassical economics is but one knowledge or information structure that leads to processing the information inhering in matter-energy in ways that are fundamentally destructive of the environment. Much of advertising, public relations, political rhetoric, courses in management and business administration do likewise. An eco-centered information policy, therefore, as discussed in the following section, must address intentional informational flows like these that continuously program and reprogram societies.

Once again, then, information/communication can be seen as basic to economy/ecosystem interaction. Information/knowledge structures or programs mediate and direct the transformation of inputs into outputs. These programs in turn are modified by incoming flows of information.

Economy/ecosystem interactions consequently comprise issues in information/communication policy. By confining attention to price and to commodity exchange as sole modes of communicatory interaction, neoclassicism casts a blind eye to the importance of information/communication in setting and maintaining economies on their course.

Toward an Eco-centered Communication Policy

The neoclassical understanding of information, and communication policy proposals stemming from that understanding, are quite inconsistent with moving in the direction of sustainable development. Assuredly, in the short term, it is better to afford pollution a positive price than it is to continue treating so much of the planet's capacity to absorb wastes as "free goods" (goods "without value"). However, from an eco-centered standpoint, the basic issue is not one of proper pricing, but rather the continued instrumental treatment of the environment per se.

As an alternative to neoclassical policy proposals, this section in rudimentary fashion explores elements of an eco-centered communication policy that strives to rebalance the present mix of communicatory modes, reducing both the relative and absolute significance of commodity exchange relations by accentuating alternatives more conducive to sustainable development. Three components of such an overall communication strategy are addressed briefly here: mass media policy, telecommunications policies in the context of globalization, and development of an economics of gift relations. Aspects of these strategies are taken up again in subsequent chapters.

Mass Media Policies

Communication/journalism scholar Everette Dennis remarked recently that "any deficiency in public understanding of the current state and probable future of the environment could be solved by continuous and massive [media] coverage." He then asked, "If it is all so simple, why don't the news media simply develop a strategic plan and make it happen?" Dennis's answer?: The public simply is *not interested* in environmental issues, and consequently the media do not cover them to the extent or in the manner that they would otherwise deserve. Environment, Dennis explained, is "a snore, a hard sell in a world where people like scandal and sensationalism, personalities and celebrity" (Dennis, 1991, pp. 55, 60).

Likewise the *Vancouver Sun*, in jettisoning from its pages ecologist David Suzuki's column, explained laconically that Suzuki had become "repetitious and boring." His column was simply no longer *in demand*.[38] Similarly the *Globe and Mail*, in pushing Suzuki off its science page, pointed to the geneticist's unduly "narrow focus" (Suzuki, 1994, p. xi).

Dennis, the *Sun*, the *Globe and Mail*, each in its own way, invoked liberal shibboleths of market demand and consumer sovereignty to explain editorial decisions restricting environmental coverage.

There are, however, other explanations.

In a classic 1977 paper political economist Dallas Smythe noted that the commodity bought and sold in the media marketplace is not the edition of the newspaper or the TV show or the radio program; rather, it is readership and audience. Newspaper editors and television station owners assemble or package readers and audiences for sale to advertisers. They bill advertisers not only according to audience and readership size, but as well on the basis of audience "quality" (income, wealth, age, location, gender, consumption patterns, "psychographics," and so on). Advertisers, for their part, are willing to pay top dollar for the privilege of gaining "access to the thoughts and emotions" of audiences (Vogel, {1986] 1990, p. 156). The "sovereign" customer, in other words, is not the gentle reader, listener or viewer, but the advertiser.

Nor are programs and news stories final products; these are, rather, costs of producing the commodity: audience attention (Smythe, 1977; see also Freiman, 1984).

Forthrightly articulating the real nature of the mass media marketplace, *Globe and Mail* publisher and editor, Roy Megarry, in 1982 wrote: "By 1990, publishers of mass circulation daily newspapers will finally stop kidding themselves that they are in the *news*paper business and admit they are in the business of carrying advertising messages" (*Editor & Publisher*, April 1982; quoted in Heinricks, 1989, p. 19). Such candor, albeit refreshing, unfortunately remains all too rare; pretensions and protestations still abound of the press as public protector, the veritable Fourth Estate.

Even more to the point, Megarry's maxim confronts Dennis's liberal contention that systematic omissions in environmental coverage (exemplified for instance by Megarry's termination of the Suzuki column), are to be ascribed primarily to minuscule reader/listener/viewer demand.

So incisive and yet self-evidently true is the Smythe/Megarry formulation of the nature of the mass media marketplace and the consequent real meaning of consumer sovereignty, that Edward S. Herman (1994), Noam Chomsky, Jacques Ellul ([1965] 1973), Nimmo and Combs (1993), and others[39] have developed full-scale media propaganda models based in part upon it. Notes Chomsky, for instance:

> The major media—particularly the elite media that set the agenda that others generally follow—are corporations "selling" privileged audiences to other businesses. It would hardly come as a surprise if the picture of the world they present were to reflect the perspectives and interests of the sellers, the buyers, and the product (Chomsky, 1989, p. 8).

From an environmental perspective, there are at present essentially two problems with regard to the mass media marketplace. First of course is the continual diffusion of mass media advertising. Mass advertising is a vital component of the present mass consumption/high waste economic order. As Galbraith pointed out so well years ago, given the inessential or non-vital character of much commodity production and consumption in industrialized countries, producers need to stimulate and manage consumer demand to avoid build-ups of inventories that on a large scale could endanger the very survival of the present economic system (Galbraith, 1967, pp. 211-218; also Schiller, 1984, pp. 53-59; Lears, 1983; Williams, 1980; Beniger, 1986, pp. 344–389). A principle means of managing or controlling consumer demand is advertising; advertising "programs" and "reprograms" individual agents, sustaining or redirecting their purchasing decisions. Indeed, the present economic system is to a large extent *defined by* the nexus of corporate commodity producers, mass media organizations, and advertisers/public relations/media relations firms and strategists. Each functions symbiotically and synergistically with the others to maintain and extend current, albeit moribund practices.

The consequences of advertising go well beyond stimulation of demand for advertised commodities. Advertising is at the very root of a "therapeutic culture" (Lears, 1983), a "magic system" (Williams, 1980) whereby purchase and consumption of material goods are proffered as means for relieving all sorts of existential angst and personal deficiencies. Advertising promotes life-style, value systems, modes of perceiving, valuing and behaving that are fundamentally anti-environment and hence anti-life.

The second problem concerns media's editorial or non advertising content. Media dependency on advertising for basic revenues skews editorial content in ways both blatant and subtle. Most obviously, the very shape, format, pace, and timing of media content are designed to accommodate advertising (Peterson, 1979; Dyer, 1982, p. 35). Less immediately obvious, perhaps, but of far greater significance, the tone, subject matter, and point of view of articles and programs are crafted to provide a climate consistent with, and indeed supportive of, the successful hawking of advertised goods to carefully targeted audiences (Barnouw, 1978; Bagdikian, 1990, pp. 105–117, 134–151). When violations of this basic axiom occur, advertisers' response can be swift. Thus, the Canadian Imperial Bank of Commerce, succumbing to the wrath of its logging industry clients, withdrew sponsorship of Suzuki's television program, *The Nature of Things*, in 1991 (Ottawa *Citizen*, 1991, p. A10).

The significance of mass media with regard to economy/ecosystem interaction is difficult to overstate. Media impart a view of the world; they construct and maintain shared paradigms through which phenomena are interpreted and valued; they select and define "reality;" they distinguish the "real" from the "illusory," "fact" from "fancy," the "possible" from the totally "impractical," the important from the trivial. Media inform us explicitly of which conditions of our economic/ecological system we should be monitoring, and by inattention implicitly as to which ones are unimportant and can safely be ignored: Should we be keeping track of oil production, or rather perhaps of oil pollution, including the regular dumping of oil into oceans to "clean" oil tankers? Should we be monitoring sales growth and daily stock market prices, or rather perhaps the logging industry's daily activity in clear-cutting? Media, by their selections, tone, emphasis, and inattentions, tell us what matters most and how it matters.

As well, media tell us what goals to set; for example, cutting the deficit, growth in trade, improvement in the balance of payments, pursuing world competitiveness, or perhaps rather curtailment of CFC and CO_2 emissions, encouragement of small scale production, phasing back of international trade, and promotion locally of economic self-sufficiency in order to help preserve ecosystem balance. In making, by necessity, selections from an infinite array of possibilities, media never are, nor can they ever be, neutral.

The concern expressed here is that media, financed by advertising, have pecuniary incentives to systematically refrain from affording due attention to conflicts and inconsistencies between the present economic order and ecological well being. Commercial mass media, after all, value manufactured goods more than they do natural ecosystem processes, and they posit reality as being centered on human interactions with commodities and institutions much more than with the ecosystem (the ubiquity of weather reports notwithstanding).

Paradigms gain authority and are maintained by constant repetition (Meadows, 1991, p. 74). Indeed the extraordinary power of commercial enterprise in our day can be attributed in no small part to the continuous barrage of commercial information and ideology by mass media.

Given media's centrality in maintaining and indeed extending the present ecologically destructive economic order, an eco-centered communication strategy needs propose alternative modes of media ownership and alternative means of media finance. In terms of ownership, taking the ecosystem seriously means removing at least substantial portions of media holdings from the private corporate sector, and expanding, at least relatively, the non profit, public, co-op, and community-based media sectors. In terms of finance, an eco-centered media strategy points to increased subsidies, grants, and membership fees for the production of content to replace advertising. It points as well to proscriptions on "persuasive" as opposed to "informative" advertising, and to imposition of heavy advertising taxes.

Precedents have already been set in terms of tobacco advertising. In Canada, advertising of tobacco products is illegal because these commodities endanger health. Ecologists know that our present high production/ high waste economic order also endangers health, possibly to the point of species' extinction. It makes sense, therefore, to legislate dramatic cutbacks to all forms of persuasive advertising.

Changes in patterns of media control and content can contribute to an on-going paradigm shift whereby manufactured products and their associated images progressively decline in social value *vis à vis* ecosystem vitality and improvements in prospects for species' survival. What is truly needed is a Change of Mind—a *metanoia*—a change difficult if not impossible to effect, however, on a wide scale given the current nexus of media/corporate power.

Telecommunications

Telecommunications are essential for the control of economic activity over space. International computer communication networks support trends apparent since the 1950's as regards the aggrandizement of transnational corporate power and concomitant erosion of national sovereignty. In a prophetic 1969 speech, Jacques Maisonrouge, then President of IBM World Trade Corporation, opined, "The world's political structures are completely obsolete; the critical issue of our time is the conceptual conflict between the global optimization [*sic*] of resources and the independence of nation states. ... For business purposes the boundaries that separate one nation from another are no more real than the equator" (quoted in Barnet and Müller, 1974, p. 14; and in Mulgan, 1991, p. 220).

Telecommunications permit markets administered from central points to be extended to international and global levels. As well, transnational communication networks provide new opportunities for businesses to shift risks from transnational investors and managers to local governments, labor, and consumers (Melody, 1991, p. 28).

For present purposes, key aspects of global telecommunications are: tendencies for markets to grow at the expense of the ecosystem through world trade, heightened global divisions of labor, and growing capacity of transnational corporations (TNCs) to thwart local environmental initiatives. (See Chapter 11, below). Advent of Free Trade Zones and Export Processing Zones point to an "horrific underside of the expanding multinational economy" (Nelson, 1989, p. 98). "Favorable business climates" in Free Trade Zones dotting the world (in countries such as Malaysia, Dominican Republic, the Philippines, Mexico, Sri Lanka, and many more) are due to incredibly low or non-existent minimum wage laws and outright prohibition of labor unions, hundred hour work weeks, minimal health and safety standards, and negligible environmental regulations (Nelson, pp. 102–107). General Motors, while closing 12 of its 21 plants in Canada and the US, by 1992 had opened 37 plants in Mexico to become the largest employer in that country's "Free Trade Zone" nestled along the US/Mexican border, a region where environmental standards are so lax that stones cast into canals of the Rio Grande release chemical stench to the air as they wend their way to the bottom (Meeker-Lowry, 1992, p. 27). Although to be expected, it is nonetheless a sad commentary on the Canadian "free press" that this Maquiladoras region in Mexico received scant media attention during negotiations and "debate" culminating in the signing of the North American Free Trade Agreement.

A second element of an eco-centered communication policy, then, entails dismantling of large portions of transnational telecommunications to help restore local and national sovereignty, and thereby open possibilities of replacing the global marketplace and global divisions of labor now controlled by transnational businesses, with local, environmentally-inspired legislation and production. "Information Highway" initiatives, in this context, are to be seen as being quite anti-environmental, and should be resisted with the utmost effort.

About fifty years ago Canadian economic historian and communication theorist, Harold Innis, elucidated the link between telecommunications and global empire, making "a plea for time." By "time" Innis meant oral, local, communal communication to provide a sense of both continuity with the past (i.e., culture) and of community in the present[40] (Innis, [1951] 1971). Innis's "plea for time" takes on added urgency in our present era, blighted by eco-damages wrought by unrestrained profit seeking.

Like recommendations made previously with regard to mass media, those presented here regarding telecommunications may seem unlikely to be pursued at present, given the momentum that has been achieved by globalization. It would, therefore, be easy to fall into despair, like Heilbroner, at prospects for human survival.[41] Nonetheless, there signs of hope—Greenpeace, Friends of the Earth, the German Green Party, and other related movements (Tehranian, 1990, pp. 208–242), making possible a cautious optimism.

Telecommunications policy, both as it unfolded historically and in the context of present "Information Highway" initiatives, is addressed again in Chapters 10 to 12.

An Economics of Person-in-Community

Over two hundred years ago, Adam Smith, patriarch of modern economics, made a great mistake (Lux, 1990). He wrote *The Wealth of Nations*, in which he lauded "self-love" and single-minded pursuit of individual gain as the surest means for attaining the common weal. Smith's ode to greed in *The Wealth of Nations*, unfortunately, has overshadowed ever since his earlier homage to empathy, addressed with nuanced comprehensiveness and abundant insight in *The Theory of Moral Sentiments*, wherein Smith declared,

And hence it is, that to feel much for others and little for ourselves, that to restrain our selfish, and to indulge our benevolent affections, constitutes the perfection of human nature (Smith, [1759] 1982, p, 25).

The subtitle of E. F. Schumacher's now-classic treatise, *Small Is Beautiful*, is "A Study of Economics As If People Mattered." Why did Schumacher feel called upon to write an economics text "as if people mattered," unless he considered that the hegemonic economics of the day, an economics that had pursued and refined the ethic of greed argued so persuasively by Smith in *The Wealth of Nations*, had meant, ultimately, that people no longer mattered; that mainstream economics had served to alienate people from one another, from their jobs, from their environment, and even (perhaps especially) from themselves?

For neoclassicism (the modern embodiment and elaboration of Smith's ethic as developed in *The Wealth of Nations*), everything—the self, the Other, Nature—is commoditizable, to be bought and sold for a price in the marketplace. Items bearing no price, according to neoclassicism, are *without value*: "Nothin' ain't nothin' if it ain't free."[42] In neoclassicism price *is* value, and for neoclassicism value does not exist apart from price.

By neoclassicism's logic, the value of the self to the self is set by the price the self can exact in commodity exchange, and hence selves subject to neoclassicism's logic will forever be selling themselves short (selling out) in attempts at market valuation, the sole means recognized for self-validation. Likewise, the value of the Other can be merely what the Other can command in a *quid pro quo*, which is to say what it can do for me or you in a commodity exchange. And the value too of the environment, of Nature, is purely instrumental, given by Nature's capacity to help yield goods for commodity exchange. "Land" and capital, after all, for neoclassicists are infinitely substitutable!

In neoclassicism, then, there is no intrinsic value, no empathy, no relatedness, no sense of the sacred, no love—in the final analysis not even "self-love," for as the Adam Smith of *Moral Sentiments* so lucidly observed:

> As to love our neighbour as we love ourselves is the great law of Christianity, so it is the great precept of nature to love ourselves only as we love our neighbour, or what comes to the same thing, as our neighbour is capable of loving us (Smith, [1759] 1982, p. 25).

So yes, Schumacher had a point. Economics indeed needs to be reformulated, because it alienates.

By contrast to neoclassicism, an eco-centered economics is one that attempts to regain the ground lost when Smith strayed from *Moral Sentiments* to pen *Wealth of Nations*. An eco-centered economics is one that endeavors to restore human relations, and relations of people with their environment. It is an economics that recognizes that human communication far exceeds the bounds of commodity exchange, and that value can far transcend mere price.

The current project of mainstream economics and of modern economies alike is, of course, to yet further commoditize matter, energy, and information. Our era has even been named the "Information Economy," indicating the markedly heightened commoditization of processes of human communication. As more and more of our communicatory activities become commoditized, however, and the "wealthier" we become as a result, the more estranged we also become—from ourselves, from one another, and from our environment.

For Herman E. Daly & John Cobb, as for Schumacher—and indeed for the Adam Smith of *Moral Sentiments*—the path from alienation to wholeness, and by implication from entropy to sustainability, is a journey from individualism to "person-in-community," from commodity exchange to gift economy, from exchange value to intrinsic value. John Donne's insight, that "no man is an island," that everyone is "a part of the main," is a lesson we need continually to bear in mind,[43] and begin again to incorporate into an economics discipline for tomorrow, to help dispel the grim warnings sounded by Heilbroner, Suzuki, Bruntland, and so many others.

Humans have been granted such marvelous gifts of communication. What a travesty that we construct models and economic systems in ways that give credence only to such reductionist and perverted forms thereof.

Notes

An abbreviated version of this chapter was delivered to the Students' Symposium on Critical Communication, University of Ottawa, October 28, 1994.

1. Per capita annual energy consumption in developed countries (26% of world population) is over eleven times that in developing countries (WCED, 1987, p. 33).

2. The Bruntland Report did not escape criticism from environmentalists, but was mostly welcomed by the business community and by governments, possibly because it proffered continued growth as the only way of alleviating world poverty. As Robert Goodland remarks, however, "the growth called for by Bruntland will dangerously exacerbate surpassing the limits [for sustainability]" (Goodland, 1992, p. 16; see also Nelson, 1989, pp. 125-147; and Suzuki, 1994).

Despite these criticisms, Bruntland nonetheless provides a suitable base for launching this chapter since, as Goodland argues, the Report is "excellent" on describing the global environmental crisis and in proposing three of four conditions necessary for sustainability (Goodland, 1992, p. 16).

3. Or as Georgescu-Roegen expressed the point, "Combination *per se*—as an increasing number of natural scientists admit—contributes something that is not deducible from the properties of the individual components" (Georgescu-Roegen, 1971, p. 116). See also Ruben (1972), and Koestler ([1967] 1975).

4. The term "sustainable development" was used, probably for the first time, by the Bruntland Commission to indicate "a process of change in which the exploitation of resources, the direction of investments, the orientation of technological development, and institutional change are made consistent with future as well as present needs" (WCED, 1987, p. 9).

5. The qualification that the effect be "direct" is important since, as Mishan notes, in an interdependent system, change in the behavior of one component will have consequences on others, even in the absence of externalities. The difference is that interdependencies in the absence of externalities work their way indirectly through the system by means of prices, whereas externalities work directly, before price changes (Mishan, 1971a, p. 2).

6. As he put it: "It is as idle to expect a well-planned town to result from the independent activities of isolated speculators as it would be to expect a satisfactory picture to result if each separate square inch were painted by an independent artist. No "invisible hand" can be relied on to produce a good arrangement of the whole from a combination of separate treatments of the parts. It is therefore, necessary that an authority of wider reach should intervene and should tackle the collective problems of beauty, of air and of light, as those other collective problems of gas and water have been tackled" (Pigou, [1920] 1932, p. 195).

7. Coase, consequently, might be thought of as a theorist writing, unwittingly, in the interests of protection racketeers. Compare Coase's analysis to that of Samuels (1971).

8. Coase's article was intended as rejoinder to Pigou, and consequently a number of his examples were drawn from Pigou, not however his one concerning the manure pile.

9. Stigler wrote: "If one is not an economist, one might well be inclined to say that Coase had a cute point, but why the excitement? A world free of transactions costs is, as you say, a farfetched state of affairs, and it should be expected that it leads to bizarre results. Think of all the odd things one could imagine of a society that did not obey the law of conservation of matter, and shrank with every bite! I must say in candor that there is some point to the remark."

Stigler then attempted to neutralize his objection by remarkng: "Theorists like new and strange constructs that create a new world or change the way of looking at the current one. ... [The Coase Theorem] immediately changes the way one looks at and studies a vast variety of economic problems " (Stigler, 1988, p. 78).

10. Coase wrote as well one other very famous article, "The Nature of the Firm" (1937). It was largely on the basis of the two articles that he was awarded the Nobel prize.

11. Here Friedman is quoting from his book, *Capitalism and Freedom*.

12. Friedman too can of course be critiqued on a number of grounds, of which three are highlighted here. First, he presumed that shareholders, customers and workers (his ordering) are as apprised as are managers of environmental degradations stemming from managerial decisions (the perfect information assumption again!). Furthermore he assumed that these groups can actually reverse environmental damages if they choose to try. These assumptions are not always (indeed generally) warranted. Corporate secrecy is such that pollution is seldom publicized until obvious and widespread damages have been done, sometimes years later. Nor are all damages reversible, for instance species become extinct, old growth forests are clear-cut, people die.

Second, Friedman claimed that "social responsibility" is a "socialist" doctrine since it recommends "political mechanisms, not market mechanisms [as being] the appropriate way to determine the allocation of scarce resources to alternative uses." Only a neoclassicist would partition economic and political processes so rigidly. "Property and law are born together, and die together," noted classical economist Jeremy Bentham "Before laws were made there was no property; take away laws, and property ceases" (Bentham, 1830, in Macpherson, 1978, p. 52).

Finally, central to Friedman's position is the contention that "There are no social values, no social responsibilities in any sense other than the shared values and responsibilities of individuals. Society is a collection of individuals and of the various groups they voluntarily form" (Friedman, [1970] 1985, p. 25). One might well ask, however, whether those whose homes were built, unbeknownst to them, upon chemical waste, or those enduring heightened ultraviolet radiation from ozone thinning, or people experiencing radioactive fall-out from reactor melt-downs, in any sense constitute collectivities formed *in freedom*.

Friedman wrote that in an "ideal" situation, "no individual can coerce any other" (Friedman, [1970] 1985, p. 25). Unfortunately, the real world of environmental degradation falls far short of Friedman's ideal. Indeed pollution *is* coercion, and in recommending that businesses not exercise voluntary restraint. Friedman in fact recommended that businesses exercise coercion to the fullest extent permitted by law.

13. They explained further: "Nature's input should now be conceived as *units of mass and energy,* not acres and tons. Now the problem is more one of manipulating the available store of iron, magnesium, aluminum, carbon, hydrogen, and oxygen atoms, even electrons. This has major economic significance" (Barnett and Morse, 1963, p. 238, emphasis added).

14. They explained, "The Conservationists' premise that the economic heritage will shrink in value unless natural resources are "conserved," is wrong for a progressive world. The opposite is true. In the United States, for example, the economic magnitude of the estate each generation passes on—the income per capita the next generation enjoys—has been approximately double that which it received, over the period for which data exist. Resource reservation to protect the interest of future generations is therefore unnecessary" (Barnett and Morse, 1963, pp. 247-8).

15. The foregoing should not be taken as mere musings from an extremist fringe of neoclassicism. Recall the epigram from Solow at the start of this chapter, and note as well the following ringing endorsement by Joseph E. Stiglitz: "One should not view equity in a narrow sense of simply looking at the division of natural resources between present and future generations; the present generation may give future generations fewer natural resources (this is inevitable in the case of exhaustible natural resources), but will give future generations a higher level of technology and more capital. One has to look at the relative welfare of the different generations and there is strong presumption that future generations may be better off than the present generation. *On grounds of equity it might be argued that we should consume even more now including more natural resources*" (Stiglitz, 1979, p. 61, emphasis added).

16. For a satiric commentary on these and like-minded views, see Mishan (1971b).

17. The first method, a per unit environmental tax, can take several forms: It can be based on damages inflicted (presuming these can be measured, certainly an important qualification), or on emissions, or on inputs used in polluting activities, or it can be levied on outputs of goods and services, the production of which generates pollution (Olewiler, 1993, p. 1). Per unit subsidies, a second method suggested for commoditizing pollution, entail payments to polluters for reducing emissions in recognition that such reductions impose costs on them, whether in terms of pollution abatement equipment, or on account of lessened output and foregone sales opportunities. While at the margin taxes and subsidies, if set at the same rate, should have "an identical impact on the amount of pollution emitted *per source*" (Olewiler, 1990, p. 2), nonetheless subsidies will normally expand industry size (number of sources), possibly increasing the amount of pollution overall. In any event subsidies will tend to impact more negatively on governmental budgets than pollution taxes. Tradable licences guaranteeing possessors rights to pollute, a third neoclassical proposal, will generate market prices equal to the marginal value to its holder from exercising the right to pollute, and in that sense set marginal cost equal to the marginal benefit. The procedure, however, quite ignores valuing environmental costs, surely the whole point of the exercise, except in the unlikely case that those afflicted by the pollution can combine (that is, overcome transactions costs) to themselves bid for licences which they, presumably, would refrain from exercising if successful in their bid.

18. The contingent valuation method (CVM) entails asking people "for their willingness-to-pay for a well defined but unpriced environmental commodity, thus creating a hypothetical market" (Dietz, van der Ploeg and van der Straaten, 1991, p. 6).

19. As demonstrated by trade liberalization, deregulation, privatizations, cutbacks in social services, drastic cuts in corporate tax rates, and so forth.

20. Consequently these authors recommended adopting a "prices and standards approach," whereby an environmental standard is (arbitrarily) fixed and thereafter in an iterative process per unit taxes (or subsidies) are established so as to generate the standard. They advised, "While it makes no pretense of promising anything like an optimal allocation of resources, the pricing and standards technique can, in some cases where external effects impose high costs (or benefits), at least offer some assurance of reducing the level of damages." See Baumol and Oates (1971).

21. The following extract from *Our Common Future* may suffice to illustrate the point: "Growing populations and the decreasing availability of arable land lead poor farmers ... to seek new land in forests to grow food. ... Deforestation most severely disrupts mountainous areas and upland watersheds and the ecosystems that depend on them. The uplands influence precipitation, and the state of their soil and vegetation systems influence how this precipitation is released into streams and rivers and onto the croplands of the plains below. The growing numbers and growing severity of both floods and droughts in many parts of the world have been linked to the deforestation of upland watersheds " (pp. 127-8).

22. Dietz and van der Straaten gave several reasons why processes in nature, and hence consequences of human interventions into these processes, "appear to be hardly predictable." First, "synergetic effects increase the impact on the environment of separate emissions." Air and water pollution are affected by a whole series of factors that react upon one another. Second, "thresholds are very common in ecosystems." For instance sudden deterioration of European forests in the 1980's ("like a bolt from the blue"), occurred once the buffering capacity of the soil that had protected trees for decades had been exceeded. "Third, many emissions have delayed effect on the environment."

Predictability aside, neoclassicism fails to "map" ecosystem relations for yet another reason: Neoclassicism assumes bidirectional time: guns can be turned into butter, and then back into guns. In ecosystems, however, events can be non-reversible, as when a species becomes extinct or an old growth forest is clear-cut. See Dietz and van der Straaten, 1992, p. 34.

23. As noted by Kapp, "The logical and practical result of using willingness to pay as a criterion [in cost-benefit analyses] would be that public parks or clean air in the ghetto sections of a large city would yield a lower benefit-cost-ratio than the marina for top management personnel" (Kapp, 1972, p. 120). As Daly and Cobb noted, neither the price system nor neoclassical economists can say "that food for the hungry yields more utility than a third TV set in a rich family's second house; nor that a leg amputation hurts Jones more than a pin prick hurts Smith" (Daly and Cobb, 1989, p. 93).

There is, in other words, in cost-benefit analysis, a built-in discrimination against the poor. As well there is the problem that preferences of future generations can be accounted for only on the basis of preferences of current generations, again a systematic bias in favor of the most powerful.

24. Note the explanation provided, for example, by Ely and Hess: "It is true that we find land in all forms provided by nature, but in economics we are not concerned with the physical supply of land as such, but with *the economic supply of land.* In all the older countries, the toil of ages has become embodied in the present usefulness and value of land. No land is economically utilizable which does not represent human toil of some kind. For example, land cannot be put to economic use unless we have access to it; and the efforts involved in creating means of access often constitute a very considerable part of the cost of making land economically utilizable; land may thus be said to be "produced," and to be the result of "stored-up effort" (Ely and Hess, 1937, p. 449; emphasis in original).

25. Whereas Marx and Engels characterized feudalism as obeying and passively acquiescing in nature, they saw capitalism as aiming to subjugate it: "[With capitalism] for the first time, nature becomes purely an object for human-kind, purely a matter of utility; ceases to be recognized as a power for itself; and the theoretical discovery of its autonomous laws appears merely as a ruse so as to subjugate it under human needs, whether as an object of consumption or as a means of production"(Marx, *Grundisse*; quoted in Parsons, 1977, p. 17).

26. Polanyi wrote: "The economic function is but one of many vital functions of land. It invests man's life with stability; it is the site of his habitation; it is a condition of his physical safety; it is the landscape and the seasons. We might as well imagine his being born without hands and feet as carrying on his life without land. And yet to separate land from man and organize society in such a way as to satisfy the requirements of a real-estate market was a vital part of the utopian concept of a market economy." Polanyi continued, "To detach man from the soil meant the dissolution of the body economic into its elements so that each element could fit into that part of the system where it was most useful. ... The aim was the elimination of all claims on the part of neighborhood or kinship organizations" (Polanyi, [1944] 1956, pp. 178-9).

27. Nor should Henry George's *Progress and Poverty* ([1880] 1930) be forgotten.

28. The distinctions made here are among "isolated systems" for which there are no throughputs, whether of matter, energy or information; "closed systems," where there is no throughput of matter, but for which energy and informational throughputs exist; and "open systems" where matter, information, and energy are taken in from outside and degraded forms thereof expelled from the system.

29. A system, as Boulding advised, is "anything that is not chaos; ... any structure that exhibits order and pattern," which is to say information (Boulding, 1985, p. 9).

30. Hence Bateson's dictum that "information consists of differences that make a difference" (Bateson, 1979, p. 99).

31. Indeed in Shannon and Weaver's "Mathematical Theory of Communication," information is a measure of entropy, and of its converse, negentropy. See Shannon and Weaver ([1949]; 1963; Darnell 1972; Ritchie 1991, pp. 1-18; and Georgescu-Roegen 1971, p. 8).

32. As the Ehrlichs and Holdren have written, "The laws of thermodynamics explain why we need a continual input of energy to maintain ourselves, why we must eat much more than a pound of food in order to gain a pound of weight, and why the total energy flow through plants will always be much greater than that through plant-eaters, which in turn will always be much greater than that

through flesh-eaters. They also make it clear that *all* energy used on the face of the Earth, whether of solar or nuclear origin, will ultimately be degraded to heat" (Ehrlich, Ehrlich, and Holdren, [1977], 1993, p. 72).

33. This is not merely the "information" of Shannon and Weaver's Information Theory, however. (On Shannon and Weaver, see Chapters 1 and 3, above). For Boulding, information "involves not only improbability of structure, but the structure's ability to 'instruct'; that is, to be a code of selection according to a program" (Boulding, 1978, p. 13).

34. The sum total of the earth's stored up energy is equivalent to but a few days' sunlight (Georgescu-Roegen, 1971, p. 21).

35. Beniger's book, *The Control Revolution*, contains no citation of Boulding.

36. He wrote, "In order to oppose entropy and put off for a time the inevitable heat death, every living thing must maintain its organization by processing matter and energy. Information processing and programmed decisions are the means by which such material processing is controlled in living systems, from macromolecules of DNA to the global economy " (Beniger, 1986, pp. 58-9).

37. French philosophers Gabriel Marcel and Jacques Ellul have given profound insight into distinctions between education (as an ideal) and propaganda. For Marcel, "an effective propagandist winds *into* the thought, and *under* the thoughts of his auditor, in order to circumvent him"; it is "the very nature of propaganda to degrade those whose attitudes it seeks to shape" (Marcel, 1978, pp. 51, 50). Education, by contrast, is (should be) direct and up-front, its aim being to uplift the learner. Likewise, for Ellul, "propaganda ceases where simple dialogue begins" (Ellul, [1965] 1973, p. 6); a propagandist, as distinct from a true educator, does not want to initiate critical thought, but rather displace it.

38. Nor was Suzuki the only victim of the *Sun's* cutback in environmental reporting. *The Sun*, at one time "a leading voice in covering the environment," by early 1991 (upon formation of the British Columbia Forestry Alliance, a "citizen's lobby" organized by the BC forest products industry upon the advice of public relations firm, Burson-Marstellar), dropped all coverage of, for example, clear-cutting in Clayoquot Sound. As a former *Sun* environmental reporter put it: "The Vancouver *Sun* has pretty much turned a blind eye to the biggest environmental story in North America, which is happening right here in its backyard, and that's the termination of the temperate rainforests." Environmental beats were relocated to the business section; today all that remains of editorial environmental reporting is confined to Greater Vancouver and the lower mainland, areas generally free of large tracks of old growth forests (Palmer, 1994; see also Nelson, 1994).

39. For instance Winter (1992); Schiller (1989); Hackett (1991); Parenti (1993); Bagdikian (1990); Barnouw (1978).

40. According to Innis, "The Western community was atomized by the pulverizing effects of the application of machine industry to communication. ... The influence of mechanization on the printing industry had been evident in the increasing importance of the ephemeral. Superficiality became essential to meet the various demands of larger numbers of people and was developed as an art by those compelled to meet the demands. ... The essence of living in the moment and for the moment is to banish all individual continuity" (Innis, [1951] 1971, pp. 79, 82, 90).

41. Heilbroner wrote: "The outlook for man, I believe, is painful, difficult,

perhaps desperate, and the hope that can be held out for his future prospect seems to be very slim indeed. Thus, to anticipate the conclusions of our inquiry, the answer to whether we can conceive of the future other than as a continuation of the darkness, cruelty, and disorder of the past seems to me to be no; and to the question of whether worse impends, yes " (Heilbroner, 1974, p. 2).

42. From the Kris Kristofferson song, "Me and Bobby McGee."

43. Donne's thoughts are so profound, and their expression so exquisite that perhaps they may be recited yet again: "No man is an island, entire of itself; every man is a piece of the continent, a part of the main. If a clod be washed away by the sea, Europe is the less, as well as if a promontory were, as well as if a manor of thy friend's or thine own were. Any man's death diminishes me because I am involved in mankind, and therefore never send to know for whom the bell tolls; it tolls for thee" (Donne, *Meditation XVII*, 1623/1624).

PART THREE

Information and Communication in Institutional and Evolutionary Economics

7

T. R. Malthus and the Origins of Communication in Economics

Oh God! to hear the Insect on the leaf pronouncing on the too much life among his hungry brothers in the dust!

—Charles Dickens (*A Christmas Carol* 1843)

Reality is, above all, a scarce resource. Like any scarce resource it is there to be struggled over. ...The fundamental form of power is the power to define, allocate, and display this resource.

—James W. Carey (1989)

Information and Evolution

God and Natural Selection

According to evolutionary biology, the primary mechanism of species' derivation and development has been *Natural Selection*, meaning that individuals and species "well-adapted" to surroundings persist (are "selected" by their habitat), while those "ill-adapted" dwindle, and perhaps become extinct (Jacob, 1973, p. 13). Natural Selection has been and remains one of this century's principle "paradigms" (Kuhn, [1962] 1970), or "myths" (see above, Chapter 5), even though (or perhaps because) it is tautological, that is to say it is "all hindsight ... [with] practically no predictive power at all" (Boulding, [1965] 1995, p. 11). Starting particularly with Herbert Spencer (1820–1903), an evolutionary perspective analogous to Natural Selection in the biosphere has been applied to such otherwise seemingly diverse phenomena as ideas, institutions, societies, laws, customs, knowledge, artifacts, and technology (Spencer, 1904; Basalla, 1988;

Veblen [1919] 1990; Boulding, 1978). (As we saw in Chapter 5, the economists' "Market" is essentially a particularization of the more generic notion of "Natural Selection." Like "Natural Selection," Supply and Demand according to neoclassical mythology are non-deliberative, impersonal, yet powerful forces rewarding the "fit" and weeding out the "unfit").

Evolution, in the sense of change, is of course pervasive in the universe. Recognizing and accepting this fact, however, need by no means entail acceptance also of the proposition that "*Natural* Selection" is or has been the sole or most basic factor motivating change. Just as critics of the notion of an impersonal Market contend that Supply and Demand result in large measure from the deliberative choices of concentrated human power blocks, including businesses and legislatures, so too do critics of "Natural Selection" point to the role of conscious human agents in affecting species' survival, and posit as well Mind as conceiving all things and as constituting the ground for all existence (Whitehead, 1929). As noted by Barbour, for instance,

> Recent authors point to both chance and law as expressions of God's overall design of the universe. Thus Polkinghorne [1987] writes, "The actual balance between chance and necessity, contingency and potentiality which we perceive seems to me to be consistent with the will of a patient and subtle Creator, content to achieve his purposes through the unfolding of process and accepting thereby a measure of the vulnerability and precariousness which always characterize the gift of freedom by love" (Barbour, 1990, p. 175).

Whether one ascribes the *most basic* explanation for existence and for change to "Chance,"[1] to "Nature," or to God—and the differences ontologically and existentially *are* indeed great—information remains meaningful and deepens insight with respect to on-going biogenetic and social transformations.

The chapters of Part 3 pursue the thought of some great economists, notably Thorstein Veblen and Kenneth Boulding, with regard to information as agent of economic change. To be true to their writings, we shall, in accordance with the practice of the authors, adopt for the most part the paradigm or myth of "Natural Selection." This is certainly not to say that information as agent of economic change is incompatible with alternative or more encompassing frameworks, and in particular with theological discourse. Simply referencing the opening chapter of *Genesis* (God spoke and it was done), and the beginning of John's Gospel demonstrates no such inconsistency.

However, insofar as the pioneering economists, beginning with Veblen and including the most devout, such as Boulding, have largely undertaken their analyses within a paradigm of "Natural Selection," so too by and large ought the chapters of this Part to adopt that convention. Taken together, the chapters of Part 3 point the way toward a more ecologically sound economics centered on person-in-community, as proposed at the conclusion of the preceding chapter.

Economics and Natural Selection

Economics foreshadowed and indeed inspired the myth or paradigm of biological evolution through Natural Selection. Charles Darwin and Alfred Russel Wallace, co-originators of the doctrine, each avowed indebtedness to Thomas Robert Malthus, a founding figure in classical political economy.[2]

Malthus was not himself, however, an evolutionary economist. Nor has mainstream economics since his time pursued to any marked degree evolutionary perspectives,[3] evidently preferring the elegance, mathematical rigor, and political congeniality of essentially static, equilibrium models such as those pioneered, for instance, by Léon Walras in the late nineteenth and early twentieth centuries. Indeed, as early as 1898, Thorstein Veblen was asking, "Why Is Economics Not An Evolutionary Science?" (Veblen, [1898] 1990). The answer emphasized in this chapter to Veblen's query is that mainstream economics' reductionist conception of information/communication minimizes analytical possibilities for acknowledging change.[4] On the other hand, within heterodox, and particularly evolutionary economics, information/communication have played more central roles. Ensuing chapters on the communication theory of Thorstein Veblen and Kenneth Boulding testify to this.

Diverging Streams in Institutional and Evolutionary Economics

Within Institutional and Evolutionary Economics there are divergent streams from what we take here to be a Malthusian origin.[5] One branch extends of course to Charles Darwin, leading as we shall see to an "evolutionary" economics of the right (Social Darwinism). A second branch, however, connects Malthus with Alfred Russel Wallace who, along with Henry George, helped forge a position consistent with a more egalitarian and pacific evolutionary economics of the left, for which Thorstein Veblen in the first quarter of this century became a prolific and influential exponent. Veblen, however, while emphasizing the vital role of *communication* in effecting economic change, did not consider explicitly *information*. More recently Kenneth Boulding and Nicholas Georgescu-Roegen particularly have gone great distance in privileging information as agent of change in economics.

Malthus as Prologue

Principle of Population

In 1798, Thomas Robert Malthus (1766–1834), as yet an unmarried cleric serving a small country parish near his parents home in Surrey, England, published anonymously *An Essay on the Principle of Population as it Affects the Future Improvement of Society*, causing economics thereafter to be renowned as "the dismal science." Affording his work the subtitle, *With Remarks on the Speculations of Mr. Godwin, M. Condorcet and Other Writers*, Malthus's intent had been to dispute "utopian" outpourings of the French Revolution that were then circulating. Primary among his targets was William Godwin (1756–1836)—pamphleteer, novelist and "philosophical Anarchist" (Cole, 1953, p. 25). Malthus took exception to Godwin's portrayal of an "illimitable vista of steady progress" (Mitchell, 1967, p. 236), and to Godwin's proffering prospects of a perfectible human nature. Moreover, Malthus disputed Godwin's contention of co-operation and communal ownership as constituting hallmarks of civilization, and as well his depiction of competition as being characteristic of barbarism. Malthus's rebuttal, prepared "on the spur of the occasion, and from the few materials which were within my reach in a country situation" (Malthus, [1803] 1992, p. 7), was primarily deductive, and proceeded from two "postulata," namely:

> First, that food is necessary to the existence of man. Secondly, that the passion between the sexes is necessary, and will remain nearly in its present state (Malthus, [1798] 1986, p. 8).

To Godwin's contention that eventually reason would advance sufficiently to reduce or restrain sexual desire and/or proclivity to reproduce, bachelor Malthus responded:

> Mr. Godwin considers man too much in the light of being merely intellectual. ... The voluntary actions of men may originate in their opinions; but these opinions will be very differently modified in creatures compounded of a rational faculty and corporal propensities, from what they would be in beings wholly intellectual (Malthus, [1798] 1986, pp. 89–93).

For Malthus, in plant and animal life alike, there is an "instinct" or propensity, uninterrupted by reason or concern for provisioning for offspring, which "impels" species to increase. Malthus's Principle of Population contended that unchecked, population would swell in "geometric ratio," as in the sequence 1, 2, 4, 8, 16, 32, whereas food supply could increase at best only in an "arithmetic ratio," as in the series 1, 2, 3, 4, 5, 6. Unchecked, therefore, population outgrows subsistence in the ratio of 32: 6 in merely five generations.

Malthus continued:

> By that law of our nature which makes food necessary to the life of man, the effects of these two unequal powers must be kept equal. This implies a strong and constantly operating check on population from the difficulty of subsistence (Malthus, [1798] 1986, p. 9).

Second and subsequent editions of Malthus's *Essay* added supporting documentation to the deductive argument of the first. Traveling and reading extensively, Malthus became by the early 1800's an "assiduous collector of information on his chosen field" (Winch, 1992, p. xii), and was thus able to present data concerning, *inter alia*, American Indians, South Sea Islanders, populations in Africa, Siberia, Turkey, Persia, England, China, Greece, Rome, Sweden, Russia and France, to support his contention that over-breeding was primarily, if not solely, responsible for evils and all forms of misery—for "bestial life, sickness, weakness, poor food, lack of ability to care for young, scant resources, famine, infanticide, war, massacre, plunder, slavery, disease, epidemics, pestilence, plague, and abortions" (Young, 1969, p. 132).

One way or another, Malthus warned, if not through human will and the exercise of self-restraint, then through natural and rather painful processes, population *would* be controlled. Two major "modes" of population control adumbrated by Malthus were: first, *preventive checks* working through marriage and/or birth rates; and second, *positive checks*, functioning through death rates. Malthus's examples of "preventive" checks included "promiscuous intercourse, unnatural passions, violations of the marriage bed, and improper arts to conceal the consequences of irregular connections" (Malthus, [1803] 1992, p. 24). Among "positive checks" he listed: "all unwholesome occupations, severe labour and exposure to the seasons, extreme poverty, bad nursing of children, great towns, excesses of all kinds, the whole train of common diseases and epidemics, wars, pestilence, plague, and famine" (Malthus, [1803] 1992, p. 23).

To an extent that can too easily be over-emphasized, second and subsequent editions of Malthus's *Essay* lightened, to a degree, the first's "melancholy hue" (Malthus, [1798] 1986, p. ii). For during the course of his empirical researches Malthus discovered that *both* mortality *and* fertility rates in Norway, Switzerland, and England had been low, making him a touch less pessimistic and deterministic concerning the human prospect than he hitherto had been. Now married, he began as well not merely acknowledging but, indeed, emphasizing the possibility of "moral restraint"[6] as a more convivial "check" to population growth, and in so doing approached, albeit gingerly, a position on human betterment not wholly dissimilar to that of arch nemesis, William Godwin. While certainly not becoming "sanguine in ... expectations of any great change in the conduct of men on this subject" (Malthus, [1803] 1992, p. 225),

Malthus nonetheless felt sufficiently encouraged to close revisions of his *Essay* in the following modestly upbeat way:

> On the whole though our future prospects affecting the mitigation of the evils arising from the principle of population may not be so bright as we can wish yet they are far from being entirely disheartening, and by no means preclude that gradual and progressive improvement in human society which before the last wild speculations on the subject [reference here being to "utopians" like Godwin and Condorcet] was the object of rational expectations (Malthus, [1803] 1992, p. 331).

Malthus Appraised

For critics like Henry George (1839–1897) the Malthusian doctrine was a "soothing and reassuring" panacea to those who "largely dominate thought." "A theory that ... justifies the greed of the rich and the selfishness of the powerful," George charged, "will spread quickly and strike its roots deep" (George, [1880] 1930, p. 100). By naturalizing or "theologizing" poverty and inequality, he continued, Malthus parried demands for reform and sheltered "selfishness from question and from conscience" (George, [1880] 1930, p. 99).

For George, Malthus's Population Principle was fundamentally flawed in two respects. First, "the reverend gentleman," George pronounced, failed to take into account the overriding "law of intellectual development." Population increases, he explained, invariably enable production of *more* food, thereby invalidating the purported mere "arithmetic" increase in means of subsistence. Humans, after all, differ from all other living creatures in being able to apply imagination, intelligence, and capital equipment to the cultivation of land to yield abundant harvests (George, [1880] 1930, p. 139). In formulating this argument George echoed Friedrich Engels who years earlier had claimed that the productivity of land could be increased "infinitely" by the application of capital, labor, and science (Engels, [1844] 1954, p. 58). For Engels, as well as for many non-Marxists of our day, knowledge "increases at least as fast as population" (Engels, 1844, in Meek, 1954, p. 63).[7]

George's general point, that increases to and changes in knowledge impact upon economic processes (and concomitantly therefore upon social structures) was well-placed, and indeed constitutes a cornerstone of Veblenian and Bouldingesque analyses. However, George's specific argument, that agricultural production can increase indefinitely through gains in knowledge, is becoming increasingly less convincing in an era now facing seemingly intractable problems of environmental degradation and resource depletion. (See Chapter 6, above).

A second rebuttal, formulated by George, however, retains full cogency for our day. George argued that Malthus completely failed to consider "social maladjustments." In countries beset by starvation, such as India, China, and Ireland, "the form of social organization shackled productive power and robbed [workers] of [their] reward" (George, [1880] 1930, p. 114). In India, for instance, working classes "since time immemorial ... have been ground down by exactions and oppressions into a condition of helpless and hopeless degradation" (George, [1880] 1930, p. 121). The very existence of vast tracts of uncultivated land for George was positive proof that "parsimonious nature" was not to blame for human misery, that attention rather should be cast upon *human* institutions, particularly the institution of private property (a theme advanced subsequently by Veblen), and to simple human greed. "Everywhere," he continued, "the vice and misery attributed to over-population can be traced to the warfare, tyranny, and oppression which prevent knowledge from being utilized and deny the security essential to production" (George, [1880] 1930, p. 123).

The aptness of George's second critique stems essentially from the paucity in Malthus's work of evolutionary and communicatory insight. Malthus assumed as given institutional arrangements (including the distribution of wealth, income, and property), and further he assumed human nature to be largely set. Moreover, he adopted an individualist mode of analysis, viewing economic agents as essentially autonomous, engaging in interaction merely through commodity exchange (and as well, of course, through conjugal relations). Nor were collectivities of people afforded much attention in his work. Stated otherwise, Malthus was largely oblivious of communicatory patterns and informational flows in establishing and maintaining organizational complexity.

Although the foregoing critique strikes hard at the Malthusian system, nonetheless Malthus can be interpreted more charitably. One hundred and sixty years after publication of his *Essay*'s first edition, Kenneth Boulding lauded Malthus's Population Principle as being "irrefutable as a syllogism," being in practice essentially correct, at least in the long run. Eventually, Boulding declared, "a stationary population *must* be reached on a limited earth." While like Henry George, Boulding too has most assuredly been cognizant of the capacity of growing knowledge to augment output, and likewise has been aware of, and concerned over, large and growing disparities in wealth between rich and poor (see for example, Boulding, 1973), nonetheless, unlike George or Engels, Boulding emphasized that at some point on the finite earth the "law of diminishing returns," and hence the Malthusian Population Principle, *must* set in.[8] Indeed, in the view of some, it has already done so (Daly, 1991).

Moreover, for Boulding, the Malthusian message, by being true, was also positive and hopeful. By "puncturing" the easy optimism of utopians, and exposing "at least one dragon which must be slain before misery can be abolished," Malthus in Boulding's opinion helped induce not despair but activity, activity "of the right kind" (Boulding, [1959] 1971, p. 142).

Finally, according to Boulding, Malthus stands "at the portal of the whole great movement of nineteenth-century evolutionary thought." "Evolution as ecological succession," he explained, is but a simple extension of the Malthusian system (Boulding, [1959] 1971, pp. 135, 139).[9]

Malthus's Dual Legacy

Stimulus to an "Evolutionary" Economics of the Right

Darwin. Malthus promoted a severe doctrine of individual responsibility for outcomes. Humans, he contended, are inherently slothful and exert themselves only under the yoke of dire necessity. "Had population and food increased in the same ratio," he mused, "it is probable that man might never have emerged from the savage state" (Malthus, [1798] 1986, p. 127). Given the parsimony of Nature, only those able and willing to work long and hard can survive. For the rest, "at nature's mighty feast there is no vacant cover. ... She tells [them] to be gone, and will quickly execute her own orders" (Malthus, [1803] 1992, p. 249).

Charles Darwin, while reading Malthus's *Essay* "for amusement," was struck with an explanation for his surmised ascent of life forms. For Darwin and Malthus alike, life was struggle. Both saw creatures as being tested for survival by a harsh, frugal environment. In the Malthusian Population Principle, Darwin detected a force in nature "selecting" living beings, but lacking in the purpose or design of plant and animal breeders. Darwin was at one accord with Malthus in contending that limited food in the face of population growth meant that only some would survive. Hence, Darwin wrote, the "Struggle for Existence" is simply "the doctrine of Malthus applied with manifest force to the whole animal and vegetable kingdoms." "For," he continued,

> in this case there can be no artificial increase of food, and no prudential restraint from marriage. There is no exception to the rule that every organic being naturally increases at so high a rate, that if not destroyed, the earth would soon be covered by the progeny of a single pair. ... Even slow-breeding man has doubled in twenty-five years, and at this rate, in a few thousand years, there would literally not be standing room for his progeny (Darwin, [1859] 1959, p. 147).

Despite manifest commonality between Malthus's Principle of Population and Darwin's Theory of Natural Selection, Darwin departed significantly from Malthus. Malthus, it will be recalled, in conceiving the Population Principle as rebuttal to Godwin, had been intent on defending the *status quo*—in nature as in society (Young, 1969, p, 116). His Population Principle depicted nature as periodically restoring equilibrium or balance, with the implication that human "interference," for instance by implementing social measures such as those proposed by Godwin and others to alleviate human suffering, was vain and misguided, merely disrupting natural cycles put in place by a beneficent Providence. By contrast Darwin's Theory of Natural Selection (or "Survival of the Fittest") advanced the doctrine of sequential and cumulative change without limit and without a prior-determined destination. It is then indeed ironic that the same natural forces that for Malthus restored equilibrium, for Darwin set in motion continuous change.

Social Darwinism. Through successive editions of his *Essay*, Malthus resolutely maintained that the poor "are themselves the causes of their own poverty," that "the means of redress are in their own hands, and in the hand of no other persons whatever," and that "it is clearly the duty of each individual not to marry till he has the prospect of supporting his children" (Malthus, [1803] 1992, pp. 229, 215). Failure to put Reason in nuptial matters ahead of Passion, the stern pastor admonished, was the single major cause of suffering on the part of the poor (Malthus, [1803] 1992, p. 221). Those foolish enough to reproduce in the absence of adequate material support, he advised, were destined to be "crowded together in close and unwholesome workhouses where a great mortality almost universally takes place, particularly among the young children" (Malthus, [1803] 1992, pp. 221, 106).

Malthus was extremely skeptical about all forms of charity, of communal provisioning, of common property, and of egalitarian social legislation. He pronounced gloomily that these could but destroy "the encouragement and motives of moral restraint," and hence "increase population without increasing the means for its support" (Malthus, [1803] 1992, p. 103). Better to let the indigent starve than to have their numbers swell through well-intentioned but misguided philanthropy.[10] "As with Intemperance in eating and drinking," he continued, so too with evils "arising from the principle of population"—all are contingent upon "palpable disobedience of [natural] law" (Malthus, [1803] 1992, pp. 209, 221).

Malthus was, then, progenitor of a movement that came to be known as Social Darwinism, espousing a doctrine summarized by Jacques Barzun as signifying that "no good thing was ever lost and that no lost thing was any longer any good" (Barzun, 1981, p. 60). Social Darwinism applied and extended Darwinian concepts of struggle, adaptation, selection, and succession to various dimensions of social life. Foremost among the movement's expositors were philosopher Herbert Spencer in England and, in the United States, the conservative economist and Episcopal minister, William Graham Sumner. It is to the latter that we turn briefly here.

For Sumner (1840–1910) "life on earth must be maintained by a struggle against nature, and also by a competition with other forms of life" (Sumner, 1963, p. 14). Under dual, divinely orchestrated ordinances, namely the Principle of Population and the Law of Diminishing Returns, "want and distress" as well as "constraint, anxiety, possibly tyranny and repression," are but normal characteristics of social relations (Sumner, 1963, p. 14). Sumner rejected adamantly all philosophy suggestive either of natural rights or of innate human freedom. To the contrary, he declared, "The human race has never had any freedom which it did not earn, or any freedom which it did not conquer" (Sumner, 1963, p. 17). The "radical error of the socialists and sentimentalists," he charged, is that they "bring forward complaints [against society] which are really to be made, if at all, against the author of the universe for the hardships which man has to endure in his struggle with nature" (Sumner, 1963, p. 17). "The law of survival of the fittest was not made by man," he explained, and "interfering with it [can only] produce the survival of the unfittest" (Sumner, 1963 p. 17). Since for Sumner "the only social element" is "the competition of life," it follows that "liberty perishes in all socialistic schemes, and the tendency of such schemes is to the deterioration of society by burdening the *good* members and relieving the *bad* ones" (Sumner, 1963 p. 17, emphasis added).[11]

Current Reformulations. The Malthusian doctrine of individualized struggle and the presumed efficacy of natural selection in comparison with ameliorative and egalitarian social policy, reappears as today's neo-conservatism. As well, Malthus's doctrine is consistent with neoclassical economics' methodological individualism, and with its emphasis on efficiency and competition. Moreover, like Malthus, modern neoclassicism ascribes equilibrium-inducing properties to competitive struggle, in marked contrast, however, to the Darwinian notion that competition and the struggle to survive lead to continuous, cumulative, and unpredictable change.

Stimulus to an Evolutionary Economics of the Left

Alfred Russel Wallace, co-originator of the doctrine of evolution through natural selection, like Darwin, paid homage to Malthus, writing that "perhaps the most important book I read was Malthus's 'Principles of Population.'" Wallace declared that Malthus's tome provided him with "the long-sought clue to the effective agent in the evolution of organic species" (Wallace, 1905; quoted in Young, 1969, p. 130).

Wallace differed from Darwin, however, in one very important respect. While accepting, indeed co-creating, the doctrine of natural selection to "explain" variation in life forms of lower species, Wallace rejected natural selection as being applicable either to the origin or to the development of the human species. His reasons for reaching this position are worth recounting.

First, Wallace pointed to the large size of the brain of pre-historic humans. Their "large and well-developed brain," he surmised, was "an organ quite disproportionate to [their] actual requirements." It was, he continued,

> an organ that seems prepared in advance, only to be utilized as [humanity progresses] in civilization. ... Natural Selection could only have endowed a savage man with a brain a little superior to that of the ape, whereas he actually possesses one very little inferior to that of a philosopher (Wallace [1870] 1973, pp. 343, 356).

For Wallace, the brain of prehistoric humans in fact pointed to "the existence of some power, distinct from that which has guided the development of lower animals through their ever-varying form" (Wallace [1870] 1973, p. 343).[12] For him, indeed, the advent of human beings inaugurated a new era, one "governed by mental and supernatural factors rather than the material ones that hitherto had been in complete control" (Gordon, 1991, p. 512).

Second, anticipating Veblen and Institutional Economics, Wallace emphasized the importance for human evolution of human artifacts. Whereas other species, according to the Theory of Natural Selection, can adapt to changing circumstances only, or at least primarily, through transformations in bodily structures—"longer nails or teeth, greater bodily strength or swiftness," for instance—humans, on account of superior mental capacities, can and do devise artifacts such as "sharper spears" and "a better bow," "a cunning pitfall" and "a hunting party to circumvent [their] new prey" (Wallace [1870] 1973, p. 314). Rather than growing warmer fur or a new covering of fat in order to adapt to the arrival of a new glacial age, humans can make "warmer clothing" and build "better houses," leaving the "natural body ... naked as before" (Wallace [1870] 1973, p. 314). Humanity, in other words, "has taken away from nature that power of slowly but permanently changing the external form and structure ... which she exercises over all other animals" (Wallace [1870] 1973, p. 315).

Third, again anticipating Institutional Economics, Wallace saw voluntarism, cooperation, and purposeful social/institutional reform as transcending natural selection and as providing thereby keys to human progress. According to Wallace, humans possess "superior sympathetic and moral feelings" compared to other species, making humans "fitted for the social state" (Wallace [1870] 1973, p. 328). Humans possess the "capacity for acting in concert for protection, and for the acquisition of food and shelter." Likewise, humankind's sense of "sympathy ... leads all in turn to assist each other." Even "in the rudest tribes the sick are assisted, at least with food. ... Neither does the want of perfect limbs, or other organs, produce the same effect as among animals" (Wallace [1870] 1973, p. 312).

Both Wallace and Henry George, then, were forebears of an evolutionary economics of the left, soon to be further developed and refined by Thorstein Veblen, and subsequently by Kenneth Boulding. Theirs was an economics that repudiated the methodological individualism of the economics mainstream, stressing rather the significance of human cognition and the role of human artifacts and institutions in human social evolution.

Recapitulation

Malthus, a seminal figure in political economy, inspired a biological theory of natural selection from whence has stemmed both Social Darwinism on the right, and Institutional and Evolutionary Economics on the left. Malthus himself, however, was far from being an evolutionary economist. He considered human nature to be largely set. Moreover, he paid scant attention to institutional change. Nor did he appreciate fully the contributions that growth in knowledge, and particularly technological change, make in transforming social and economic structures. Neither was he appreciative of the significance for human organization of communication.

Emphasizing individual struggle and downplaying communicatory interaction, Malthus most directly inspired Social Darwinism, an "evolutionary" economics of the right, maintaining that *decline* in human prospects can be averted, and the human condition perhaps even improved, only if "Natural Selection" is left unfettered of amelioratory and collectivized human interventions. Otherwise, "evolutionary" economists of the right contend, the "unfit" will proliferate to the point where the "quality" of species deteriorates.

Social Darwinists and other "evolutionary" economists of the right, it is to be noted, proffer a very circumscribed depiction of human/societal evolution. Concentrating on biogenetics and heredity[13] they perceive societal institutions and basic parameters of the political, social, cultural, and economic system as unchanging, indeed as being perhaps unchangeable.

Malthus also inspired, however, an evolutionary economics of the left which indeed recognizes and attempts to account for changes in human nature, institutions, and societal parameters. Exponents posit human cognition and institutional change as superseding and rendering insignificant both "Natural Selection" and individual human struggle as factors underlying and motivating human/societal evolution. Alfred Russel Wallace and Henry George were early expositors of this view.

The amount of attention afforded *communication* is crucial in distinguishing between "evolutionary" economics of the right and evolutionary economics of the left. Communication is the transmittal and exchange of knowledge and information, and hence is necessarily the means whereby individuals constitute groups and whereby groups attain and maintain coherence. Communication is also the means whereby individuals influence and mutually transform one another, and their institutions. Communicatory considerations, therefore, undermine the assumed autonomy of economic actors, as postulated by economists of the right. One suspects, therefore, that it is primarily on account of the logical (and empirical) inconsistency of individual autonomy *vis à vis* communication, that has induced the economics mainstream to proffer such reductionist treatments of information/communication. Simply put, methodological individualism is belied by fully-textured communicatory interaction.

By comparing treatments of information/communication on the part of Malthus, Social Darwinists, and other conservative economists, with treatments afforded information/communication by economists of the left, the importance of communicatory processes for economic change and organizational development becomes clearly evident.

Notes

1. "Chance" is a name afforded processes that have not been explained, and that are presumed to be unexplainable. "Chance," then, is yet another of the secular mythologies addressed in Chapter 5.

2. The others most often cited of course are Adam Smith and David Ricardo.

3. At the turn of the century Alfred Marshall recommended incorporating evolutionism into marginal analysis. He declared that human nature, far from permanent, is subject to transformation through interaction with its environment. Furthermore, according to Marshall, the social world, like the organic one, is subject to simultaneous and dialectical processes of dissolution and integration (shades of Herbert Spencer!), resulting in greater specialization and complexity, and *parri passu*, in greater interdependence (Marshall, [1890]1920, pp. 240-9). Despite such insights, Marshall was unable to follow through on his own recommendation (Boulding, 1981, p. 84).

One who did try, years later, to marry neoclassicism and evolutionism was Armen Alchian. In his endeavor Alchian dismissed neoclassicism's myth of the omniscient entrepreneur, concomitantly jettisoning as well its vaunted moral stance whereby rewards are presumed to accrue solely to the prepared and skilled, explaining perhaps why the Alchian synthesis receives scant attention these days within neoclassicism.

Alchian proposed refocussing attention from the individual economic agent (the profit maximizing firm or entrepreneur), onto the economic environment as the agent that selects individuals. According to Alchian, corporate decision-making is akin to chance biological mutations: "Sheer chance is a substantial element in determining the situation selected [by firms and individuals] and also in determining its appropriateness or viability" (Alchian, 1950, pp. 213-4).

Note that by retaining the individualist methodology of Malthus and of neo-classicism, albeit in this case in the context of Natural Selection, Alchian gave short shrift to communication. In privileging Chance, rather than information or communication, as the causal agent for change, Alchian became in the end, however, tautological. Chance, by definition, denotes that which is not or cannot be explained. Alchian's "theory," therefore, in the end, like all evolutionary "theories" relying on Chance, is bereft of predictive power, even in a probabilistic sense.

4. More fundamental, however, are political economy answers.

5. As Ian Parker in private correspondence has noted, it would be quite possible to select origins other than the Malthusian one. James Steuart, for example, a mentor of Adam Smith, developed the core of an evolutionary, economic-historical framework and mode of analysis which Smith himself adopted, particularly in Book III of *The Wealth of Nations*. Smith's fundamental theorem, that the division of labor is limited by the extent of the market, according to Parker, is a basic maxim of evolutionary economics, indeed "one of the most profound evolutionary theses in the history of economic thought."

Nonetheless, the "origin" of evolutionary and communicatory economics selected here is Malthusian. The direct lineage from Malthus to bio-evolutionary theory (Darwin and Wallace) and thence to subsequent evolutionary social theory, justifies this choice. Moreover, the clarity with which Malthus's thought depicts the consequences of employing but rudimentary conceptions of information/communication for interpreting social phenomena gives added justification.

6. Malthus wrote: "By moral restraint I would be understood to mean restraint from marriage from prudential motives, with a conduct strictly moral during the period of this restraint. ... When I have wished to consider the restraint from marriage unconnected with its consequences, I have either called it prudential restraint, or a part of the preventive check, of which indeed it forms the principal branch" (Malthus, [1803] 1992, p. 23, n. 4).

7. Marx and Engels took great (and bitter) exception to Malthus. Marx called him "the mountebank-parson" and the "shameless sycophant." Like Godwin, Wallace, and George, Marx and Engels too argued that it is, or at least should be, the *reduction* in the struggle for survival that distinguishes humans from other forms of life. Engels wrote: "Free competition, the struggle for existence, which the economists celebrate as the highest historical achievement, is the normal state of the animal kingdom; only conscious organization of social production, in which production and distribution are carried out in a planned way, can lift mankind above the rest of the animal world as regards the social aspect, in the same way that production in general has done this for men in their aspect as species" (Engels, in Meek, 1954, p. 185).

8. One cannot grow the world's food supply in a flower pot, Boulding was fond of remarking, which would be possible in the absence of a law of diminishing returns (Boulding, 1981, p. 110).

9. Boulding, however, usually distinguished "ecological succession" from true evolutionary change By ecological succession he meant "patterns of succession of short-run equilibrium states. ... The lake fills up and becomes a swamp, finally a prairie, and then a forest" (Boulding, [1966] 1995, p. 11). Evolutionary systems, in contrast, "involve the processes of genetic mutation *and* ecological selection in the biological field, and parallel phenomena involving the growth of knowledge and organizations, cultures and societies, techniques and commodities, in the social field" (Boulding, [1966] 1995, p. 11, emphasis added).

10. Malthus was at least incipiently an eugenicist, writing, "If distress be made the sole measure of our liberality, it is evident that it will be exercised almost exclusively upon common beggars, while modest unobtrusive merit struggling with unavoidable difficulties, yet still maintaining some light appearance of decency and cleanliness, will be totally neglected. We shall raise the worthless above the worthy; we shall encourage indolence..., and, in the most marked manner subtract from the sum of human happiness" (Malthus, [1793] 1986, pp. 135-6).

As noted by Scott Gordon, eugenics in the first third of the twentieth century captivated some of the most distinguished minds in America and Britain: George Bernard Shaw, Sidney and Beatrice Webb, Alfred Marshall, John Maynard Keynes, Harold Laski, Havelock Ellis, H. G. Welles, Winston Churchill, Theodore Roosevelt, Alexander Graham Bell, Oliver Wendell Holmes. Only with abhorrence at the Nazi euthanasia and eugenics programs before and during World War II did enthusiasm for eugenics wane (Gordon, 1991, p. 522).

11. We may note here some remarks by Kenneth Boulding on Social Darwinism, which may find applicability as well for the thought of Malthus. Boulding maintained that Social Darwinists espoused a "profoundly erroneous view" of evolutionary processes, and that in attempting to justify a "politics of unbridled competition" they underestimated the complexity of ecological interactions, placing too strong an emphasis on competitive aspects of natural selection (Boulding, 1981, p. 18). According to Boulding, "In biological evolution, *cooperative* behavior often paid off very well, and indeed the principle of the "survival of the *fitting*" can easily be translated into the principle that the meek—that is, the adaptable—inherit the earth. The tough and the unadaptable either kill each other off or do not survive changes in the environment" (Boulding, 1981, p.18).

Furthermore, Boulding wrote, Social Darwinists ignored "the role of government and political structure in the social evolutionary process" (Boulding, 1981, p. 18). Through political processes, Boulding continued, the entire system changes (Boulding, 1978, p. 23).

More generally, it was Boulding's conviction that human artifacts and human activity of all types have affected and continue to affect profoundly the course of human evolution. See Chapter 9, below. Note also the consistency of Boulding's thought with that of Henry George and Russel Wallace.

12. As noted by Arthur Koestler, Darwin responded to these thoughts by letter to Wallace: "I hope you have not murdered completely your own and my child." But, Koestler remarked, Darwin had no satisfactory response to Wallace's critique, "and his disciples swept it under the carpet" (Koestler, 1978, p. 274).

13. The following extract from neoclassical economists, Rose and Milton Friedman, illustrates the preponderant focus by neoclassicists on individual

characteristics and demonstrates an affinity between neoclassicists and Malthus with regard to social policy: "If we took [fair shares] seriously, youngsters with less musical skill should be given the greatest amount of musical training in order to compensate for their inherited disadvantage and those with the greater aptitude should be prevented from having access to good musical training, and similarly with regard to all other categories of inherited personal qualities "(Friedman and Friedman, 1980, p. 136).

An implicit critique of the Friedmans' position will be found in the main body of this chapter where the thoughts of George and Wallace are addressed, and as well in the next chapter, which reviews Veblen's contribution to evolutionary economics (see particularly note 3). For present purposes it is perhaps sufficient to note in addition that "egalitarian" social policy, far from striving to eradicate all differences, typically attempts merely to ensure decent minimum living standards for all.

8

The Communication Theory of
Thorstein Veblen

Society not only continues to exist by transmission, by communications, but it may fairly be said to exist in transmission, in communications.

—John Dewey (1915)

Veblen's Ontology

Methodological individualism, characteristic of neoclassicism, imposes a highly circumscribed notion of information and communication on analyses of human interaction. Methodological collectivism, conversely, by emphasizing the radical interdependencies of individuals and the importance of groupings in the political economy, gives greater sway to the complexities of communicatory interaction.

One who recognized the centrality of communication to economic processes, and who therefore eschewed the methodological individualism of the dominant economics discourse, was Thorstein Veblen (1857–1929). Writing during neoclassicism's formative years, Veblen viewed society and its institutions as evolving entities, comprised of individuals certainly, but of individuals *in communication*. Moreover, Veblen afforded prominence in his writings to organized bodies of information—to knowledge, customs, habits of thought, belief, rituals, artifacts, inventions—maintaining that these informational structures on the one hand motivate, and on the other hand issue out of, societal change.

Veblen, however, was something of a tragic figure. With penetrating insight and satiric wit, he pierced the social veil, "seeing through" society's conventions and rituals, through its distinctions, knowledge, "common sense" and belief systems, adjudging them all to be mere social constructions, "true" for a time in the sense of being accepted and perhaps useful within a given culture, but of no enduring consequence. In "seeing through" so much, nothing for Veblen remained opaque. In a sense, he "abolished" himself (Lewis, [1943] 1978; also Grant, 1969) as his ontology was unable to substantiate or render valuable even for him his own keen and penetrating intellect. For Max Lerner, Veblen "was a man living in a shell formed by long years of alienation and hurt, and perhaps also by the glimpses of terror he had when he probed into the nature of institutions and the course of history" (Lerner, 1950, p. 48).[1]

For some, reading Veblen can be displeasing (see note 24): his penchant for irony and his capacity to see through so much meant that, in the end, he "saw" Nothing. Yet, despite his avowed agnosticism and an apparent nihilism, Veblen can be interpreted differently, as being indeed in some respects a profoundly, albeit radically incomplete, religious figure. (But then, are not we all in one sense or another radically incomplete?). Veblen was the archetypal sojourner in a foreign land, both literally and figuratively but, unlike Bunyan's Pilgrim, one who retained little hope or expectation of finding eventually a more congenial home. In his scholarship Veblen was scrupulously honest, describing , indeed satirizing, the foibles of the world as he saw them, irrespective of personal consequences. He was also humble, keenly aware of his own as well as of humanity's limitations or "fallenness," albeit unable to accept a doctrine of redemption or forgiveness. Finally, and certainly much more than the religious figures whose views on society he scorned—particularly those of Malthus and Sumner— Veblen perceived a fundamental unity for all things, a sense of connectedness being perhaps the most basic of all religious experience.

Intellectual Forebears

Continuing in the same vein as Henry George and Russel Wallace, Veblen contributed to the development of an evolutionary economics of the left, combating thereby his era's Social Darwinism.[2] According to his biographer and former student, Joseph Dorfman, Veblen's first book, *The Theory of the Leisure Class*, satirically invoked Spencerian principles to show that evolutionism implies socialism, not capitalism (Dorfman, 1932).[3] While insisting that economics needed to become more "Darwinian,"[4] Veblen rejected utterly, however, the Malthusian/Social Darwinist dogma of individualized struggle as the sole, or even as a primary agent of human/societal evolution.[5] He denied, in other words, that individuals are inheritors only of genetic information, biochemically fixed upon conception. More significantly, Veblen opined, people are inheritors of *culturally generated* information that changes continually and cumulatively, and to which Darwinian-type principles of selection apply (Veblen, [1914] 1964, p. 138).

For Veblen, therefore, there was no such thing as *homo economicus*—the isolated, self-sufficing individual. All production, he wrote, is "in and by the help of the community, and all wealth is such only in society" (Veblen, [1898] 1964, p. 33). Knowledge and technology, Veblen claimed, constitute a social endowment, society's "common stock." Barred access to this common informational pool, every person, irrespective of genetic endowment, would be rendered quite "helpless" (Veblen, [1914] 1964, p. 138).

In addition to Darwin and Spencer, another seminal influence on Veblen was Charles Sanders Peirce, a colleague during Veblen's sojourn at the University of Chicago. Peirce was a founding figure in American semiology, the study of the generation of meaning from signs, and of pragmatism, a philosophical school whose most famous exponents have been William James and John Dewey (Dorfman, 1934, pp. 40, 41). Peirce maintained that "the whole function of thought" is to produce the rules of behavior ("habits of action," he called them) that help organisms survive. "Habits of mind," according to Peirce, guide behavior of all kinds, including research and inquiry. For Peirce, "thought is an action" that leads in turn to further thought (Dorfman, 1934, p. 41). "What a thing means," Peirce claimed, "is simply what habits it involves" (quoted in Wright, 1988, p. 101). As well, Peirce attacked what he called the "greed philosophy" of conventional economics, the conviction that "all acts of charity and benevolence, private and public ... degrade the human race'" (quoted in Dorfman, 1934, p. 94). Peirce's thoughts, as we shall see, resonate in the writings of Veblen.

Inveighing against the static nature of classical economics, Veblen's critical analysis remains pertinent for the present era as a dynamic alternative to static neoclassicism, largely bereft of communicatory considerations. Veblen, like Wallace and George, and like Boulding who is addressed in the next chapter, helps point us in the direction of an economics that incorporates expansive conceptions of information and communication, an economics that can encompass both individual and social/institutional change.

Veblen and Institutional Economics

Institutions

"Habits of thought," that is, routinized presuppositions and modes of thinking, were basic for Veblen; they undergird understanding and constitute every culture's (or subculture's) premises, or ground, upon which cognition and interpretation are formed (Veblen, [1906] 1990, p. 10).

Anticipating by several years the more famous formulation (quoted above) by John Dewey,[6] another illustrious colleague at the University of Chicago, Veblen declared:

> The cultural scheme of any community is a complex of the habits of life and of thought prevalent among the members; it makes up a more or less congruous and balanced whole, and carries within it a more or less consistent habitual attitude toward matters of knowledge (Veblen, [1908] 1990, p. 39).

Routine activities ("habits of life," Veblen called them) engender "habits of thought," what we might term "common sense," accepted uncritically by most people most of the time. These taken-for-granted, perhaps unconscious, even subconscious, "habits of thought," Veblen surmised, have as their bases vague and mutable propensities or "instincts," but are given their specificity through interaction within society (i.e. communication).[7]

In Veblen's view, if in a given social environment an individual's particular mode of thought or of action secures advantage (or fitness for survival), it becomes sedimented as "habit" for that individual. Likewise, group modes of thought or of action, if bestowing a survival advantage, congeal as "institutions." "Habits" and "institutions," then, issuing primordially from "instincts," but moulded (mutated) by the natural and, significantly, social environments, for Veblen were adaptive strategies on the part of individuals and groups respectively.[8,9]

Furthermore, Veblen maintained, "the fabric of institutions intervenes between the material exigencies of life and the speculative scheme of things." While, as just noted, institutions *derive from* the habits or customs of individuals interacting to sustain material existence, they furthermore impose on individuals "conventional standards, ideals, and canons of conduct," thereby constituting "the community's scheme of life" (Veblen, [1908] 1990, p. 44). "The scheme of life, within which lies the scheme of knowledge," Veblen remarked, "is a consensus of habits in the individuals which make up the community" (Veblen, [1908] 1990, p. 38).

Institutions, Social Construction, and Power

Individual conduct, and hence habits of thought, Veblen contended, are "fostered by the more impressive affairs of life," which is to say institutions of wealth and power (Veblen, [1906] 1990, p. 10). They are, in other words, part and parcel of the distribution of power and the organizational structure of society. "Canons of knowledge" inevitably take on "the same complexion" as the ruling institutions. During transitional periods, for example from hunter-gatherer to agricultural, or from agricultural to industrialized society, habits of thought perforce change in conformity with new economic and social arrangements. Whereas in normal times they constitute "common sense," in times of transition habits of thought can comprise loci of struggle or tension. On the other hand, vestiges of thought patterns characteristic of previous eras can also co-exist alongside, albeit inconsistently with, those of the newer order.

More generally Veblen, following Peirce and anticipating as well Boulding and other, modern communication theorists, maintained that meaning resides not only in the symbolic constructs or messages, but also in interpretation. Interpretations differ, however, according to the particular system of decoding that individual readers (receivers) apply to messages. Systems of decoding, in turn, while derived in part perhaps from unique individual life experiences, more generally and more powerfully are based on cultural or subcultural habits of thought.

Causal Sequence

For Thorstein Veblen, the implicit "postulate" of evolutionary science is the "notion of sequence, or consecutive change, in which the *nexus* of the sequence ... is the relation of cause and effect" (Veblen, [1908] 1990, p. 32). "Cumulative change" Veblen conceived as being self-continuing, self-propagating, and without final term or goal (Veblen, [1908] 1990, p. 37).[10] When one conceives of processes, whether physical, biological, or social, as comprising unbroken sequences of cumulative change stemming from the interplay of natural forces and purposive human action, in Veblen's eyes that one is "Darwinian," "matter-of-fact," "modern." Systems of thought positing a "final term" toward which things inevitably progress, by contrast, he termed "animistic," "teleological," "archaic," "pre-Darwinian" (Veblen, [1899] 1990, pp. 82-99). To his credit, while opting for the former view, Veblen acknowledged the choice to be a matter of belief or of faith: "[The] ultimate ground of knowledge is always of a metaphysical character. ... [The] endeavor to avoid all metaphysical premises fails here as everywhere"[11] (Veblen, [1900] 1990, p. 149).

Artifacts and Evolution

Human artifacts for Veblen are not merely outcomes of human evolution; they also in turn impact on human knowledge, on economic processes, and hence on the course of social development. He defined artifacts both as "items in a process of cumulative change" as humans work on them, and as "items in the scheme of life" which impact on human knowledge and on economic processes (Veblen, [1898] 1990, p. 71). The microscope, for example, was produced through application of human knowledge, but in turn its invention affected the subsequent course of human knowledge, and perforce of economic processes. Bi-directional causality, Veblen contended, typifies many artifacts. Being, on the one hand, "facts of human knowledge, skill, and predilection," artifacts also "enter into the process of industrial development" (Veblen, [1898] 1990, p. 71).

Veblen contrasted his "genetic" or "evolutionary" perspective respecting human artifacts and their two-way interactions with people and cultures, with the classical or "pre-Darwinian" treatment, whereby inert matter was "scheduled and graded by the economists under the head of capital," conceived merely as "a mass of material objects serviceable for human use." While this might be "well enough for the purposes of taxonomy," Veblen remarked, "it is not an effective method of conceiving the matter for the purpose of a theory of the developmental process" (Veblen, [1898] 1990, p. 71). Years later, Kenneth Boulding expounded at length on this, as on many other of Veblen's thoughts.

Individual Psychology and Institutional Change

In Veblen's view, the mainstream economics of his day incorrectly proposed an "immutably given," hedonistic,[12] essentially "passive and substantially inert" human nature (Veblen, [1898] 1990, p. 73), a most grievous error in his opinion, as this robbed economics of dynamic potential. For economics truly to become an "evolutionary science," Veblen opined, a mutable and evolutionary psychology needed to be incorporated within the discipline. While people certainly are creatures of habit and of propensities, he wrote, they *do* change. As he explained:

> The economic life history of the individual is a cumulative process of adaptation of means to ends that cumulatively change as the process goes on, both the agent and his environment being at any point the outcome of the last process. His methods of life to-day are enforced upon him by his habits of life carried over from yesterday and by the circumstances left as the mechanical residue of the life of yesterday.
>
> What is true of the individual in this respect is true of the group in which he lives. All economic change is a change in the economic community—a change in the community's methods of turning material things to account. The change is always in the last resort a change in habits of thought (Veblen, [1898] 1990, pp. 74–75).

More generally, Veblen maintained that mainstream economists took too much for granted and too much as given—indeed the very things (such as the distribution of income, wealth and power)[13] that are the very heart of the matter. Economists, Veblen charged, like other "animistic" or "teleological" thinkers, transform "the [culturally] accepted ideal of conduct [into] a canon of truth," thereby legitimizing established arrangements. In this way, "habits of thought" become transformed into instruments of social control.

Communication and Social Evolution

In Veblen's schema, social history has consisted of three major eras: *peaceful savagery,* accounting for "by far the greater portion of the life-history of mankind" (Veblen, [1906] 1990, p. 25); *predatory barbarism* (sometimes subdivided into "lower barbarism" and "higher" or "mature" barbarism); and *civilization,* or *industry* (also subdivided into "lower-civilized" and "higher-civilized"). In contrasting these three epochs, Veblen drew particular attention to, and contrasted, the nature of belief and knowledge systems and the institution of property—in other words, individual and societal habits of thought and modes of communicating. The following summarizes Veblen's analysis of these three eras.

Savagery

Veblen believed that the human genetic endowment had largely stabilized by the conclusion of the neolithic era, making savagery or tribalism "in a sense, native to man" (Veblen, [1914] 1964, pp. 36, 20). Social life during this "golden age," according to Veblen, had few sharp class divisions. Nor was there "an unremitting endeavor of one individual or group to get the better of another" (Veblen, [1906] 1990, p. 24). Rather, "the ruling institutions [were] those of blood-relationship, descent, and clannish discrimination" (Veblen, [1906] 1990, p. 10) and life, "with [but] sporadic predation," was primarily peaceable (Veblen, [1906] 1990, p. 10).

Significantly, "property rights [were] few, slight and unstable" during savagery (Veblen, [1908] 1990, p. 47). In his essay, "The Beginnings of Ownership," Veblen (in contradistinction to some later and speculative anthropological works such as Robert Ardrey's *Territorial Imperative*) maintained that property is neither "natural" nor a given, but rather that it is mere social construction, a human institution.[14] As noted by Eff (1989), Veblen differed markedly from Herbert Spencer in his analysis of property, and hence also in assessing property's role in evolution. For Spencer, private property had always existed and, he claimed, augmented market activity could but serve to break down traditional hierarchies and stimulate industrial progress. Property for Veblen, in contrast, was the primary source of human aggression and predation, transforming a peaceable instinct of workmanship into invidious emulation (Edgell and Tilman, 1989, p. 1008).

In the era of "peaceable savagery," Veblen declared, knowledge arose primarily from a basic human instinct that he termed "idle curiosity," akin to play. Knowledge issuing from idle curiosity, he added, is constructed not for practical application but is merely a "response to stimulus," an attempt to render coherent the "sequence of activities going on in the observed phenomena." It is humankind's attempt to "tame the facts thrown in its way ... and to break them in under a scheme of habitual interpretation" (Veblen, [1908] 1990, p. 40).

Knowledge stemming from idle curiosity in the savage era Veblen depicted as "romantic and Hegelian rather than realistic and Darwinian" (Veblen, [1906] 1990, p. 25). In describing this knowledge as "romantic and Hegelian," Veblen meant that the era's knowledge presumed that dramatic clashes of opposites would bring about new syntheses, tending toward a final state or goal. By "realistic" and "Darwinian," on the other hand, he referred to knowledge that is cumulative rather than dialectical, and that points to no final or predetermined end. Knowledge in "peaceable savagery" for Veblen was "naive," "crude," "animistic ," and "dramatic," taking the form of myths and legends (Veblen, [1908] 1990, p. 40).[15] The test of validity for "dramaturgic knowledge" arising from idle curiosity, according to Veblen, is "dramatic consistency" (Veblen [1906] 1990, p. 8).

The second source of human knowledge, not so apparent during savagery or lower barbarism but nonetheless always running "along by the side of these dramaturgic life-histories, and underlying them," Veblen termed "pragmatic attention" or "expediency," giving rise later on to science (Veblen, [1908] 1990, p. 41). Here again the consistency of Veblen's thought with that of C. S. Peirce (and, for that matter, John Dewey) is apparent. "There is no range of knowledge that is held more securely by any people," Veblen declared, than "matters of fact; and these are generalizations from experience; they are theoretical knowledge ... and they ... underlie the dramatical generalisations" (Veblen, [1908] 1990, pp. 41–42).

Being prior to the emergence of a scientific method, however, pragmatic attention in the era of savagery was unable to build incrementally on what had gone before. Therefore, Veblen maintained, the pragmatic knowledge of savagery's earliest years differed little in character from that of its most mature phases.[16] According to Veblen the test for pragmatic knowledge is simply its "usefulness."

The bifurcation of knowledge that characterized the savage era—on the one hand "a higher range of theoretical explanations of phenomena, an ornate scheme of things," *vs.* on the other "an obscure range of matter-of-fact generalisations," has continued, Veblen opined, through the course of human history:

> In all succeeding phases of culture, developmentally subsequent to the primitive phase supposed above, there is found a similar or analogous division of knowledge between a higher range of theoretical explanations of phenomena, an ornate scheme of things, on the one hand, and such an obscure range of matter-of-fact generalisations as is here spoken of, on the other. And the evolution of the scientific point of view is a matter of the shifting fortunes which have in the course of cultural growth overtaken the one and the other of these two divergent methods of apprehending and systematising the facts of experience (Veblen, [1908a] 1990, pp. 42-43).

Barbarism

The second era Veblen termed "barbarism," denoting particularly feudalism and the Middle Ages. Veblen associated barbarism with class distinctions arising from the spread of private property. Ownership, for Veblen, was "an accredited discretionary power over an object on the ground of a conventional claim" whose tenure is "by prowess, on the one hand, and by sufferance at the hands of a superior, on the other" (Veblen, [1898] 1964, pp. 42–3). The further back in history the origins of property are traced, he added, the "more immediate and more habitual ... the recourse to prowess as the definitive basis of tenure" (Veblen, [1898] 1964, p. 43).[17]

For Veblen the emergence of property was not only "a concomitant of the transition from a peaceable to a predatory habit of life"[18] (Veblen, [1898] 1964, p. 44), it furthermore coincided with "the emergence of a leisure class" (Veblen, [1899] 1953, p. 33). According to Veblen "the possession of wealth confers honor ... [and] it becomes indispensable to accumulate, to acquire property, in order to retain one's good name" (Veblen, [1899] 1953, pp. 35, 37). Other characteristics of predatory barbarism, likewise issuing from the institution of private property, include: "mastery and servitude, gradations of privilege and honor, coercion and personal dependence," and war (Veblen, [1906] 1990, p. 10).[19]

With regard to the pattern of knowledge in barbarism Veblen contended, somewhat inconsistently,[20]

A culture whose institutions are a framework of invidious comparisons implies, or rather involves and comprises, a scheme of knowledge whose definitive standards of truth and substantiality are of an animistic character; and, the more undividedly the canons of status and ceremonial honor govern the conduct of the community, the greater the facility with which the sequence of cause and effect is made to yield before the higher claims of a spiritual sequence or guidance in the course of events.

With the coming of barbarism, he wrote, knowledge, whether derived from idle curiosity or from expediency, changed in conformity with "conventionalized relations of fraud and force ... of mastery and subservience" (Veblen, [1906] 1990, p. 10). Habitual distinctions, he continued, became ones of "personal force, advantage, precedence, and authority." "A shrewd adaptation to this system of graded dignity and servitude," Veblen explained, "becomes a matter of life and death, and men learn to think in these terms as ultimate and definitive" (Veblen, [1906] 1990, p.11). Consequently, "pragmatic attention," as exemplified for instance by alchemy and astrology, imputed degrees "of nobility and prepotency" to objects" (Veblen, [1906 1990, pp. 11-12). Likewise knowledge deriving from idle curiosity, albeit still typically "animistic" and organized into myths and legends, also evinced important transformations, including the weakening of tribal or family loyalties and altered conceptions of the Deity. As Veblen explained:

> The postulates of the dramaturgic theories and the tests of theoretic validity are no longer the same as before the scheme of graded servitude came to occupy the field. The canons which guide the work of idle curiosity are no longer those of generation, blood-relationship, and homely life, but rather those of graded dignity, authenticity, and dependence. ... The cosmologies of these higher barbarians are cast in terms of a feudalistic hierarchy of agents and elements, and the causal nexus between phenomena is conceived animistically after the manner of sympathetic magic. The laws that are sought to be discovered in the natural universe are sought in terms of authoritative enactment. The relation in which the deity, or deities, are conceived to stand to facts is no longer the relation of progenitor, so much as that of suzerainty (Veblen, [1906] 1990, p. 11).

Industry

Veblen's third epoch—civilization, or industry, or modern times— began with the handicraft economy prior to the onset of the industrial revolution. During this period the artisan, "more or less skilled and with more or less specialist efficiency, [became] the central figure," setting the very "tone" of the whole era (Veblen, [1919] 1990, p. 13). This inaugural period of civilization Veblen saw as characterized by a heightened sense of *workmanship*, whose salient features included personal skill, initiative, diligence, and efficiency (Veblen, [1908] 1990, p. 50). According to Veblen, "the new organum" became the "hegemony of workmanlike efficiency, under the style and title of the 'law of causation' or of 'efficient cause'" (Veblen, [1908] 1990, p. 51).

During the handicraft era hierarchy flattened in practical affairs as "conceptions of authentic rank and differential dignity [grew] weaker" (Veblen, [1906] 1990, p. 13). Indeed, so important did the artisan and the accompanying conception of workmanship become, that even "concepts of the scientists came to be drawn in the image of the workman" (Veblen, [1906] 1990, p. 14). Workmanship, in other words, supplanted differential dignity as the "authoritative canon of scientific truth" (Veblen, [1906] 1990, p. 14).

In later modern times—the industrial revolution and beyond—formulations of causal sequence grew ever more impersonal, objective and matter-of-fact, in keeping with the proliferation of large factories and standardized machine processes such as the assembly line, and a concomitant displacement of workers by capital investments. Machine processes, in other words, became the linchpin of the economy, and also a new archetype. Increasingly habits of thought entailed notions of process rather than workmanship, and phenomena came increasingly to be interpreted impersonally as cumulative, incremental, and consecutive (Veblen, [1908] 1990, p. 54).

Industry, industrial processes, and industrial products, then, in Veblen's view,

> progressively gained upon humanity, until … it is not too much to say that they have become the chief force in shaping men's daily life, and therefore the chief factor in shaping men's habits of thought. Hence men have learned to think in terms in which the technological processes act (Veblen, [1906] 1990, p. 17).

Machine processes "act" in terms of "standardization," "brute causality," "impersonal sequence," taking "no thought of human expediency or inexpediency," or of "human nature or preternatural agencies" (Veblen, [1906] 1990, pp. 17–18). The post-Darwinian scientific outlook, Veblen remarked, accords well with such technological perspectives: both view processes as impersonal, sequential, cumulative, "opaque and unsympathetic" (Veblen, [1906] 1990, p. 17).

While passages such as the foregoing point to a doctrine of technological determinism on Veblen's part (see Chapters 5 and 10 of this volume), at other times Veblen was quick to disassociate himself from such a position, as attested to by the following:

> It is in the *human* material that the continuity of development is to be looked for; and it is here, therefore, that the motor forces of economic development must be studied if they are to be studied at all (Veblen, [1898] 1990, p. 72, emphasis added).

A Veblen Appreciation and Critique

In this section we draw critical attention to some of Veblen's major contributions as they relate to information/communication in evolutionary economics.

Communication and the Sociology of Knowledge

By maintaining that each stage of societal development is typified by an archetypal system of preconceptions, socially constructed and grounding reality, and in emphasizing the communal or collectivist underpinning of knowledge, Veblen extended Marx[21] and anticipated writers such as Walter Lippmann (1922), Thomas Kuhn ([1962] 1970), and Peter Berger & Thomas Luckman (1966), who explored at greater length the sociology of knowledge. In proposing modes of social-economic interaction wherein habits of thought come to be revised in light of new information or exposure to competing systems of knowledge,[22] Veblen anticipated also writers such as Kenneth Boulding ([1956] 1961) and Friedrich Hayek ([1952] 1976). In perceiving that the technological system infiltrates consciousness, changing people's very minds, Veblen extended Marx and anticipated writers as diverse as Harold Innis ([1950] 1972, [1951] 1971), Lewis Mumford (1962), and Jacques Ellul ([1954] 1964).

Regarding the interplay of machine culture and human consciousness, for instance, Veblen wrote:

> The discipline exercised by the mechanical occupations, in so far as it is in question here, is a discipline of the habits of thought. It is, therefore, as processes of thought, methods of apperception, and sequences of reasoning (Veblen, [1904] 1950, p. 339).

In this regard Veblen also anticipated writers as diverse as Marshall McLuhan and Kenneth Boulding, both of whom have viewed human artifacts ("media," McLuhan called them) as "extensions of man" (McLuhan, 1964). Veblen declared that "the accumulation of goods already on hand conditions [a person's] handling and utilization of the materials," while conversely "the changes that take place in the mechanical contrivances are an expression of changes in the human factor" (Veblen, [1898] 1990, p. 71). Just as McLuhan argued that persons might become "numbed" by technological extensions, Veblen perceived that "as a workman, laborer, producer, breadwinner, the individual is a creature of the technological scheme" (Veblen, [1914] 1964, p. 144).

Despite these remarkable achievements, Veblen's seminal contributions to the economics and sociology of knowledge were not unflawed. He maintained, it will be recalled, that property inevitably breeds invidious distinctions, and that economies premised on the same will, in turn, breed "animistic" ways of thinking. But, by Veblen's own account, "peaceable savagery," which was both egalitarian and based on communal organization, was highly "animistic." Furthermore, Veblen appears to have been forgetful, on occasion, of the radical egalitarianism of early, pre-Constantinian, Christianity (an "animistic" belief, in his view), and particularly of the teachings of its founder who welcomed women, outcasts, sinners, children, cripples, and tax collectors to his banquet table, and who cautioned strongly against making friends with unrighteous Mammon. (See also, however, Veblen, [1910] 1950). In thoroughly materialist or "scientific" cultures invidious distinctions certainly need not be absent; indeed, they are most unlikely to be absent. People's worth (even sense of self-worth) in such cultures is all too often gauged by their material possessions (their "net worth"), a schema for evaluation that can easily be "justified" ontologically through the materialist doctrine of the survival of the fittest, as the Social Darwinists well understood. In such circumstances, an "animistic" or "teleological" belief that all are fundamentally equal on account of their common creation in the image of God, can help mitigate or counter invidious distinctions in material disparities.[23]

Dynamic Systems Approach

Another major contribution of Veblen, like that of Russel Wallace, was a holistic, systems approach to understanding, anticipating thereby such writers as Ludwig von Bertalanffy (1981), Norbert Wiener ([1950] 1967), and Kenneth Boulding (1978). Veblen believed that knowledge and artifacts comprise part of the ecosystem as much as do organisms and other natural factors. For him people live in an environment at once natural and artifactual. In turning "the material means of life to account," Veblen wrote, people utilize and transform not only climate and topography, but also "customs, conventions, and methods of industry," and are in the process themselves altered or transformed (Veblen, [1899] 1964, p. 22).

In Veblen's view, since machine processes and the concomitant matter-of-fact mode of perception yield greater outputs than did handicraft methods and animistic ways of thinking, in the struggle for survival the former inevitably displace the latter. Changes in the mode of production invariably have their correlates in alterations in individuals' discourse, transforming habits of thought and of action, and thereby social relations.

For Veblen, all institutions and social processes, including knowledge and belief systems, epistemology, science, production, modes of ownership, war and peace, social stratification, technology, exchange, money, custom, and ceremony, constitute interdependent elements that interact bi-directionally to produce an evolving sequence of cumulative change through the principle of cause and effect.

An Evolutionary Economics of the Left

Along with John R. Commons, Thorstein Veblen is generally credited with inspiring Evolutionary and Institutional Economics (Samuels, 1987, pp. 864–866; Ramstad, 1994)). Even those few evolutionary economists, such as Kenneth Boulding, who have disavowed indebtedness to Veblen,[24] actually trod very much the path he blazed, albeit perhaps in a gentler, more endearing manner.

Veblen described and analyzed social-political-economic systems in flux, systems both dynamic and comprised of components engaged in interdependent interactions. For Veblen systems and institutions, more importantly than individuals, are "selected" for survival by the supra-systems for which they constitute components, and in being "selected" they in turn modify their suprasystems. Modes of production, patterns of perception, and ways of interacting, according to Veblen, are "selected" if and when they increase the chances of survival of their practitioners. Moreover, changing modes of production and changing patterns of perception/interpretation impact upon one another in a seamless and indeterminate sequence of cumulative change.

Through his discourse, then, Veblen countervailed the prevailing Social Darwinism of his day. Redirecting his readers' attention from biogenetically inherited characteristics of individuals to the "selection" of institutions,[25] Veblen helped recast human development as a social process rather than as an outcome of individual struggles for survival. Veblen thereby helped restore ameliorative social policy to intellectual respectability.

Veblen's methodological collectivism, as manifested in the attention he afforded institutions, necessarily privileged communicatory processes as agents of social organization and of social change. For this reason, he is to be considered a founder of the discipline of Communication Studies, as well as progenitor of Institutional and Evolutionary Economics. Although writing for a former era enthralled by the likes of Herbert Spencer and William Graham Sumner, Veblen's writings nonetheless remain highly pertinent in our day as counterpoint to neoconservative and neoclassical thought.

Notes

1. Veblen's final impoverished years were spent by choice alone, and in low spirits at his cabin at Palo Alto (Reynolds, 1989, p. 94). Unsigned and written in pencil, probably within a week of his death, Veblen decreed: "It is my wish, in case of death, to be cremated, if it can conveniently be done, as expeditiously and inexpensively as may be, without ritual or ceremony of any kind; that my ashes be thrown loose into the sea, or into some sizable stream running to the sea; that no tombstone, slab, epitaph, tablet, inscription, or monument of any name or nature, be set up in my memory or name in any place or at any time; that no obituary , memorial, portrait, or biography of me, nor any letters written by me be printed or published, or in any way reproduced, copied or circulated" (quoted in Dorfman, 1934, p. 505).

2. Veblen had, in fact, been well imbued with Social Darwinist thought. As a student at Carleton College in the late 1870's he had read Herbert Spencer, whom he continued to admire grudgingly. Veblen's biographer, Joseph Dorfman, quoted Veblen as declaring that Spencer's critics "stand on his shoulders and beat him about the ears," while Harold Innis noted that Veblen "regarded himself in some sense as a disciple of Spencer" (Innis, [1929] 1956, p. 18). At Yale he was a student of William Graham Sumner whom Veblen "admired" and with whom Veblen shared a "zest for discovering the futility of human action" (Riesman [1953] 1960, pp., 19–20).

3. The opponents of socialism, Veblen once noted, argued incorrectly that

evolution constantly accentuates inequality among individuals, whereas social-ism demands equality. Veblen's rejoinder, summarizing an argument by Enrico Ferri, was that socialism demands merely equality of opportunity, not identity of function or of the details of life. A second conservative argument, also recounted by Veblen, contrasted the comfort and fullness of life for *all* demanded by social-ism, with Darwinian struggle entailing destruction of the "unfit" in order to fur-ther the progress of the species; here Ferri's rejoinder, again approvingly reproduced by Veblen, was that social evolution requires contest among institu-tions and groups, not among individuals, and since struggle pits class against class, group solidarity in fact is a requisite of social advance. Finally, to the argu-ment that the struggle for existence entails replacing the unfit by the superior, Veblen responded that only by injecting "wholly illegitimate teleological meaning into the term 'fittest' as used by Darwin and the Darwinists [is] the expression 'survival of the fittest' made to mean a survival of the socially desirable individu-als" (quoted in Dorfman, 1934, pp. 142-43).

4. It is to be noted that for Veblen "Darwin" and "Darwinian" were "catch-words," summarizing a nineteenth century movement in science. Use of Darwin's name," Veblen stated, "does not imply that this epoch of science is mainly Darwin's work" (Veblen, [1908] 1990, p. 36). According to Innis, "With Darwin he [Veblen] was obviously impressed with the importance of evolution but he was not convinced of the finality of materialism and mechanism" (Innis, [1929] 1956, p. 18).

5. On occasion, however, primarily in the final three essays of *The Place of Sci-ence in Modern Civilization* ([1919] 1990), Veblen did argue on the purported deri-vation of race through biological natural selection.

6. Dewey's statement continues: "There is more than a verbal tie between the words common, community, and communications. Men live in a community in virtue of the things they have in common; and communication is the way in which they come to possess things in common" (Dewey, 1915, p. 4).

7. According to Alan Dyer (1986), Veblen could have benefited to an even greater extent than he did from the thought of C. S. Peirce. Peirce's semiology, Dyer declares, if more fully incorporated, would have allowed Veblen to dispense with his (to Dyer) problematic instinct theory.

8. Habits and institutions, Veblen added, can lag social or environmental change (Veblen, [1925] 1964, p. 5), in which case institutions can become "imbecile" (Veblen, [1914] 1964, p. 25).

9. In a remarkable, and in a sense perhaps somewhat autobiographical, pas-sage in *Essays in Our Changing Order* ([1919] 1964, p. 227) Veblen expressed the view that those standing outside a culture are best able to spot its inconsistencies and inadequacies, presumably on account of their different codes or interpreta-tive systems. "The intellectually gifted Jew," he wrote,"is in a peculiarly fortunate position in respect of this requisite immunity from the inhibitions of intellectual quietism. But he can come in for such immunity only at the cost of losing his secure place in the scheme of conventions into which he has been born, and at the cost, also, of finding no similarly secure place in that scheme of gentile conven-tions into which he is thrown. He becomes a disturber of the intellectual peace, but only at the cost of becoming an intellectual wayfaring man, a wanderer in the

intellectual no-man's land, seeking another place to rest, farther along the road, somewhere over the horizon. They are neither a complaisant nor a contented lot, these aliens of the uneasy feet."

10. Therefore, Veblen declared, science can never come up with final answers; indeed, he mused, "it is something of a homiletical commonplace to say that the outcome of any serious research can only be to make two questions grow where one question grew before" (Veblen, [1908] 1990, p. 33).

11. Elsewhere Veblen remarked: "The postulate of the scientist is that things change consecutively. It is an unproven and unprovable postulate —that is to say, it is a metaphysical preconception" (Veblen, [1908a] 1990, p. 33) .

12. With regard specifically to the hedonistic psychology developed by Jeremy Bentham (a mainstay of neoclassicism) Veblen wrote wryly: "A gang of Aleutian Islanders slushing about in the wrack and surf with rakes and magical incantations for the capture of shell-fish are held, in point of taxonomic reality, to be engaged on a feat of hedonistic equilibration in rent, wages, and interest" (Veblen, [1908b] 1990, p. 193).

Another famous and related passage is the following: "The hedonistic conception of man is that of a lightning calculator of pleasures and pains, who oscillates like a homogeneous globule of desire of happiness under the impulse of stimuli that shift him about the area, but leave him intact. He has neither antecedent nor consequent. He is an isolated, definitive human datum, in stable equilibrium except for the buffets of the impinging forces that displace him in one direction or another. Self-imposed in elemental space, he spins symmetrically about his own spiritual axis until the parallelogram of forces bears down upon him, whereupon he follows the line of the resultant. When the force of impact is spent, he comes to rest, a self-contained globule of desire as before. Spiritually, the hedonistic man is not a prime mover. He is not the seat of a process of living" (Veblen, [1898] 1990, pp. 73-74).

13. Classical and neoclassical economic theory shows how total income is apportioned among factors of production in exactly the proportions that each "deserves," i.e. according to their "marginal productivities." Classical economics in Veblen's view was characteristically apologetic of existing power relations.

14. He wrote: "No concept of ownership, either communal or individual, applies in the primitive community. ... It is not something given to begin with ... something which has to be unlearned in part when men come to co-operate in production and make working arrangements and mutual renunciations under stress of associated life—after the manner imputed by the social contract theory. It is a conventional fact and has to be learned; it is a cultural fact which has grown into an institution in the past through a long course of habituation, and which is transmitted from generation to generation as all cultural facts are" (Veblen, [1898] 1964, pp. 39, 42).

15. According to Veblen, in savagery "Facts [were] conceived in an animistic way, and a pragmatic animus ... imputed to them. ... Knowledge ... of the phenomena of nature ... [was] of the nature of life-histories. Procreation, birth, growth, and decay constitute[d] the cycle of postulates within which the dramatized processes of natural phenomenon [ran] their course. Creation [was] procreation ... and causation [was] gestation and birth" (Veblen, [1906] 1990, p 9-10).

16. Veblen wrote: "Its highest achievements in the direction of systematic formulation consist of didactic exhortations to thrift, prudence, equanimity, and

shrewd management—a body of maxims of expedient conduct. In this field there is scarcely a degree of advance from Confucius to Samuel Smiles" (Veblen, [1906] 1990, p. 9).

17. On the other hand, "property rights sanctioned by immemorial usage," Veblen teased, "are inviolable, as all immemorial usage is, except in the face of forcible dispossession; but seizure and forcible retention very shortly gain the legitimation of usage, and the resulting tenure becomes inviolable through habituation. *Beati possidentes*" (Veblen, [1898] 1964, p. 43).

18. He wrote: "Wherever the institution of private property is found, even in a slightly developed form, the economic process bears the character of a struggle between men for the possession of goods" (Veblen, [1899] 1953, p. 34).

19. Veblen related property and war, social stratification, and a leisure class in the following passage: "Throughout the barbarian culture, where this tenure by prowess prevails, the population falls into two economic classes; those engaged in industrial employments, and those engaged in such non-industrial pursuits as war, government, sports, and religious observances. In the earlier and more naive stages of barbarism the former, in the normal case, own nothing; the latter own such property as they have seized, or such as has, under the sanction of usage, descended upon them from their forbears who seized and held it. At a still lower level of culture, in the primitive savage horde, the population is not similarly divided into economic classes. There is no leisure class resting its prerogative on coercion, prowess, and immemorial status; and there is also no ownership" (Veblen, [1898] 1964, p. 43).

20. See below, the section entitled "A Veblen Appreciation and Critique."

21. While certainly appreciative of the consistency of the Marxian system ("There is no system of economic theory more logical than that of Marx ..."), nonetheless Veblen was critical of Marx's Hegelianism. By applying a "transmuted framework of Hegelian dialectics" to his work, Marx cast himself "immediately and uncompromisingly into contrast with Darwinism and the Post-Darwinian conceptions of evolution" (Veblen, [1906] 1990, pp. 410–11, 413–14). For Veblen, "it is not the Marxism of Marx, but rather the materialism of Darwin, which the socialists of to-day have adopted" (Veblen, [1907] 1990, p. 432).

On the decidedly non-dialectical nature of evolutionary change, Veblen and Kenneth Boulding were in full accord. See Boulding (1970).

22. In a cogent passage Veblen declared that a culture's "binding convictions of what is true, good, and beautiful in the world ... [are] binding only so far as the habitual will to believe in them and to seek the truth along their lines remains intact. That is to say, only so long as no scheme of habituation alien to the man's traditional outlook has broken in on him, and forced him to see that those convictions and verities which hold their place as fundamentally and eternally good and right within the balanced scheme of received traditions prove to be, after all, only an ephemeral web of habits of thought" (Veblen, [1919] 1964, p. 228).

23. See particularly Adler (1981, pp. 228–243).

24. For Kenneth Boulding, Veblen was a dissenter "of the sourest kind, whose weapons [were] sarcasm and sardonic innuendo" (Boulding, [1957] 1971, p. 90). Veblen, Boulding continued, did not really understand evolutionary processes very well. "What he was looking for," Boulding contended, "was a kind of celes-

tial mechanics of society, a set of stable parameters uniting events of successive time periods" (Boulding, 1981, p. 23).

It is difficult, however, to reconcile Boulding's critique with Veblen's position that evolutionism's fundamental premise is cumulative and unpredictable change through cause and effect toward no particular end or goal. As Boulding himself remarked, "Evolutionary theory is all about hindsight; it has practically no predictive power at all" (Boulding [1966] 1995, p. 11).

25. Such is the main thrust of Veblen's writings, notwithstanding the final three chapters of *The Place of Science in Modern Civilization.*

9

The Communication Theory of
Kenneth E. Boulding

In the act of creation, a man brings together two facets of reality and, by discovering a likeness between them, suddenly makes them one.
                                                    —Jacob Bronowski ([1956] 1972)

Kenneth E. Boulding (1910–1993)—poet, peace activist, environmentalist, Quaker, co-founder of general systems theory—was author of more than thirty books, many of them positioning information/communication at the very heart of an innovative, evolutionary economics. Of them all perhaps the most significant were *The Image,* the book he felt to be his most influential, completed by dictation in but nine days, and *Ecodynamics,* which he termed his "manifesto about the universe" (Boulding, 1992, p. 81).

Born at Liverpool, England to a working class family,[1] Boulding studied first at Oxford, then at the University of Chicago under Frank Knight, and briefly at Harvard under Joseph Schumpeter. Another important influence was sociologist Robert Park, whom he met while teaching at Fisk University. Boulding recounted how a "half-hour conversation [with Park] about social ecology ... quite changed my life, beginning my interest in ecological and evolutionary theory" (Boulding, 1992, p. 74).

Never earning an advanced degree, Boulding nonetheless was recipient of more than thirty honorary degrees. He taught at universities in some seven countries and served as president of six learned societies, including the American Economics Association and the Society for General Systems Research, of which he was co-founder. Through his life and works Boulding maintained passionately that "There is such a thing as human betterment—a magnificent, multidimensional, complex structure—a cathedral of the mind—and [that] human decisions should be judged by the extent to which they promote it" (Boulding, 1992, p. 83).[2]

If Malthus sowed seeds for an evolutionary economics, and if Veblen interleaved expansive notions of communication into economics, thereby inaugurating Evolutionary and Institutional Economics, Kenneth Boulding was the one most fully to isolate and explore *information* as an agent of economic organization, change and development.

Production as Communication

Production

For Kenneth Boulding *production*, "whether of a chicken from an egg or of a house from a blueprint," is a process whereby "some kind of information or knowledge structure is able to direct *energy* toward the transportation, transformation, or rearrangement of *materials* into less probable structures than those existing at the start of the process" (Boulding, 1978, pp. 12, 34; emphasis added). When a seed germinates in the ground, for example, its informational structure (DNA) utilizes and directs stored energy to draw selectively upon nutrients or "building materials" in the soil to produce its *phenotype* (the plant). Likewise for animals, *genomes* (that is, the total inherited genetic information) utilize energy and materials in directing processes of growth and development. Similarly, a housing contractor studies a blueprint, and from the knowledge or instructions embedded therein (the analogue of a genome) utilizes energy to assemble construction materials, which he/she rearranges to produce a more complex or improbable structure than had existed previously.

For Boulding, production is defined as the realization of phenotypes from genotypes (Boulding, 1981, p. 25), and for him it is not merely metaphorical to view genes as *knowing how* to construct organisms out of surrounding materials. Rather, he affirmed,

> There is clearly know-how in the genome, not only how to make a leg but how to make it the right length and how to stop building when it is long enough; these are pretty subtle instructions, especially for anything as speechless as DNA, which does not seem to have much capacity beyond four-letter-words (Boulding, 1978, p. 106).

In Boulding's eyes, while there are important similarities between organic and inorganic processes of production, there are also important differences. Genes, for example, while imparting organization to surrounding materials and constructing organisms out of them, are themselves slow to change. ("The gene," he joked, "is a wonderful teacher; it is, however, a very poor learner.") According to present theories (as distinct from those implicit in the works of Lamarck),[3] genes "learn" nothing and change only through "chance" (i.e., unexplained or unexplainable mutations).

By contrast, many organic *phenotypes* do learn, which is to say that interactions with their environment change their images or knowledge structures, i.e., the informational patterns encoded in their nervous systems. Boulding believed that growth in the knowledge possessed by phenotypes follows a pattern "closely related to the life pattern itself." Since knowledge is a structure, he explained, its "present form always limits its possibilities of growth, ... [resulting in] the phenomenon of 'readiness' for certain kinds of knowledge at different stages of life" (Boulding, [1966] 1995, p. 14).

In addition to organic genomes and learned structures, Boulding viewed material artifacts also as constituting knowledge structures. Human artifacts (or "social species," as Boulding often referred to them), are produced by applying human learning and energy to matter; they therefore embody and manifest human knowledge. Just as the genome "in a favorable environment is capable of creating a teleological process to produce the appropriate phenotype" (Boulding, 1970, pp. 21–2), so too can human knowledge in a favorable environment produce artifacts, or social species. In both instances, improbable informational structures (or "know-how") direct "energy toward the transportation and transformation of materials into equally improbable structures of the phenotype or product" (Boulding, 1978, p. 106). So universal indeed is this process of production that Boulding, as we saw previously, recommended replacing economics' traditional triad of land-labor-capital as prototypical factors of production with the triad, energy-materials-information.[4] According to Boulding, economics' traditional classification is far too "imprecise."[5]

All production, whether organic or inorganic, according to Boulding, entails *selections*. Through sequences of behavior, knowledge structures "recognize" and correct divergence between actual and ideal states (Boulding, 1978, p. 108). These sequences he referred to as homeostatic or cybernetic mechanisms. Embryology is the study of such mechanisms in developing organisms, but for Boulding analogous are conscious processes of human decision-makers when producing social species. Decision-makers, Boulding wrote, bring mental contexts or "images" to production processes. These images are comprised of two parts, the first being a system of ideal values, goals or preferred states, and the second a notion of actual values or of actual states. The goal of decision-makers is always to reduce differences between these two images (Boulding, 1958, p. 93).[6]

Production of Artifacts ("Social Species")

Boulding distinguished among three main types of human artifacts or "social species," namely: *material artifacts,* that is material structures and objects such as buildings, machines, and automobiles; *organizational structures,* that is human institutions, ranging from extended families and hunting bands to transnational corporations, governments, and churches; and *biological artifacts,* under which heading Boulding included not only plants and animals altered by domestication, selective breeding and genetic engineering, but as well human beings.

Humans, Boulding declared, are to a considerable extent artifactual. While every person is, of course, produced *biologically* in accordance with information inherent to the genetic structure of the original fertilized egg, people are "produced" also in the cultural sense of acquiring learned images, knowledge, language, skills, and so forth (Boulding, 1981, p. 24). Moreover "there is also an important internal learning process in which human beings help to create themselves" (Boulding, 1985, p. 72).

Despite remarkable similarities between biological and social processes of production, there are also, however, important differences. Whereas biological reproduction (birth) is occasioned by sexual union between two members of the same species, production of artifacts stems from "intercourse among a large number of artifacts of different kinds." Automobiles, for example, are compound entities consisting of myriad parts, each with its own informational ("genetic") structure. Whereas biological populations tend, eventually at least, toward zero growth in accordance with the Malthusian Population Principle and the "law of diminishing growth,"[7] no such tendency is apparent, according to Boulding, for human artifacts (social species) due to their multiparental, asexual origin (Boulding, 1978, p. 68).[8] Furthermore, unlike biogenetic information, knowledge of how to produce social species exists outside the phenotype, for instance as blueprints, plans, templates, maps, chemical equations, books, and in human memory; Boulding averred that this "extrinsic nature of the genome" permits and encourages rapid evolution, adding that specialized components of artifacts are particularly subject to continuous change as humans focus attention and work upon them (Boulding, 1981, p. 26).

A further important dissimilarity between organic and social processes of production concerns the introduction, reintroduction, or perhaps affirmation[9] of "teleological" elements in evolutionary processes. Noogenetic[10] processes of teaching and learning, while in some ways similar to biogenetic processes of mutation and selection, were for Boulding unique in terms of obvious or manifest deliberation and purposefulness. "The human race," he wrote, "is not merely pushed by past events or present circumstances, but it is also pulled by its own images of the future into a future" (Boulding, 1978, p. 132). Humans, in other words, are "niche-expanders," unlike most other organisms that usually simply occupy niches and expand to fill them up.

Communication

Communication, for Boulding, is "any process that transfers some kind of significant structure or pattern from one system to another" (Boulding, 1985, p. 133). Physical systems (such as air, light, wires, paper, cables, invisible portions of the electromagnetic spectrum, and so forth), are "agents of communication," enabling this transfer. Communication takes place when images or information structures, encoded by physical carriers, reach their destination.

Production for Boulding, then, is a *communicatory* process. Production entails an image or information structure being "carried over" so as to bring about a higher order of complexity elsewhere. In *biogenetic production*, genetic information (or "know-how") is transmitted by genes from one generation to the next. In *noogenetic production*, "learned structures in central nervous systems or their equivalents ... [are transmitted] by a learning process" (Boulding, [1979] 1995, p. 27). Parallels to the thought of Veblen in these matters are readily apparent.

Information, whether transmitted biogenetically or noogenetically, can be subject to alteration in transmission, a change often termed *evolution*. Boulding defined evolution as "a process of cumulative change of know-how" (Boulding, [1983] 1995, p. 47). *Biogenetic evolution* occurs when genetic information (or know-how) undergoes mutation, the mutant phenotype then being subject to selection processes in its environment. *Noogenetic evolution*, on the other hand, occurs when knowledge transmitted from one generation to another undergoes change and becomes subject to cognitive social selection processes (Boulding, [1979] 1995, p. 27).

For Boulding, "because human knowledge creates know-how—and know-how is the genetic factor of production that produces human artifacts—the growth of knowledge has irreversible effects" (Boulding, [1983] 1995, p. 51. Boulding saw the cumulative growth in know-how as constituting a primary explanation of "time's arrow," that is the unidirectional or non reversible property of time.

Social Species and the Ecosystem

Organic species and social species alike constitute components of *ecosystems*, defined by Boulding as "interacting populations of different species in which the birth and death rates of each population are a function of its own size and the size of the other populations with which it is in contact" (Boulding, 1985, pp. 23–4). Species, whether organic or social, occupy *niches*, defined by Boulding as the equilibrium populations of phenotypes in their ecosystems (Boulding, [1979] 1995, p. 27).

Social species are similar to organic species in the sense that both are "selected" for occupancy of niches. Commodities, for instance, at any moment have a population or stock that increases through production and decreases through consumption and, like biological species, they interact continuously, influencing each other's birth, growth and death rates.

Modes of species' interaction are various. Petroleum and automobiles, for Boulding, are in continuous symbiotic interaction, whereas inter-city trains and buses tend to interact competitively. Social artifacts may also be competitive with organic species (for example, automobiles with horses), or co-operative with them (for instance, chemical fertilizers with domesticated crops). Boulding also analyzed predator-prey relations, and host-parasite relations (Boulding, [1962] 1963).

For him, "the fundamental principle of ecological evolution" is that "everything depends on everything else." This, he wrote, means that "there is no such thing as 'environment,' if by this we mean a surrounding system that is independent of what goes on inside it" (Boulding, 1978, pp. 224, 31).

Commoditized and Non-Commoditized Species

Commoditized and non-commoditized species (whether biological or social), while alike in engaging in ecological interaction, differ by definition in the extent to which the price system, at least directly, mediates their ecological interactions. According to Boulding, "the niche of a commodity is determined mainly by the demand for it—that is, the willingness of people to purchase it" (Boulding, 1981, p. 61), whereas the niche for non-commoditized biological species is determined by their ability to produce surviving offspring. The distinction, however, is by no means absolute: non-commoditized biological species are increasingly subject to ecological pressures stemming from markets; chain saws displace non-commoditized species living in rain forests, for example. As noted in Chapter 6, "environmental economists" recommend in principle that all non commoditized species should be made over into commoditized species.

Information and Knowledge Structures

The Information Concept

We have seen how Boulding characterized production as the activation or functioning of a knowledge structure to bring about a more improbable material structure than had existed at the start of the process. Production, then, entails communication, since production means the carrying-over of a knowledge structure to a new location, and the fulfillment of its potential there. Utilizing potential inhering in knowledge structures does not necessarily mean, however, simply "the mechanical following of a previously known plan with all the potential present at the beginning." It can entail also "the creation of new potential under the stimulus of events that could not be predicted" (Boulding, [1983] 1995, p. 42).

Knowledge structures, or know-how, relate closely to *information* of course, and Boulding's typification of information contributes to our understanding of the correspondence between production and communicatory processes. "Information is not," he wrote "a simple physical event such as a noise or a shape on a piece of paper." Rather, "it is an event in a context." And the context is the thing that really determines the significance, that is the meaning or information-content, of the event (Boulding, 1958, p. 89).

Conceptually there are at least two contexts to consider in order to discern how meaning or significance is gleaned from stimuli, messages or events. One concerns the physical stimuli surrounding the information or event in question. "A word is not so much a *thing* as a *place* in a sentence," wrote Boulding (1958, p. 88); a word's meaning depends upon its context in its own sentence, and upon its place within the larger message or system of messages. Likewise, the "meaning" of a gene (the effect it produces) depends upon the complete genome.

Second, message recipients bring context to messages and events. Messages, comprised of signs and symbols, are decoded by means of the particular language or decoding system that the message recipient applies to them. Codes or languages, however, are social constructions ("institutions," or "habits of thought," in Veblen's terms). A given symbol, therefore, can connote different meanings to different message recipients, depending upon which "language" or "dialect" the particular respondent applies to it, which will depend *inter alia* upon the culture or subculture within which the message recipient is immersed, and as well on his/her unique life experiences.

According to Boulding, therefore, information distinguishes *living* processes from purely mechanical ones. Whereas in mechanical processes a particular physical event always produces identical responses, for living systems there can be "varying responses to constant physical stimuli, depending on the 'significance' of the stimuli in an informational setting" (Boulding, 1958, p. 87). Boulding maintained that mainstream economics is too mechanical in its interpretation of life processes; consequently, he upbraided the discipline on the one hand for maintaining impoverished conceptions of information, and on the other for applying deterministic models to human (living) processes.

Knowledge

Boulding distinguished mere *information* from *knowledge*, the former term denoting sensory inputs (stimuli or messages) received by the brain, the latter implying structure. *Structure* Boulding defined as "a very complex and frequently quite loose pattern, almost like an enormous molecule, with its parts connected in various ways by ties of varying degrees of strength." Knowledge, for Boulding, is "mental structure" (Boulding, [1955] 1974, p. 23). Knowledge, or "image," or "information structure," for Boulding, derives from experience: "Part of the image is the history of the image itself" (Boulding, [1956] 1961, p. 6).[11]

At any moment, information (that is, sensory stimuli) bombards a person's knowledge structure. Messages in a sense are "shot into" the image. Behavioral psychologists, in attempting to reduce behavior to mere stimulus-response, Boulding suggested, commit a grievous error in failing to consider the knowledge structure, and "especially images of the future," which for him are decisive (Boulding, 1978, p. 109).

When an organism confronts messages or sensory stimuli there are, according to Boulding, not one but four possible consequences for image or knowledge structure. First, information may pass right through the knowledge structure's interstices, leaving it quite unaffected.

Second, messages can "stick" to the knowledge structure (what he called "addition"), leaving however the basic organization intact. Rote learning, he suggested, would be an example of "addition."

Third, and more interestingly, message reception can cause reorganization, whether great or small, in the knowledge structure. For Boulding, as for Marshall McLuhan, "the meaning of a message *is* the change which it produces in the image" (Boulding, [1956] 1961, p. 7, emphasis added). Likewise *learning* Boulding defined as a change in the knowledge structure or image (Boulding, 1970, p. 9). If a message "hits some 'nucleus' that knocks the props out of a large area of the structure," he explained further, there will result "a very radical reorganization of the mental structure" (Boulding, [1955] 1974, p. 24). Such fundamental reorganizations, he believed, are rare. Usually people resist information fundamentally at odds with their knowledge structure.

Finally, the fourth possibility concerns dimensions of certainty and uncertainty, of probability and improbability, of clarity and vagueness. Elements of the knowledge structure are not uniformly certain, probable, or clear. Informational stimuli, therefore, can either clarify or obscure images; they can make things previously regarded as less certain more certain, and vice versa (Boulding, [1956] 1961, p. 10).

Stability (resistance to change) of a knowledge structure, Boulding wrote, depends in part upon its internal consistency and its arrangement.

As with some crystals and molecules, minimizing internal strain lends stability to knowledge structures (Boulding, [1956] 1961, p. 13). Boulding raised the difficult question of the optimal tradeoff between stability and adaptability of knowledge structures. Clearly, on the one hand, stability (that is, insensitivity to, or critical appraisal of, message inputs) is required as otherwise "the world would dissolve into a heap of incoherent impressions—"automobiles would get bigger as they approached us, rooms would change shape as we walked through them." On the other hand, however, survival also requires that knowledge "map" adequately the outside world, that it adapt as changes occur in the environment.

Boulding noted also that the concept of "an optimum degree of sensitivity of the knowledge structure, useful as it may be, begs some of the ultimate metaphysical questions" (Boulding, [1955] 1974, p. 27).

Information, Perception, and the Sociology of Knowledge

Boulding on occasion distinguished also mere information (any and all messages or sensory inputs registered on the brain) from "signals." A *signal* he defined as "a non-random event set in the middle of a succession of random events (noise)." Since "all events, however, are events," there arises the problem of discriminating between signals and noise. Boulding proposed four possibilities. First, the signal receiver ("signal detector") may correctly recognize a signal as a signal (a "hit"); second, he/she may mistake a random event for a signal (a "false alarm"); third, the receiver may mistake a signal for a random event (a "miss"); fourth, the detector may correctly perceive a random event for what it is (a "negative hit," or a "correct rejection").

For any given intensity of signal relative to noise (signal to noise ratio), there is, according to Boulding, a mathematical function "relating the probability of a hit with the probability of a false alarm under 'optimal' behavior" (Boulding, [1955] 1974, p. 25); this function he termed the "signal detection curve." Cautious receivers score few hits but also give few false alarms, whereas reckless receivers attain many hits but give also more false alarms. Furthermore, payoffs and penalties for hits and false alarms respectively influence the positioning of a signal detector on the signal detection curve: "The detector will be more reckless the greater the intrinsic probability that the signal is present, the smaller the rewards for correct rejections and the smaller the penalties for false alarms, and the greater the rewards for hits and the penalties for misses" (Boulding, [1955] 1974, p. 25).

The implications of this theory of signal detection, according to Boulding, are several and startling. With regard to the theory of perception, for instance, "the notion of a clear psycho physiological 'threshold' of signal intensity above which the signal is perceived and below which it is not," is questioned since, in Boulding's model, "all perception is only probable, and the greater the probability of hits the greater the probability also of false alarms" (Boulding, [1955] 1974, p. 25).[12]

As well the theory has implications for the problem of the validity of knowledge. Boulding's "organic theory of knowledge," he attested, challenges the purported 'objectivity' of science, since "perception of anything cannot be divorced from the valuations which surround the act of perception." Indeed, he declared, "the whole concept of a 'fact' really disappears: all that is left are messages in noisy channels, and the interpretation of these messages as 'facts' depends in part on the value system of the observer" (Boulding, [1955] 1974, p. 25).[13]

In saying this, however, Boulding did not contend that images are purely private or subjective. To the contrary, he wrote,

> Part of our image of the world is the belief that this image is shared by other people like ourselves who are part of our image of the world. In common daily intercourse we all behave as if we possess roughly the same image of the world. ... Where there is no universe of discourse, where the image possessed by the organism is purely private and cannot be communicated to anyone else, we say that the person is mad (Boulding, [1956] 1961, pp. 14-5).

Boulding, then, continued in, and amplified, the tradition known as the sociology of knowledge developed by Veblen. Like Veblen, he too posited a "selection process" whereby images interact with environment, a continual testing to segregate and eliminate the ones not "fit" for survival (Boulding, 1978, p. 20).

Knowledge for Boulding was an "organic structure"[14] that grows, mutates, is selected, even dies. Like all structures, knowledge has an "embryology," starting off simple, then growing and developing, becoming increasingly complex. At each stage of development there are only certain alternative paths open; everything builds on what has gone before (Boulding, [1956] 1961, p. 95). As Boulding expressed it, "The tree of knowledge unfolds in good order and proper succession, first the blade and then the ear, first the trunk and then the branch." Growth in this "tree of knowledge," however, is also profoundly affected by outside conditions—it is "bent by storms or encouraged by sunshine in one direction or another."

Boulding noted as well an important difference between the "metabolism" of knowledge and biogenetic metabolism: The former does not obey the laws of thermodynamics, that is the law of conservation and the law of entropy. For Boulding this distinction is most significant, and is addressed below.

Constituents of Communicatory Processes

Signs and Symbols

In communicatory processes signs and symbols are carried by media ("agents of communication") to the destination. *Signs*, Boulding defined, as information that alters an organism's image of its immediate surroundings. For Boulding all life participates at some level in communication through signs. Plants, for instance, lean in the direction of the sun while social insects communicate with one another through signs (Boulding, [1956] 1961, p. 45). In contrast, *symbols* impact upon the "image of the image, on the image of the future, on the image of the past, on the image of the potential or even the image of the impossible" (Boulding, [1956] 1961, p. 44). When someone speaks, our image of our surroundings changes as we receive *signs* that someone is present; but in comprehending what is said the content of our imagination also is affected, and this "same" information becomes a *symbol*. What distinguishes human society from all other animal life, according to Boulding, is the high level of symbolic communication.

Media

Modes of communication (i.e., media) carry signs and symbols to the destination. Physical systems, then, are "agents of communication." In biogenetic systems the agent or carrier is DNA, genetic information being encoded in a double helix of carbon atoms with attached atoms of oxygen, hydrogen, nitrogen and carbon. In human social systems, by contrast, modes of communication (media), change through time and these changes, for Boulding (as for others such as Harold Innis), lie at the very heart of societal evolution.

In non-literate societies, for example, "noogenetic" communication is limited to verbal rituals, poems, legends, ceremonies, and so forth. Writing, however, inaugurated what Boulding called the "disassociated transcript" (Boulding, [1956] 1961, p. 65), expanding enormously the temporal and spatial dimensions of communication and learning (Boulding, 1981, p. 122). Without records, complex organizational continuity from place to place and generation to generation would have been impossible. Nor could decision-makers have transmitted instructions as effectively to distant peripheries. With writing, the "total body of human knowledge potentially accessible to an individual grew constantly, as each generation left its deposit. ... It was no accident," Boulding concluded, that [western or modern] science comes along with printing" (Boulding, 1981, p. 128).

Inventions subsequent to printing (for instance cameras and sound recordings), Boulding further opined, permit direct,[15] as opposed to symbolic, transcription of aspects of life and experience, although large portions thereof—smell, taste, touch, emotions, feelings—must still be stored and transmitted "through the crowded channels of symbolic representation" (Boulding, [1956] 1961, p. 65).

Innovations in media were, for Boulding, at the heart of the "organizational revolution," by which he meant the "great rise in the number, size, and power of organizations of many diverse kinds, and especially of economic organizations" (Boulding, [1953] 1968, p. xiii). He maintained that evolving media enable organizational growth in two principal ways. First, media help overcome external constraints. Revolutions in transportation (for example, railroads, steamships, automobiles, airplanes) and in communication (telegraph, telephone, radio) "pushed back the limitations of the environment [enabling organizations] to expand farther into [their] environment" (Boulding, [1953] 1968, p. 25). Second, media like typewriters, duplicators, calculators and computers facilitate internal communication (Boulding, [1953] 1968, p. 26). Without changes in media technology, internal communication for growing organizations would become increasingly difficult: relaying information from organizations' contact points with their environment to their decision-making centers, and as well transmittal of accurate instructions from centers to their peripheries, become more difficult as the number of messages increase exponentially with firm size. Evolving media, however, alleviate such internal constraints on organizational growth by increasing both the speed of message transmittal and organizations' capacities to process information (Boulding, [1953] 1968, p. 23).

Indeed communication media help alter fundamentally geo-social/cultural structures. Over the past couple of hundred years "the world has changed from being a set of a considerable number of fairly isolated social systems … into something approaching a single social system" (Boulding, 1985, p. 148). Initially ocean transport enabled transoceanic migrations and world trade; subsequently the telegraph, telephone, transoceanic cables, radio, television, communication satellites, and optical fibres "played an overwhelmingly important role in this transformation into a single world system" (Boulding, 1985, p. 148). Transmissions of knowledge structures have affected profoundly "architecture around the world, tastes in food and clothing, music and art, and dancing," eroding local cultures and substituting in their place "superculture" (Boulding, 1985, p. 151).

Ways of Communicating

Moreover, as noted at the close of Chapter 3, Boulding often invoked a triad of communicatory modes consisting of threat, exchange, and love to typify instances of human communication. He affirmed, "All social organizations without exception are built by processes that can be classified into these three general types... ." (Boulding, 1970, p. 27).

It was Boulding's position that market exchanges are necessarily rooted either in systems of love and integration, or in systems of threat; hence, he distinguished between "economies of love " and "economies of fear" (Boulding, 1973). Understanding the social system "as a total pattern, of which economics is only a part," led Boulding to depart from economic orthodoxy, and to conceive all human communication, including the traditionally "economic," as bearing elements of threat and love. Even the *grants economy* of one-way transfers, he noted, issues from these two different motivations—love giving rise to "gifts," and threat giving rise to "tribute" (Boulding, 1973, pp. v–vi).

Information, Entropy, and Evolution

Laws of Conservation, Entropy, and Evolution

Boulding declared that evolution "is not a determinate system like celestial mechanics because it is not an equilibrium system."[16] Rather, it involves inherently unpredictable changes in parameters on account of "the long-run importance of improbable events" (Boulding, 1981, p. 69).

Mechanical and equilibrium processes, he explained, are predictable or determinate because they involve matter and energy alone, and consequently physical (mechanical) laws apply to them. Matter and energy, for example, are subject to the Law of Conservation, also known as the First Law of Thermodynamics, which states that matter/energy can neither be created nor destroyed, only rendered more or less useful.

Information structures, on the other hand, are not likewise constrained. Knowledge alone is what can really increase; it is the only thing not conserved (Boulding, 1978, pp. 224–5). Since information transcends physical laws, for Boulding information constitutes the very essence of evolutionary processes.

In thus distinguishing matter/energy on the one hand from information/knowledge on the other, two opposing forces or tendencies become evident. On the one hand is the Law of Entropy, known also as the Second Law of Thermodynamics, which states that increased disorder or randomness results from any process, that there is a tendency for states to become more probable, more chaotic, less ordered, less differentiated (Boulding, 1978, p. 10). The end of the universe, according to the Law of Entropy, is a but a "thin soup without form." The counter-tendency, however, is the Law of Evolution, the capacity for complexity, organization, differentiation, and structure to increase over time (Boulding, 1978, p. 10). Recall that Boulding defined *production* as processes that increase material complexity (Boulding, 1978, p. 34). Evidently production, and therefore information and communication, are inherent to the Law of Evolution.

Production and changes in processes of production, according to Boulding, are possible over the long term only because of the properties of information and knowledge, and in particular the inapplicability to information/knowledge of the Law of Conservation. Unlike matter and energy, knowledge can be reproduced without limit, can be shared simultaneously by many, and can grow both incrementally and suddenly. (See Chapter 1 and 3 of this volume). Boulding declared, "It is a powerful and accurate metaphor to see the whole evolutionary process from the beginning of the universe as a process in the increase of knowledge or the information structure" (Boulding, 1978, p. 33).

Knowledge and Economic Development

Economic development from Boulding's perspective consists of two processes "which go in opposite directions" (Boulding, 1981, p. 73). First is the using up of known stocks of matter and energy; second is "replenishment," by which he meant "the constant growth of knowledge and discovery" (Boulding, 1981, p. 73). Discovery of so-called fossil fuels, for instance, "represented [an] enormous expansion of the energy inputs into human societies and temporarily at least expanded the human niche to the point where we find it today" (Boulding, 1981, p. 72). Since scarcity of energy and materials constrains economic development, whereas increments to knowledge serve to "push back" constraints, Boulding concluded that:

> In interpreting history one should look for the points at which knowledge rose to the point where new energy sources and new materials were captured for the productive process. The domestication of both crops and animals typified such occasions of fundamental change, increasing the efficiency of the capture of solar energy for human purposes. The development of the steam engine was a similar step forward (Boulding, 1978, p. 225).

On the other hand, Boulding perceived those nations mired in underdevelopment as lacking the means of storing and distributing knowledge. Indeed, in his view, the world is quickly separating into two cultures. Those individuals and countries able to adapt to and utilize modern technology are growing richer, while those unable to adapt and utilize the new media are experiencing not only the collapse of their traditional cultures due to the onslaught of the "technical superculture," but, as well they are becoming ever more "disorganized, delinquent, anemic and poor" (Boulding, [1966] 1995, p. 20).

Evolutionary Directionality

Evolutionary processes, while inherently unpredictable, display distinct directionality toward "complexity and toward noogenetics and consciousness" (Boulding, 1978, p. 22). Boulding regarded the universe as having undergone three great stages of development: first was *physical evolution*, culminating in the appearance of DNA; second came *biological evolution*, giving rise to life forms of increasing complexity, culminating in human beings; and finally, *societal evolution*. As Boulding noted, "these three great evolutionary processes ... are not independent of each other [but] constantly interact" (Boulding, 1978, p. 30).

The "sociosphere," consisting of humans, their organizations, and artifacts, interacts profusely with the biosphere, causing for instance extinction of some species and domestication of others. Human knowledge and evaluations have even produced "very substantial rearrangements of existing genetic material." Boulding therefore conjectured, "It may well be that biological evolution is approaching its end and that it will be succeeded by an evolutionary process wholly dominated by noogenetic processes directed by human values" (Boulding, 1978, p. 22)

Human activity has also profoundly affected the earth's physical evolution:

It has built dams, diverted rivers, dug mines, bulldozed mountains, eroded soil, and even created earthquakes; it has polluted the atmosphere, rivers, lakes and oceans; it has cut down forests and substituted agriculture; it has changed climates, at least over small areas, and perhaps over the whole earth; it has even gone to the moon and left its improbable artifacts (Boulding, 1978, p. 31).

For Boulding, we live in the middle time, the epoch of "civilization," an intermediate state for humankind separating "pre-civilization" from "post civilization." "It is furthermore a rather disagreeable state for most people living in it, and its disappearance need occasion few tears" (Boulding, [1964] 1965, p. 2).

Boulding believed that throughout the epoch of civilization there has arisen "a slowly rising stream of knowledge and organization" of a quality different from that of the civilized society within which it has grown (Boulding, [1964] 1965, p. 5). Hence, he contended, humanity is entering a new era—*Post-civilization*—an epoch based on knowledge, on science and on technology, as opposed to the mechanical and industrial processes of civilization (Boulding, [1956] 1961, p. 37).

While the human niche "expanded enormously" during the neolithic period, "from perhaps ten million to hundreds of million" (Boulding, 1978, p. 17), the rise of science over the past five hundred years is expanding it dramatically once again (Boulding, 1978, p. 171).

How far this expansion can continue, however, is a moot question, insofar as part of the expansion is attributable to the discovery and utilization of non renewable resources. And, as noted in Chapter 6, there is now a continual build up of wastes.

"Post-civilization," then, must entail new awareness, altered perceptions, and transformed goals. In the previous industrial (or "cowboy") economy, the earth was perceived as boundless, both in its supply of resource inputs and its capacity to absorb waste. In our day, high production engendered by the harnessing of scientific knowledge to industry has, however, rendered that perception obsolete and dangerous. For post-civilization the requisite image is that of "spaceship earth," our island home, where both resource inputs and the capacity of the earth to absorb waste are recognized as being finite.

This new vision carries with it altered values. In post-civilization, consumption and production are no longer to be perceived as being good in and of themselves. To the contrary, they are to be regarded as things to be minimized. As Boulding advised, in the post-civilization, spaceship-earth economy, value needs to center on the nature, extent, quality, and complexity of the total capital stock, which should be maintained using as few resource inputs as possible, rather than on production, consumption, and throughputs. This is a lesson, he added, that is "very strange to economists, who have been obsessed with the income-flow concepts to the exclusion, almost, of capital-stock concepts" (Boulding, [1966] 1970, pp. 281–2).

Usually quite buoyant, Boulding on occasion entertained dark thoughts with regard humankind's future. In his view technological modes of communication and emerging world "superculture," carry high risks. He wrote:

> There are ... profound dangers. [And particularly] there is danger ... due to the lack of isolation. All systems face eventual catastrophe, that is death. The evolutionary process has survived the death of innumerable individuals and species because of isolation and diversity, but a single world system might face universal and irretrievable catastrophe. One world could lead to no world. The one source for hope is the unexhausted potential of the human mind and the unexhausted potential of the evolutionary process itself. Any species, the human race not excepted, from an evolutionary point of view is a transmitter of the process of increasing complexity. When its work is done, it passes from the scene. How long the human race will last, we do not know. At the rate at which we have speeded up the evolutionary process, the life span of all species may be diminishing markedly. We may not have long to go. If we produce our evolutionary successor, however, we will not have been wasted (Boulding, [1979] 1995, pp. 37–38).

Recapitulation

According to Kenneth Boulding:

The pattern of human development is ... an extension, enlargement, and acceleration of the pattern of biological development, operating through mutation and selection. Selection is ecological interaction constantly creating new niches and destroying old ones; mutation takes the form of invention, discovery, expansions of the noosphere and the human noogenetic structure (Boulding, 1978, p. 18).

Malthus, Veblen, and Boulding

Thomas Robert Malthus maintained that important parameters, such as the Law of Population and the Law of Arithmetic Food Increase, are most difficult to alter. The perceived intractability of these two "laws" for the Malthusian system, as we have seen, flows from the scant attention Malthus paid to information/communication. Communication in the Malthusian system was confined largely to commodity exchange relations and to conjugal acts of reproduction that he perceived were instinctual (mechanical), giving rise to the "law" of population. It is true that Malthus, in revisions to his first *Essay*, significantly modified his pessimism and determinism by acknowledging the possibility that the "instinct" to reproduce could be countered by "moral restraint," a possibility stemming from the human capacity to teach, learn and communicate. In the Malthusian system, therefore, we indeed detect an incipient theory of information/communication, giving rise to the possibility (albeit an improbable one, in Malthus's view) of fundamental shifts in society's basic parameters.

Thorstein Veblen seized and elaborated upon the notion that through communication all things can change, and do so unpredictably. Veblen defined institutions as "habits of thought." For him changes in habits of thought are intrinsic to social/cultural change. Successive generations of individuals differ little in intellectual capacity or in amorphous instinctual propensity, but ways of seeing and of doing (habits of thought and of action) can and indeed do undergo cumulative change. Through his concept of institution, therefore, Veblen substituted collectivities for Malthus's individuals. Furthermore, he privileged communication in his social analysis rather than individual struggle and biologically inherited traits. In so doing he opened up possibilities for fundamental social and individual change.

Evolutionary economics awaited the abundant and seminal work of

Kenneth E. Boulding, however, before information, that which flows in communicatory processes, was made a primary subject of economic analysis. Through the body of his vast work Boulding has no peer in examining information as evolutionary and organizing agent. For him only "know-how," or its equivalent in the form of improbable genetic structures, grows or evolves, thus making knowledge and information crucial for evolutionary theory and for economic dynamics. Whereas matter and energy, quantifiable and subject to the Law of Conservation, are frequently amenable to mainstream (static, equilibrium) economic analyses, of the basic factors of production (as reformulated by Boulding), only information and knowledge can increase and be negentropic. Privileging knowledge and information shifts economics from a static, equilibrium, non-evolutionary mode to an evolutionary, developmental paradigm. This is one of the fundamental implications of information for economic analysis, and a summary of Boulding's immense contribution.

Malthus, Veblen, and Boulding, each in his own way, provide a counterpoint to today's prevailing neoclassicism. Malthus demonstrated that human activity, particularly biological reproduction, can outgrow the sustaining capacity of the ecosystem. Therefore, he recommended that communication, in the form of education and moral instruction, attempt to alter otherwise ineluctable social parameters. Veblen went several steps further, arguing that no social parameters are intractable; they only seem to be fixed on account of our present-mindedness due to our immersion in the present social order and its singular "habits of thought." Kenneth Boulding elucidated on information as the agent transforming social parameters and undergirding all evolutionary processes.

These three great economists give us insight as to how information/ communication can be more fully incorporated into an economics for the late twentieth and early twenty-first centuries, into an economics that will be no longer apologetic for a crisis-prone and markedly inegalitartian order, but one rather that helps usher in a new era—more just, ameliorative, and ecologically sound.

Notes

1. He has mused that he was probably the first in his family to go beyond the eighth grade (Boulding, 1992, p. 69).

2. Similarly he declared that his professional life was spent studying two questions: "First, what does it mean to say that things have gone from bad to better rather than from bad to worse? Second, how do we get to better?" (Wright, 1988, p. 295).

3. Lamarck maintained that characteristics of the genotype are modified by the phenotype it creates, now a generally discredited view with regard to biogenetic processes. According to Boulding, however, the greater the noospheric (or knowledge-based) component of evolutionary processes, the more analogous to

Lamarckian-type processes evolution becomes. *Biogenetic* mutations, that is "changes in the structure of the genes and DNA" are "highly Mendelian," wrote Boulding, whereas *noogenetic* change, that is changes in "learned structures in organisms that are transmitted from one generation to the next by a learning process" are Lamarckian, making evolution in our day, in Boulding's view, "extremely Lamarckian" (Boulding, 1985, p. 66).

4. This is not the "information" of Shannon and Weaver's "mathematical theory of communication," however. For Boulding, information "involves not only improbability of structure, but the structure's ability to 'instruct'; that is, to be a code of selection according to a program" (Boulding, 1978, p. 13).

5. Boulding's proposal, if accepted more widely, would affect dramatically "images" of economic processes. Consider, for example, implications for the Marxian theory of class struggle, and as well for neoclassical economics and its taxonomy of factor returns into rent, wages, and interest.

6. When messages confirm that a discrepancy exists between actual and ideal states, ensuing action can be of three types. Action can modify internally the ideal image, bringing it more in line with the existing state of affairs (one becomes more "realistic"). Alternatively energy may be expended on the external environment with the intent of bringing that more in line with the ideal. As a third, and probably most common possibility, action can modify both the ideal and the real. In any event, decisions or actions stem not merely from the flow of sensory stimuli, as would be the case with purely mechanical systems of cause and effect, but from "the change in context which that information provides" (Boulding, 1958, p. 90).

7. All *biological* species, Boulding maintained, are subject to the "law of diminishing growth" whereby growth rates eventually decline to zero (Boulding, 1981, p. 11). Populations that are increasing continually will normally face the spectre of overcrowding, lack of food, conflict, or other degradations, at which point birth rates will fall or death rates rise, establishing eventually an "equilibrium" where these two rates are equal, unless and until parameters of the niche change. The economists' famous "law of diminishing returns" is, then, but a special instance of this more general law, whose proof is established merely by noting the impossibility of growing the world's food supply in a flower pot (Boulding, 1978, p. 110).

8. On the other hand, Boulding acknowledged, populations of artifacts and organic species are alike in expanding or contracting in accordance with changes "in the total condition of the system" (Boulding, 1978, p. 69).

9. Boulding, unlike Veblen, certainly did not dismiss the possibility, or even likelihood, of teleological elements being inherent in the universe. He wrote that this, however, is an item of speculation or of faith, a proposition that cannot be confirmed "scientifically."

10. *Noogenetic* is a term Boulding derived from *noosphere*, a term first used by the Jesuit, Pierre Teilhard de Chardin, whose *Phenomenon of Man* ([1955] 1970) was for Boulding particularly influential. Boulding distinguished between *biogenetic processes*—those producing phenotypes, through inherited genetic structures, and *noogenetic processes*—which refer to structures within the central nervous system of the individual organism that must be learned from parents or other environments (Boulding, 1978, p. 14).

11. He elucidated further as follows: "At one stage the image, I suppose, con-

sists of little else than an undifferentiated blur and movement. From the moment of birth, if not before, there is a constant stream of messages entering the organism from the senses. At first, these may merely be undifferentiated lights and noises. As the child grows, however, they gradually become distinguished into people and objects. The conscious image has begun" (Boulding, [1956] 1961, p. 6).

12. Nonetheless, as Ian Parker in private correspondence has noted: "Notwithstanding the probabilistic character of perception, the "threshold" notion is not necessarily obsolete. In the first place, there *are* psycho physiological limits on perception: e.g. dog whistles. Second, signals can be intensified and enhanced to sharpen the differentiation between them and noise, if it is technically feasible and economically advantageous. Third, "noise" filters can perform the same function, and/or more redundancy or repetition built into the system. Fourth, apart from all of the above, there is (in hearing experiments, for instance) a range of volumes or intensities such that a signal will *never* be reported [at low intensities or low signal-noise ratios], and *always* be reported (correctly) [at high intensities or high signal-noise ratios]." In Parker's view, Boulding described an intermediary range between the extremes beyond which, on the one hand, it is impossible to detect signals due to high noise, and on the other where signals will always be detected.

13. Elsewhere Boulding wrote that science is a subculture for direct testing of new ideas, serving thereby to increase dramatically humanity's capacity for knowledge growth. Science, however, is quite restricted in the types of ideas it can test. "We cannot do experiments on unique events, and we cannot experiment on the past." Scientific testing applies only to systems that are "stable, repeatable and divisible" (Boulding, 1981, p. 10). As with all images, scientific knowledge to survive must be born anew into the minds of each succeeding generation through the selective processes of teaching and learning (Boulding, 1970, pp. 9-10).

14. Boulding used the word "organic" to describe open systems which maintain their structure even while taking things from their environment and depositing other things into it (Boulding, [1956] 1961, p. 33). He wrote: "When I say that knowledge is an organic structure, I mean that it follows principles of growth and development similar to those with which we are familiar in complex organizations and organisms" (Boulding, [1956] 1961, p. 17).

15. As Ian Parker has noted, however, the distinction between "direct" and "indirect" is complex and ambiguous. Parker writes: "I would lean toward the view that "cameras and sound recordings" generate *indirect, symbolic* messages (cf. Walter Benjamin *et al)* especially once one allows for the editing process."

16. To help explain inherent evolutionary trends toward complexity and order, Boulding classified processes as being: *equilibrium processes,* in which disturbances result in dynamic processes to restore equilibrium; *cyclical processes,* in which patterns are repeated time and time again; and *cumulative processes,* where there is never a return to a previous position but in which nonetheless a consistency in the pattern of change can be detected. Most teleological processes are cumulative, as are evolutionary processes (Boulding, 1970, p. 15).

PART FOUR

Policy Applications

10

Emergence and Development of Canadian Communications: Dispelling the Myths

Whatever changes occur in the ideal membership of the technical élite, there is always one group excluded from the list—the great mass of men in society.

—Langdon Winner (1977)

Introduction

Dispelling Myths

This chapter provides an historical account and analysis of the emergence and development in Canada of three communication sectors: the telegraph, the telephone, and broadcasting; of their relationship to the associated industrial arts or technologies;[1] and of related government policies. The chapter extends and illuminates Chapter 5 by focusing on two widely-held myths of technological dependence (Kroker, 1984): "technological imperative" and "technological determinism."

Technological imperative is the doctrine maintaining that most, if not all, technological developments ("technological evolution") are necessary and/or inevitable. Stated otherwise, it holds that human choices are severely constrained, if not indeed illusory. *Technological determinism* contends that all important human phenomena—cultures, distribution of power, belief systems, industry structures—are produced by Technology, which, in accordance with the doctrine of technological imperative, grows and develops almost independently of human will.

Technological imperative and technological determinism each exemplify myth in the Barthesian sense of the term. According to French semiologist Roland Barthes, myth deprives the object of which it speaks of all History. He emphasized that in myth,

> history evaporates. ... Nothing is produced, nothing chosen: all one has to do is to possess these new objects from which all soiling trace of origin or choice has been removed. This miraculous evaporation of history is another form of concept common to most bourgeois myths: *the irresponsibility of man* (Barthes, 1972, p. 151)

In the North American political economy there are deep-seated tendencies to mythologize technology, with governments, industry, and academics alike being culpable in this regard. Consider, for example, the following from Francis Fox, formerly Canadian Minister of Communications and recent Chair of the Social Impacts and Access Committee of the Canadian federal government's Advisory Council on the Information Highway :

> Canada has *no option* but to vigorously embrace the development and dissemination of these [new communication] technologies. The alternative would be to delay their introduction and find ourselves falling farther and farther behind in the international race to improve productivity of all sectors of the economy (Canada, Fox, 1983, p. 10, emphasis added).

Likewise, Shirley Serafini and Michel Andrieu, senior civil servants in the Canadian federal Department of Communications, wrote starkly in their widely-read report, *The Information Revolution and Its Implications for Canada:* "Like the industrial revolution, the information revolution is unavoidable" (Canada, Serafini and Andrieu, 1980, p. 13).

Technological imperative has been given vent by Industry Canada in its promotion of an "Information Highway":

> If Canada is to succeed in a global economy based on the creation, movement, storage, retrieval and application of information, our communications networks *must* be knitted into a *seamless and powerful* information infrastructure serving all Canadians. If Canada does not match the efforts of its competitors in accelerating infrastructure developments, opportunities for network, product and service development ... will be seized by firms in other countries (Canada, Industry Canada, 1994a, p. 5, emphasis added).

Technological imperative is promulgated not only by government, but also by private industry, as the following from Stentor (a consortium of Canada's major telephone companies) illustrates:

> To not act on this vision [of inaugurating a Canadian Information Highway] is to sabotage our future. If we do nothing, we risk alienating the country from developments taking place around the world. Canadians will be disenfranchised of a strong economic, social and cultural entry into the next millennium (Stentor, 1993a).

Canada must act now or get left behind. It is a simple question of *survival* in this fast changing world. .... Technology is changing at a breath-taking speed, calling into question the viability and utility of existing industry structures, regulations and policies (Stentor 1993b, p. 8, emphasis added).

Appeals to Technological Imperative are often accompanied by invocations of Technological Determinism, the doctrine that Technology is all-powerful. The Canadian federal Department of Communications, in *Instant World*, official harbinger of the Information Revolution in Canada, proclaimed for example:

Technology has fundamentally transformed the human condition twice before [reference being to the Agricultural and Industrial Revolutions]. .... How the third technological revolution *will shape our ends* is still far from clear but its nature and substance are already becoming familiar. ... Ours is ... a society built upon and shaped by technology (Canada, Department of Communications, 1971, pp. 24-25, emphasis added).

Likewise Industry Canada has opined that a Canadian Information Highway (which, of course *must* be introduced), "will have broad and tranformative effects throughout the Canadian economy" (Canada, Industry Canada, 1994a, p. 1). In a similar vein communication scholar Ithiel de Sola Pool charged:

Examining the impact of changing technologies of communication on society seems to imply a belief in some powerful causality and even determinism. But is technology in command? Certainly it stirs powerful social forces. Whether or not the technologies with which we do our work and conduct our business will control our destinies in the end, they certainly create a massive current (de Sola Pool, 1990, pp. 17–18).[2]

Finally, from a book devoted precisely to the topic:

As the literature of modernization makes clear, the process of change that accompanies technological innovation touches every dimension of society. All varieties of customs, habits, attitudes, ideas, and social and political institutions are caught up in its flow, altered, and set on a new foundation. Nothing is left untouched (Winner, 1977, p. 103).

Less sweeping, perhaps, but still in keeping with the doctrine of technological determinism are claims that industrial structures hinge on underlying techniques (the doctrine of natural monopoly,[3] for example); and as well the claim that publishing, telegraphs, telephones, and broadcasting for years constituted separate industries *because* of unique, underlying technologies; and finally that autonomous technological developments ("technological evolution") are now forcing a convergence among these activities. (See for example, Industry Canada, 1994, p. 4; also Canada, CRTC, 1994, p. 49).

In brief, the dual doctrines of technological dependence—the techno-logical imperative and technological determinism—posit Technology to be active and humans, including regulators and legislators, as being pas-sive, implying that at best one can only adapt, a notion that Jacques Ellul has aptly termed the "insidious ethics of adaptation." Ellul wrote with irony:

> Since technique is a fact, we should adapt ourselves to it. Consequently, anything that hinders technique ought to be eliminated, and thus adapta-tion itself becomes a moral criterion (Ellul, 1980, p. 243).

Power and Technological Dependence

One of the consequences, then, of mythologizing "Technology," particularly in terms of the dual doctrines of technological dependence, is to divert attention onto "Technology" and away from corporations and governments that actively research, subsidize, introduce, deploy, and promote particular techniques. By thus mythologizing, dominance and dependencies stemming from control over and utilization of technologies are obfuscated and basic issues concerning, for instance, the distribution of economic, political, cultural, and communicatory power remain une-laborated and undebated.

On the other hand, once the industrial arts ("technologies") are alternatively and more realistically viewed as being in the first instance means for attaining, exercising, and aggrandizing power, and once élites responsible for their introduction and deployment are identified, then a dialectic of political dominance and political dependence substitutes for myth. Awareness of "the soiling trace of origin or choice" politicizes and de-mythologizes technology, permitting groups disadvantaged by "tech-nological evolution" (for instance, labor displaced by capital, customers and suppliers disadvantaged by "natural monopolies," nations subjected to foreign cultural hegemony; producers and users of public services mar-ginalized by producers and users of private commodities), to become more strident and confident in their opposition.

This chapter, in presenting historical evidence on the emergence and structuring of sectors of Canadian communication, is intended to reaffirm the importance of political economy and historical analyses in media and policy studies. These analytical modes help dispel the dual myths of technological dependence. A companion chapter on the Canadian Infor-mation Highway follows.

Emergence and Development of Industrial Structures

This historical section provides the focus of the chapter. It contains three parts, dealing respectively with the telegraph, the telephone and broadcasting. Each part in turn comprises two subparts, of which the first treats the emergence and subsequent segregation of one technology or industry from another—telegraph from publishing, telephone from telegraph, broadcasting from telephone; the second deals with the structuring and restructuring of the industry in question once the segregation had been accomplished. Throughout a central theme is the absence of a technological imperative in Canadian communication. Rather, emphasis is on power, the quest for it, its distribution and deployment. The analysis throughout emphasizes also that Canadian decisions were made within the context of U.S. influence, and often indeed of U.S. control.

The Telegraph Industry

Segregation from Publishing. For over sixty years the Canadian telegraph and daily press were highly integrated. In his authoritative history of the newswire service, Canadian Press, M. E. Nichols, for example, wrote: "From the day that poles and wires went up in Canada [1846] and the keys clicked in the operating rooms, telegraph companies collected and sold news to the newspapers and the newspapers were glad to get it" (Nichols, 1948, p. 10). Newspapers depended almost totally on telegraph companies, not only for transmission services, but also for the news items transmitted. Apart from a few professional journalists in the larger cities, the only news correspondents until 1910 were telegraph operators (Rutherford, 1982, p. 95).

While all major telegraph companies collected and sold news to win the lucrative and vital press transmission business, by 1895 the field was dominated by Canadian Pacific Telegraph Company. In that year CP procured Canadian rights to the American Associated Press newswire, and thereafter, as a practical matter, virtually every daily newspaper in Canada was required to subscribe to CP's news service and to use its transmission facilities, bundled together so that newspapers could not obtain one without the other. On at least one occasion CP Telegraph disciplined a rebellious newspaper for having published stories critical of Canadian Pacific, cutting the paper off from press dispatches (Nichols, 1948, pp. 38–9). Arbitrary price increases eventually induced newspapers in Winnipeg to start up a rival press service in 1907.

Telegraph companies continued to dominate the newsgathering and reporting field until 1910, when the Canadian Railway Commission ruled that CP Telegraph's charges to Winnipeg dailies were discriminatory and hence unlawful.[4] Thereupon Canadian Pacific abandoned newsgathering, as did its main rival, the Great North Western Telegraph Company, and the era of the communication common carrier was begun.

This brief account shows that separation of content and carriage (of publishing from telecommunications) was initiated in Canada by a regulatory ruling. Prior to 1910 there had been extensive integration between these fields. In no sense were the underlying "technologies" of the telegraph and of publishing responsible.

Industry Structuring. Similarly, the structuring of the telegraph industry should not be ascribed to underlying technology. Rather, American ownership and control, government subsidy, exclusive franchises, and restrictive trade practices were the chief factors. The following provides a brief overview.

Until 1881 the largest and most powerful telegraph company in Canada was the Montreal Telegraph Company. Receiving a federal charter in 1847, it soon embarked on an aggressive campaign of acquisitions, collusive deals and predatory practices, all serving to establish, by the mid 1850's, its hegemony in Ontario, Quebec, and sections of the northeastern United States. Restrictive covenants concluded with the railways gave Montreal Telegraph exclusive rights to construct lines along railroad rights-of-way (Hopper and Kearney, 1962, pp. 160, 161; *Monetary Times*, Vol. 25, pp. 1429, 1489), to the distinct disadvantage of rivals. Predatory rate battles helped monopolization too; by reducing prices along competitive routes and cross-subsidizing losses through revenues earned on monopolized ones, Montreal Telegraph eliminated a number of hapless competitors, including the Grand Trunk Telegraph Company (linking Buffalo and Quebec City) in 1855, and the British North American Telegraph Association, (connecting Montreal and Woodstock, N.B.) in 1856 (*Monetary Times*, Vol. 25, p. 1398). In addition, in 1858, Montreal Telegraph joined an international cartel which allocated its members exclusive territories for North America. Montreal Telegraph was assigned portions of some north eastern states as well as Ontario and Quebec. Where there was duplication of routes amongst cartel members, revenues were carefully prorated. Moreover, no new competing lines were to be constructed. Furthermore, telegraphic interconnections were provided among the signatories alone, except insofar as existing contracts with other companies had to be fulfilled. The cartel made provisions for arbitrating disputes among signatories before a tribunal comprised of its members (Thompson, 1947, pp. 314–330).

One of Montreal Telegraph's more persistent and enduring competitors, the Dominion Telegraph Company, was started in 1868 to link up with the Atlantic and Pacific Telegraph Company, a rival of Western Union in the U.S.A. Until 1881 the Dominion and Montreal Telegraph companies engaged in sometimes bitter competitive struggles (duplicating industrial conduct in the United States), by which time the lines of both Canadian companies had been taken over by Western Union through a newly-organized subsidiary, The Great North Western Telegraph Company (GNWT) (Hopper and Kearney, 1962, p. 448). Western Union, already in possession of virtually all telegraphic facilities in the Maritimes, thereupon held virtually a complete monopoly over all Canadian telegraphy until the entry of Canadian Pacific Telegraph Company four years later.

A beneficiary of extensive government-built telegraph lines in Western Canada running from Fort William (now Thunder Bay, Ontario) to Edmonton, Alberta, as well as generous public funds to build the transcontinental railway, Canadian Pacific began its commercial telegraph service in 1885 between the Rockies and Lake Superior (Innis, 1923, pp. 133–4). In the following year, after acquiring several railways and associated telegraph facilities in Ontario, it expanded its commercial telegraph to connect important towns in Ontario with the West (MacGibbon, 1917, p. 43; *Monetary Times*, Vol. 26, pp. 945–6). Connections to the U.S.A. were provided through the Postal Telegraph Company (Innis, 1923, pp. 133–194). By 1890 the CPR had extended its telegraph lines to Saint John, New Brunswick, and by 1916 to Nova Scotia, in competition with Western Union.

Whereas the Canadian Pacific Telegraph Company was conceived through a gift of lines constructed by the federal government, Canadian National Telegraph Company (a crown corporation) was constituted when the federal government took over and amalgamated several bankrupt private companies. One of these was the Canadian Northern Railway and its telegraph subsidiary, Canadian Northern Telegraph Company, which had acquired Western Union's Canadian subsidiary (GNWT) in 1915. Subsequently other railway and telegraph operations were taken over as well, and in 1923 Canadian National Railway Company and Canadian National Telegraph Company were formed.

For many years Canadian National and Canadian Pacific Telegraph companies competed directly, the duopoly in Canada mirroring the industry structure in the U.S.A. In the 1940s, however, the two telegraph companies started amalgamating services, choosing to cooperate rather than compete. In 1943 CN began offering international lease wires jointly with CP while in 1947 the pooling and prorating arrangement was extended to domestic lease wires as well. By the mid fifties the two carriers were constructing microwave systems on an integrated basis and in 1956 they jointly launched Telex, a switched teletypewriter service. Despite such coordination among services and facilities, the two companies continued providing public message telegraph services on a competitive basis until 1967, at which time they agreed reciprocally to abandon offices.

Three factors are of particular importance in explaining the increased cooperation between CN and CP Telegraphs. First, in 1932 the major telephone companies established the nationally-interconnected Trans

Canada Telephone System (today known as Stentor Telecom Policy Inc.), thereby increasing competition in the field of private line services. Second, in 1943 Western Union took over the failing Postal Telegraph Company, thereby establishing a telegraphic monopoly in the United States (Borchardt, 1970, pp. 26, 47). Third, in the postwar years the traditional telegraph market went into a decline.

In 1980, cooperation between the two Canadian telegraph companies culminated in the formation of a partnership, CNCP Telecommunications, jointly owned by Canadian National Railway Company and Canadian Pacific Limited (Sutherland, 1978, p. 15; partnership agreement, 1980). In 1988 Canadian Pacific acquired the shares in CNCP owned by Canadian National, and in turn sold a minority interest in the company, now named Unitel Communications, Inc., to Rogers' Communications, a major provider of cable TV and other communication services in Canada. Subsequently American Telephone and Telegraph (AT&T) procured minority holdings as well. Unitel today is the principle alternative provider of long distance telephone circuits. As this chapter was being revised it appeared that Canadian Pacific and Rogers might both sell their shares in Unitel, which was experiencing serious financial difficulty.

The Telephone Industry

Segregation from Telegraphs. The pioneers of Canadian telephony were telegraph companies. In February 1879, less than three years after the introduction of the telephone to Canada by Alexander Graham Bell's father, Melville Bell, the Dominion Telegraph Company was granted a five-year exclusive licence to work the Bell telephone patent. Dominion Telegraph began constructing telephone lines and establishing exchanges in leading communities (Fetherstonaugh, 1944, p. 115).[5] Meanwhile, Montreal Telegraph worked rival patents for the telephone held by Western Union, extending thereby telegraphic battles into the emerging field of telephony (Fetherstonaugh, 1944, p. 115). Cut rates, even gratuitous service, characterized this early competitive period.

Financially strapped, Dominion Telegraph was unable to raise, in June 1879, $100,000 needed for outright purchase of the Canadian telephone patent. Shortly thereafter the patent was sold to National Bell of Boston, Massachusetts, at the time also holder for the U.S.A. of the Bell telephone patents (Fetherstonaugh, 1944, pp. 52–53, 63). In this way Canadian telephony fell under U.S. control less than four years after its inception.

Segregation of telephones and telegraphy in both the United States and Canada followed swiftly. Western Union, sorely troubled by telegraphic incursions from the newly established American Union Telegraph Company and facing law suits for telephone patent infringement, sold both its telephone plant and its patents to the Bell patent holders in November 1879, agreeing never to re-enter the telephone business (U.S.A., Federal

Communications Commission, 1939, p. 85). In return, the U.S. Bell agreed not to enter the telegraph field. In 1880 a similar agreement was signed in Canada, signaling Western Union's departure from Canadian telephony. Also in 1880, U.S. Bell appointed its new Canadian subsidiary, The Bell Telephone Company of Canada, to work its telephone patents. By 1881 Bell of Canada had acquired all remaining telephone plants in Canada.

The possibility of entry into telephones by yet another telegraph company, namely Canadian Pacific Telegraphs, was not put to rest until 1902, however, at which time Canadian Pacific granted The Bell Telephone Company of Canada the exclusive right to construct telephone lines along Canadian Pacific Railway's rights-of-way and to place telephone instruments in CPR's premises. A factor inducing CP to so agree was Bell's purchase, in about 1900, of the federally-chartered North American Telegraph Company which offered telegraph service in the Kingston, Ontario region and which was entitled by federal charter to provide telegraph service throughout Canada. Although Bell Telephone was precluded by its own charter from offering telegraph service, Bell increased its leverage against CP Telegraph by threatening to enter the telegraph business on a wide scale, albeit indirectly through this newly-acquired subsidiary (Canada, House of Commons, 1905, pp. 251-253). The 1902 agreement signaled a longstanding truce.

Industry Structuring. In 1885 the federal government made void the Bell patent on grounds of importation and refusal to sell telephone instruments,[6] opening the way for incursions by independent telephone companies. Nonetheless, despite its loss of patent, Bell still possessed important advantages. Under the provisions of its charter it was empowered to construct telephone lines along any and all public rights of way, even in the absence of municipal or provincial authorization. Independent telephone companies, on the other hand, needed consent from appropriate levels of government before constructing systems.

Bell's response to the cancellation of its patent, and the accompanying threat of competition, was swift. First, it focused its energies on Ontario and Quebec, the most lucrative territories, abandoning the Maritimes and British Columbia, although retaining ownership interest in the local companies in the east to which it sold out.[7] Next, it undertook rapid construction of long distance lines to link major communities within a 500-kilometre radius of Montreal (Fetherstonaugh, 1944, p. 80); these facilities gave Bell an advantage over independents lacking long distance connections. Third, when faced by direct competition, the telephone company frequently engaged in predatory rate battles. In this way the Dominion Telephone Company, centered in Sherbrooke, Quebec, was eliminated in 1886, a year after the decisive patent ruling, when Bell offered one year's free telephone service on a three-year contract (Canada, House of Commons, 1905, pp. 159–161, 806). In Peterborough,

Port Arthur, and Fort William, too, Bell Telephone offered service free of charge to reduce subscriptions to competing systems (Canada, House of Commons, 1905, pp. 77–98, 680). In Winnipeg Bell covertly set up a subsidiary to undercut the local company and drive it out of business (Surtees, 1992, p. 76).

Finally, Bell negotiated exclusive privileges with municipalities and railroads, again serving to reduce or eliminate competition. As far as the municipalities were concerned, by 1905 it attained 30 exclusive franchises, giving in return money and promises not to raise rates during the life of the agreement (Canada, House of Commons, 1905, p. 660). With the railroads, between 1891 and 1905, it negotiated 14 contracts that prohibited non-Bell telephones in railway stations and non-Bell telephone equipment on railroad rights-of-way and other property. These agreements were nullified by the Board of Railway Commissioners for Canada only in 1909.

Agitation[8] for control over the Company's affairs induced the Laurier government in 1906 to subject the company's tolls and connecting agreements to the oversight of the Board of Railway Commissioners for Canada. Deeming this measure inadequate, the three provincial governments on the prairies bought up Bell's operations between 1908 and 1909, thereby forming the Manitoba, Alberta, and Saskatchewan Government Telephone companies (Britnell, 1934). In Bell's remaining territory of Ontario and Quebec, regulation by the Railway Board initially led to a flood of small entrants into the telephone business, many competing directly with Bell. In Ontario alone some 676 independent telephone companies were established between 1906 and 1915 (Grindlay, 1975, pp. 254–305). So dramatic was the growth of independents that, by 1915, they accounted for nearly one third of Ontario's telephones.

With regulatory approval and compliance, however, Bell halted, and then reversed, the growth of independents, first through its long distance interconnection and pricing policies, and then subsequently through its local exchange pricing policies. Ultimately most independents were absorbed. Between 1950 and 1959, the dominant company bought up 160 independents in Ontario, while between 1960 and 1979 an additional 218 companies were taken over, thereby reducing independent telephones in that province to about five percent of the provincial total by 1975 (Ontario Telephone Service Commission, 1977, p. 186).

It is worth examining telephone pricing policies during this era. Prior to about 1920 Bell claimed to be providing long distance service at a loss, cross subsidizing it through high local rates.[9] However, forced by the regulator to interconnect independent telephone companies to its long distance lines (Board of Railway Commissioners for Canada, Order No. 375, 1923), the company found it advantageous to begin "rebalancing" its rates. From the 1920's to the present the company has claimed to be losing money on local exchange services, recouping the losses through the now-lucrative long distance business.[10]

The initial rate rebalancing disadvantaged independent telephone companies lacking their own toll lines (Ontario, 1953).[11] Under the "board-to-board" method of toll settlements, independent companies received no share in long distance revenues for providing telephone instruments, local distribution facilities, and local exchanges. Even long distance billing expenses were declared to be non-compensable. This, coupled with frequently lucrative take-over offers (Ontario, 1977)[12] explains the gross diminution of the independent telephone industry in Ontario and Quebec.

"Rate rebalancing" also created pressures for entry into the long distance market by independents. While an application by the then independent Northern Telephone Company to provide long distance service between Kenora and Fort William was denied by the regulator in 1964 (Board of Transport Commissioners for Canada, 1964, pp. 436ff), CNCP Telecommunications was more successful in 1979, gaining access to Bell's local switched network for certain data and private line voice services (CRTC, Telecom Decision, 1979, p. 11). That decision was subsequently extended by several others, of which two stand out.

In 1992 the Canadian Radio-television and Telecommunications Commission (CRTC) broadened the parameters of the 1979 decision to encompass public long distance voice service, permitting as well resale and sharing of long distance lines, giving rise to a plethora of long distance resellers and value added carriers (CRTC, 1992). In September 1994, the CRTC published its "Review of Regulatory Framework" decision, intended to "increase flexibility for the telephone companies on the one hand, while removing barriers to entry and adopting conditions to safeguard competition on the other" (CRTC, 1994, p. 14). According to the decision, "principles such as open entry and open access ... should govern *all* telecommunications services" (CRTC, 1994, p. 46, emphasis added). Of the decision's provisions, two are most significant: first, restrictions on the participation of telephone companies in emerging information and transactional telecommunications service markets are to be eased; second, restrictions on local competition are to be removed. According to the CRTC, "open access and interoperability principles among networks" [i.e., "Information Highway" principles] are to be promoted (CRTC, 1994, pp. 16–17). In the late autumn of 1994, the federal Cabinet ordered the CRTC to reconsider aspects of this decision and as well to conduct a special hearing on the convergence of media; hearings were held in March 1995.

The foregoing should suffice to put to rest doctrines of technological dependence in telecommunications. The segregation of telephone and telegraph plant and services into two, distinct industries was in no sense an outcome of mere technology. Rather, corporate powerplays provide a full and ample explanation. Likewise, industry structuring subsequent to segregation is fully explainable by corporate and governmental policies, without need to invoke a technological imperative.

The Broadcasting Industry

Segregation from Telephones. Although we have become accustomed to using the telephone for two-way, point-to-point communication, in contrast to point-to-multipoint services, such was not always its exclusive use. As early as 1879, sermons, operas, news, and other programs were "broadcast" over telephone lines in Europe, the United States and Canada (Montreal *Daily Star*, 26 July 1881). In 1893 in Budapest, for example, a comprehensive news and entertainment service was inaugurated for 6000 telephone subscribers, each of whom was provided with a timetable of programs which included "concerts, lectures, dramatic readings, newspaper reviews, stock market reports, and direct transmission of speeches by members of Parliament" (Kern, 1983, p. 69). The Budapest telephone system was even equipped with emergency signaling capability, allowing the "station" to ring every subscriber when special news broke. In America, the 1896 presidential election returns were reported over the telephone system, a contemporary report noting that "thousands sat with their ear glued to the receiver the whole night long, hypnotized by the possibilities unfolded to them for the first time" (quoted in Kern, 1983, p. 70). In Canada too, live music was transmitted to households over the telephone system (Hamilton *Evening Journal*, Nov. 30, 1877).[13]

Indeed, what we perceive today as "broadcasting" (the radiation of signals by a transmitter over a broad geographic space) was at one time seen exclusively as an extension of telegraphy and telephony. Until the end of the First World War, radio telegraphy and radio telephony were only important militarily. It was not until the armistice that leading American and Canadian manufacturers of radio transmission and receiving equipment, perceiving lucrative military markets to be collapsing, struck upon the notion of selling radio receivers to households. To induce consumer sales, Westinghouse Electric and Manufacturing Company inaugurated a daily program service (KDKA) out of Pittsburgh in November 1920. The station's first programming covered presidential election returns (Barnouw, 1978, p. 9). Yet KDKA was not the first station to broadcast for general reception by the public. XWA in Montreal, owned by another equipment manufacturer, Canadian Marconi, had legally inaugurated regular programming in May 1920[14] under authority of a radiotelegraph licence issued by the Department of Naval Service (Troyer, 1980, p. 25).

KDKA and XWA (or CFCF) were overnight successes, and thus the radio broadcasting industry was born. Suddenly the very meaning of "radio" was changed: for the military it had meant the transmission of intelligence and orders; subsequent to the War it represented a coming age of entertainment and perhaps even enlightenment (Barnouw, 1978, pp. 14–20).

However, divergence between telecommunications and the new radio broadcasting industry had not yet been accomplished. In the U.S.A., American Telephone and Telegraph announced in 1922 that it would open a new kind of radio station and network, applying principles of common carriage (long associated with telephony) to broadcasting. Just as one could enter a telephone booth, deposit a coin and talk to a friend, so too, AT&T announced, could persons or groups interested in reaching an audience lease time on the company's "toll broadcasting stations." AT&T planned to provide no programming of its own, but merely rent out channels through which content providers could diffuse their own messages. In August 1922 AT&T opened its first toll station, WEAF in New York City, followed in 1923 by WCAP in Washington, D.C., linked by wire to WEAF (Barnouw, 1978, pp. 14–20; Danielian, [1939] 1974, pp. 122–126).

AT&T's Canadian subsidiary, The Bell Telephone Company of Canada, also entered radio in 1922 when licences for stations CKCS, Montreal and CFTC, Toronto were issued by the Department of Marine and Fisheries. These one-year licences were not renewed in 1923, however, and in its *Annual Report* for that year the Directors of Bell Telephone explained why:

> An agreement has been concluded with the Canadian General Electric Company, the Northern Electric Company, the Marconi Wireless Telegraph Company, the Canadian Westinghouse and the International Western Electric Company, covering the use by all for radio purposes of the respective patents of each concern. Under the terms of the agreement, each of the companies agrees to the use of its patents within the natural field of such other company.
>
> The Marconi Company will have the use of all the patents for wireless telegraph purposes; The Bell Telephone Company of Canada for the purposes of public telephone communication; and the manufacturing companies, including the Marconi Company, for the purposes of manufacture and sale (Bell Telephone Company of Canada, 1923, p. 8).

In the United States, Bell's parent firm, AT&T, did not leave broadcasting until 1926 when, also through a patent pooling arrangement, it sold its broadcasting stations to RCA, agreeing never to re-enter radio broadcasting (Danielian, [1939] 1974, pp. 108-137).

In conclusion, it is to be emphasized that the Canadian patent pooling and market exclusivity contracts of 1923 resembled arrangements of 1920 and 1926 in the U.S.A. Furthermore, signatories to the Canadian agreement were all subsidiaries of foreign parents, again pointing to the high degree of foreign influence shaping Canadian communications.

Industry Structuring. Three distinct phases in the structuring of Canadian broadcasting can be discerned (Babe, 1979, p. 23).[15] The first, lasting from 1920 to 1932, saw the dominance of unregulated market forces. In this era Canadian broadcasters concentrated on playing recorded music and popular American programs, the noteworthy exception being the radio service provided by Canadian National Railways, a crown corporation.[16] The second phase was inaugurated in 1932 when the federal government, responding to recommendations of the 1929 Aird Royal Commission on Radio Broadcasting, created the Canadian Radio Broadcasting Commission (CRBC), both to engage in broadcasting and to regulate private broadcasting. In 1936 the CRBC was superseded by the Canadian Broadcasting Corporation (CBC). Despite overt and covert politicking by private sector interests, the CBC was preeminent in Canadian broadcasting for over twenty years, a status reaffirmed by successive parliamentary committees during the period and by the 1951 Massey Royal Commission on National Development in the Arts, Letters, and Sciences.

Looking, however, toward the age of television, Massey was prescient, forecasting that high programming costs could well create immense pressures on the private sector to become "mere channels for American commercial material." Consequently, Massey recommended that no private television stations be licensed until CBC had firmly established itself in the field, and thereafter any and all private stations should be required to affiliate with CBC and be regulated by it.

Public broadcasting began its decline in 1958 when the government created the Board of Broadcast Governors (BBG), separate from the CBC, to regulate most aspects of broadcasting. In addition, the government authorized the creation of a second television network (CTV) to be made up entirely of private stations. This third phase has seen a steady increase in the relative importance of the private sector, and a relative diminution of the public. The CRTC, which replaced the BBG in 1968, has devoted much of its activities to administering this change.[17]

The CRTC has had the responsibility of incorporating new technologies into the broadcasting system—first cable television, then satellite communications, and now an "Information Highway," defined as a "network of networks" converging hitherto separate communication sectors, in the view of some rendering obsolete past goals and policies based on distinct communication industry sectors. (See Babe, forthcoming).

Conclusions

From the historical section three main conclusions stand out. First, media of communication in Canada have seldom been controlled within the country. The Canadian telegraph industry was fully integrated through cartel arrangements and by ownership with the U.S. industry from the mid 1850s; it did not emerge into predominantly Canadian hands for another 60 years. Likewise, the telephone industry fell under American control in 1880, where it remained, whether through ownership or through patent licensing arrangements, for decades. In terms of program content, the Canadian broadcasting industry is still largely dominated by the U.S. entertainment industry.

Second, the historical record belies the doctrine of a technological imperative in Canadian communications. The three sectors discussed here—publishing, telegraphs/telephones, and broadcasting—had common roots and diverged only on account of agreements dividing markets and government policy. Likewise, subsequent industry structurings were part and parcel of the struggle for power by contending interests. It therefore follows that the convergence, or to be more precise, reconvergence, taking place today, is not technologically-induced either, but stems rather from corporate and/or governmental powerplays.

Third, communication technologies are highly flexible (c.f. Nora and Minc, 1980; and Williams, 1974). Those in control of technologies can do with them largely what they wish. Once goals have been formulated, technologies can be deployed to pursue certain ends. The "insidious ethics of adaptation," as Ellul suggested, is a product of our imaginings, albeit often assisted by the mass media of persuasion and indoctrination.

For those who wield technologies to further their own power positions, an ethics of adaptation can indeed be useful to propagate. Propagation of this ethic is allied closely to the mythification of Technology.

Notes

This chapter is republished, with revisions, by permission of Kagan and Woo Limited, from *Communications Canada: Issues in Broadcasting and New Technologies*, edited by Rowland Lorimer and Donald Wilson, 1988, pp. 58–79. An expanded version of the material presented here can be found in Robert E. Babe, *Telecommunications in Canada: Technology, Industry and Government* (Toronto: University of Toronto Press, 1990).

1. The word "technology" is fraught with difficulty. From the 17th century it meant merely the study of the practical or mechanical arts. By the 20th century the term had been expanded in both denotative and connotative meanings to embrace such diverse phenomena as "tools, instruments, machines, organizations, methods, techniques, systems and the totality of all these and similar things in our experience" (Winner, 1977, p. 8). For the purpose of this chapter "technol-

ogy" means simply an industrial art or system of industrial arts applied to a particular field, such as telegraph "technology."

2. In similar vein Manley Irwin wrote, for example: "*Technology* is dissolving industry boundary lines, assaulting geographic demarcations and softening global artifacts" (Irwin, 1984, p. 3, emphasis added).

3. As recently as 1978, Bell Canada, then still enjoying virtually an end-to-end monopoly in telecommunications, asserted: "The public switched telephone network as it exists today constitutes a clear and workable boundary of the basic natural monopoly of Bell Canada in telecommunications. Only services not connected to the public switched telephone network should be ... tested in the marketplace. ... The existence of economies of scale, scope and technology ... make Bell Canada a natural monopoly" (Bell Canada, Argument, CNCP Interconnection Case, 29 May 1978, Part II, Tab 4, p. 6).

4. For example, the flat rate charged clients in Saskatoon for CPR's combined news/transmission service from Montreal was $200 a month, compared with $467 a month charged for transmission only (of the same wordage) to Saskatoon from Winnipeg. See Nichols (1948, p. 55).

5. Dominion's facilities had been used by telephone interests previously. For example, in August 1876 Alexander Graham Bell set up the world's first long distance telephone call using lines of the Dominion Telegraph Company to connect Brantford and Paris, Ontario, about ten kilometres apart. The Dominion Telegraph Company is also credited with supplying the lines for the first telephone communication between Montreal and Quebec City, about 250 kilometres, in September 1877. See Patten (1926, pp. 10-14,17, 59); Quinpool (1936, p. 172); and Bell Canada Telephone Historical Collection, Montreal, Catalogued Document 27636.

6. Bell leased, and did not sell, telephone instruments.

7. Bell bowed out of PEI in 1885, selling its interests to the Telephone Company of Prince Edward Island. In 1887 it left Nova Scotia and New Brunswick, selling out to a competitor, the Nova Scotia Telephone Company. See House of Commons (1906, pp. 554, 344–345). In 1889 Bell Telephone withdrew also from British Columbia. See R. C. Fetherstonaugh (1944, p. 190). The origins and development of the British Columbia Telephone Company, not treated in this chapter, are described in Elaine Bernard (1982).

8. In 1901, 104 petitions from municipal governments were received by Parliament, while in 1905 195 counties and municipalities petitioned Parliament, requesting some form of control be imposed on telephone operations. In 1905 the Union of Canadian Municipalities petitioned that telephone systems be acquired by the government. *Journals of the House of Commons*, 1901, 1905.

9. The Railway Board accepted this contention in 6 *Cdn. Ry. Cas* 327, as did the Supreme Court in 53 *Can. S.C.R* 503 (1915).

10. In 1979, for example, Bell claimed that it cost $1.32 to produce each dollar in local service revenues, but only $0.31 to produce $ 1.00 from toll. See CRTC, *CNCP Telecommunications: Interconnection With Bell Canada*, Decision CRTC 79-11,17 May 1979, p. 216.

11. See in particular Rural Telephone Committee of the Hydro-Electric Power Commission of Ontario (1953).

12. See testimony of G. D. Inns, Executive Vice-President of Bell Canada, before

the Ontario Telephone Service Commission, 3 August 1977, Transcript, pp. 10, 37–49, 65–67, 112, where Mr. Inns agreed that high prices were paid to acquire independents which in and of themselves would remain unprofitable unless rates were more than doubled. See also Board of Transport Commissioners for Canada, *Judgements, Orders, Regulations and Rulings*, Vol. XLI, No. 15, 1 November 1951; also Vol. XLIV No. 9, 1 August 1954; and John McManus, (1973, pp. 403–408).

13. See also Montreal *Gazette*, December 1879; Bobcaygeon *Independent*, 16 November 1877; Woodstock *Times*, 2 November 1877.

14. T. J. Allard reported that "the Marconi Wireless Telegraph Company of Canada Limited opened operations in September 1919 with XWA. A year later, its activities were legalized by issue of a licence under the call letters CFCF" (Allard, 1976, p. 1).

15. The three phases are discussed at greater length in Babe (1979, pp. 11–23).

16. Canadian National Railway's radio department was set up in 1923 to gain an upper hand on its arch rival, Canadian Pacific. CN equipped its parlour cars with receiving sets so that passengers could settle back comfortably in their seats and enjoy "Romance of Canada" (a series of plays on Canadian themes); the Toronto Symphony Orchestra; condensed versions of great operas, operettas and musical comedies; "The Nation's Business" (a discussion program involving leading politicians); and indeed "Amos N' Andy". CN's program service was diffused over its own transmitters sprinkled across the land.

17. For example, CRTC Committee on Extension of Service to Northern and Remote Communities (1980, pp. 1–2); and Department of Communications (1983).

11

Telecommunications Policy: *Real World* of the Canadian Information Highway

There is a lot of talk about global crises and "our common future." However, there is far too little discussion of the structuring of the future which global applications of modern technologies carry in their wake. What ought to be of central concern in considering our common future are the aspects of technological structuring that will inhibit or prevent future changes in social and political relations.
—Ursula Franklin (1990)

"Broad And Transformative Effects"

Information highway initiatives are now being pursued vigorously by several industrial nations including Japan, the United States, and members of the European Union. Canada is no exception.

In October 1993 Stentor Telecom Policy Inc., a consortium of Canada's major telephone companies, announced its "Beacon Initiative," a plan to build "a national Information Highway capable of carrying voice, text, data, graphics and video services to and from all Canadians" (Stentor, 1993, p. 5). In contemplating the integration of networks "owned and operated by different service providers," this "Beacon Initiative" departed significantly from previous telephone company recommendations. During the 1970's, telcos had been intent on securing permission to implement a "Single Integrated Network" (SIN) whereby all telecommunications capacity, including cable TV capacity, would be owned by them. The plan at the time was to lease bandwidth to various parties (such as cable TV companies) who would become, in effect, "value-added carriers." In the 1980's, telcos renamed their proposal ISDN ("Integrated Services Digital Network"), to emphasize the digitization of communication transmission. Still, however, their ultimate design was to own as completely as possible cable TV and all other telecommunications distribution facilities.

In the 1970s and more so in the 1980s, however, regulatory agencies in Canada, the U.S., and elsewhere were intent on inducing competition in telecommunications. By the early 1990's it had become quite evident that governments and regulators were unlikely to sanction cable system takeovers that would result in single networks in major locales.

Being denied SIN and ISDN to transmit cable-type services over their own facilities on behalf of licensed cable companies, telephone companies grew increasingly restive since, under the existing regulatory régime, they were barred also from themselves entering the broadcasting and cable TV industries. They were required, that is, to act solely as common carriers, merely transmitting on a non discriminatory basis content originated by others. They were, in fact, precluded by federal policy from attaining broadcasting (including cable TV) licences.

By the early 1990s, therefore, the bifurcation of broadcasting and telecommunications described in the preceding chapter, had become disadvantageous in the telcos' view, given especially the growth potential of video-on-demand and other pay-per content services that cable companies increasingly were being allowed to provide. Telcos therefore cast about for ways to throw off regulatory shackles, in the end settling for "convergence" in the guise of an "Information Highway" initiative. Convergence and Information Highway *mean* the collapse of industry boundaries and hence *require* a revised regulatory régime. Hence, the "Beacon Initiative."

So persuasively did the telcos package their proposal that throughout 1994 Canadians could scarcely escape hearing or reading about the imminence of an "Information Highway;" *The Globe and Mail* alone published 513 articles during the year (as of 24 December) containing the words "information highway" (Keenan and Pitts, 1994, pp. B1, B15).

Telephone companies were also remarkably successful in enlisting the support of the federal government. The January 1994 Speech from the Throne announced its intention to develop a federal strategy for an Information Highway. Soon thereafter Industry Minister, John Manley, established an Information Highway Advisory Council, consisting of nineteen business persons and eleven other representatives, whose deliberations have all been *in camera*, harbinger perhaps of the type of information access a future Information Highway will provide. In September 1994 the CRTC issued its Review of Regulatory Framework decision, designed particularly it would seem to help telephone companies put in place an Information Highway.[1] On October 11, the Governor in Council issued Order in Council P.C. 1994-1689, outlining the Government's current policy framework with respect to new communication technologies, ordering also the CRTC to report "on a number of wide-ranging questions covering three broad areas, namely facilities, content and competition." In ordering this review the Government stated that "the convergence of media as well as technologies has huge implications for both Canadian culture and our economy" (*Canada Gazette, Part 1,* 29 October 1994, p. 4321).

Government and industry plan to spend between eight and ten billion dollars over the next decade to provide the high capacity, bi-directional fiber/coaxial connections that will integrate all domestic telecommunication networks, serve between 80 and 90 percent of all businesses and homes in Canada, and enable Canadians in their homes to bank, to order movies, video games, and other cultural products, to participate in video conferences, to summon up data banks and educational services.[2] According to the government, as noted previously,

> If Canada is to succeed in a global economy based on the creation, movement, storage, retrieval and application of information, our communications networks must be knitted into a seamless and powerful information infrastructure serving all Canadians. ... Canada's information highway must be linked and integrated with the networks of our trading partners as part of *a seamless, global information infrastructure.* This global reach will allow businesses and individuals to access information, markets, clients and partners around the world (Canada, Industry Canada, 1994a, pp. 5, 25, emphasis added).[3]

On the other hand, the government has also acknowledged that an Information Highway "will have broad and transformative effects throughout the Canadian economy" (Canada, Industry Canada, 1994a, p. 1). Therefore, it cautioned, implementation "must be consistent with our overall social and economic goals—including long-term growth and job creation."

The delineation of "broad and transformative effects" is indeed germane to full comprehension of "Information Highway." However, to date, important issues and probabilities have been afforded but scant public articulation. Focusing on presumed benefits, Information Highway zealots have all but obfuscated *The Real World* of the Information Highway (c.f., Macpherson, 1965; and Franklin, 1990).

Real World

In our day geopolitical realities mean globalization and globalization's concomitants: neo-Darwinism; enfeebling of nation states (Melody, 1991; Mulgan, 1991; Hepworth, 1990); augmented transnational corporate power (Barnet and Müller, 1975; Barnet and Cavanaugh, 1994); less encumbered international movements of capital, goods, and services, including information (Mattelart, 1994); widening gaps, domestically and internationally, between rich and poor; breakdown of solidarity and of community (Daly and Cobb, 1989); and of course the neoconservative policy agenda of privatization, deregulation, user-pay; and the collapse of public space (Schiller, 1989a). It is in the context of these trends and issues that the *Real* World of the Information Highway is to be understood.

Powerplays and Transnationals

Information Highway supports trends apparent since the 1950's as regards the aggrandizement of transnational corporate power and the concomitant erosion of national sovereignty. As the quote in Chapter 6 from Jacques Maisonrouge, then President of IBM World Trade Corporation indicates, advanced computer/telecommunications permit transnationals to administer, in real time, activities of foreign divisions from central locales by gleaning information and monitoring electronically activities, dispensing orders, and exploiting international divisions of labor. Furthermore, they use the same brands, by and large the same marketing strategies, the same production processes and research in their various global marketplaces (Anderson, 1984). Improvements in telecommunications make more pronounced these practices, indeed to such an extent that transnational managers today can rather hastily relocate production sites to non-unionized locales, to zones offering more favorable tax treatments, to jurisdictions with lax but "business-friendly" environmental regulations, and to zones proffering "pro-business" health and safety legislation (Suzuki, 1994; Melody, 1991).

Information Highway will continue and exacerbate trends already observed by further enhancing transnational corporate power and diminishing that of governments. Consider the following as illustration. With financial services on-line to the home, banks headquartered anywhere on the globe turn the home, in effect, into a "branch." Money, of course, is increasingly transmitted electronically, making it digitally indistinguishable from other data, and hence less amenable to government control. It is increasingly difficult to enforce laws pertaining to but one type of information (here monetary) without, at the same time, affecting all other types. In these circumstances foreign banks become indistinguishable from domestic ones and monetary policy falls prey to transnational bankers as opposed to national governments (c.f., Smith, 1980, pp. 140–7).

In its 1994 review of Canada's foreign policy, Canada's Special Joint Committee of the Senate and House of Commons opined that "globalization is erasing time and space, making borders porous, and encouraging continental integration." Globalization means, the report continued, that "national sovereignty is being reshaped and the power of national governments to control events, reduced" (Canada, Special Joint Committee,

1994, p. 1). Inducing globalization, in the view of the Joint Committee, has been an "explosion of technology ... a revolution in transportation, communications and information processing." But behind these technologies, the Joint Committee remarked, stand the transnational corporations. As the Committee affirmed,

> Non-governmental actors have become major international players. The primary agents of globalization are in fact the transnational corporations (TNCs) (Canada, Special Joint Committee, p. 4).

Of course, "free trade" deals and Information Highway initiatives would, on the surface, seem to give governments at least *some* measure of responsibility for globalization, but behind government stand the TNCs. Among the areas over which government is in fact abdicating measures of sovereignty in pursuit of globalization, according to the Committee, is foreign policy. The Committee states:

> Another feature of the changing scene in Canada is the growing *democratization* [sic] of foreign policy. The range of foreign policy actors has expanded beyond the federal, provincial and even municipal governments to include private sector associations, academics and professional institutions and NGO's, and they are contributing increasingly to both policy development and program delivery. Foreign affairs are less and less an exclusive concern of the federal government and more and more a "Team Canada" [sic] effort. Moreover, the media plays a powerful role in determining how these matters appear on the policy agenda (Canada, Special Joint Committee, pp. 6–7, emphasis added).

The idea that "Team Canada" is forming policies, such as free trade and information highway initiatives, makes a lot of sense once it is realized (as the Special Joint Committee seemed to do) that the beneficiaries of such initiatives are predominantly "Team Canada's" transnational corporate members. The federal government certainly does not gain directly except insofar as it has been captured by, and views the world exclusively through the eyes of its transnational "Team Canada" corporate masters; after all, it is giving away its sovereignty! Nor do Canadian citizens gain. As The Joint Committee noted,

> The transnational mobility of capital generates pressures for deeper harmonization of national policies. In the competition for comparative advantages governments must deal with pressures to cut back on social and environmental programs that may raise the cost of producing goods and services, and to lower corporate taxes (Special Joint Committee, 1994, p. 4).

That the Joint Committee could understand and state so clearly what is happening, *and yet celebrate these developments*, shows just how far the gap has grown between those in power and the populace at large, and how little those at the center of wealth and power empathize with the average citizen.

Despatializing Business and "Culture"

"Information Highway" facilitates direct marketing by organizations "located" on-line, acutely targeting appeals based on proprietary transactional data, eliciting sales through electronic responses, and adding thereby to the body of the transactional record (Wilson, 1988). As noted by Canada's Privacy Commissioner, Bruce Phillips, transactional information derivable from a pay-as-you-use Information Highway raises profound personal privacy questions for a society that some deem already to be "panoptic" (Canada, Privacy Commissioner, 1994, pp. 8–10; also Canada, Department of Industry, 1994b; and Gandy, 1993). Indeed, the Canadian Information Highway projected by the government as but a component of "a seamless global infrastructure" (Canada, Industry Canada, 1994a, p. 25), makes domestic-only privacy laws quite unenforceable.

Information Highway, furthermore, will emphasize communication designated for audiences defined by factors other than geography—for example, by income, class, occupation, hobbies, sex, age, race, tastes, type of accommodation, specialized knowledge, and so forth. Nation states, neighborhoods, and legislative processes, by contrast, are all defined on the basis of geography. "Information Highway," therefore, by expanding transmission capacity to the home, will aid in the further break down of local or indigenous communication, substituting "cyber-community," with definite political economy implications (Franklin, 1990, pp. 35–54). Unfortunately transnational business benefits from eroding geographically-based communities and coalitions since pseudo-communities "located" in cyber-space are unlikely to interfere much with the *global optimization* (Maisonrouge, 1969) of resources. Nor will they object to merely *local* environmental degradations. Neither will they protest corporate tax holidays specific to a nation, province or region. The world is becoming a stage on which individuals and organizations delimited geographically (for instance national governments) are increasingly powerless.

Once again the Canadian Joint Committee was perceptive, this time in quoting from a United Nations report:

> A substantial share of global output is being reorganized under common governance of TNCs. ... In the process, the nature of the global economy is undergoing a fundamental change: from being a collection of independent national economies linked primarily through markets, the world economy is becoming for the first time *an international production system* (Canada, Special Joint Committee, 1994, p. 4, emphasis added).

Weakening of Labor

Labor's strength flows from solidarity, so of course it too is suffering from enhanced transnational corporate power as enabled by advanced telecommunications. With advent of a "seamless" Information Highway, globally interconnected, employers can be expected to encourage "tele-commuting"—that is on-line work from the home. Workers then may be required to invest in computer/telecom work stations simply to remain employable. On-line telecommuting makes piece work both likely and profitable. As well unionization becomes problematic for workers never in contact with one another; conceivably a company's tele-commuting work pool will be scattered throughout the world, members merely connected to the same host computer (Garson, 1989). Termination of employment in such circumstances can be effected by merely disconnecting the party from the host computer.

Advanced telecommunications have not been unrelated to the closure of unionized plants and the movement of job opportunities to "Free Trade Zones" and "Export Processing Zones" scattered about the globe where salary, working, and health conditions are utterly satanic.[4] Trends already established by free trade agreements—job losses, plant closures and relocations, deindustrialization, substitution of Third World for domestic labor—will not merely continue, but will be extended and deepened by advent of a world-interconnected Information Highway.

The Information Commodity

We live both in the Information Age and in the Golden Age of Global Capitalism, the veritable New World Order. But, these "ages" are contradictory. Information's characteristics are fundamentally inconsistent with commodity treatment: information is infinitely reproducible at very low incremental cost; it can be used by some without reducing availability for others; information is immaterial in the sense that it pertains to the shapes or forms that matter/energy assumes, as opposed to comprising matter/energy per se.

Information/knowledge therefore historically have been treated as public goods and as community resources, not as mere commodity: folklore, public education, libraries, museums, access to information legislation, sponsorship of the arts, public broadcasting, freedom of the press and of speech—all these exemplify this non-market tradition of information as community resource and as public good, as well as fundamental human right.

Information Highway, however, enhances the powers of those who would further commoditize information by channeling electronic information onto a "seamless," global, "network of networks." Information Highway makes it much more feasible to deliver specific bundles of information to target audiences, and to charge for each unit delivered. Just as in-home laborers may well *be paid* by the "bit," so too in-home consumers will *pay* by the "bit." Ability to pay will surely come to be of even greater importance in future years, and thus we contemplate yet sharper divisions between information rich and information poor. The poor face the risk of being more stringently ghettoized unless steps are taken to *de*commoditize information—steps that are, however, incongruent with the very logic of an Information Highway.

Heightened commoditization of information is potentially devastating with regard to continuance of human community, even civility. In industrial society people became accustomed to paying, and hence charging, for material items that flow between people. Of course, there are always exceptions, as friends and neighbors exchange "gifts," but, by and large, industrial economy means the increase of commodity relations with respect to material artifacts, and concomitantly also for labor power. Citizens need to sell their labor power in order to be able to purchase commodities.

In the emerging information economy, however, as people are increasingly required to pay, and become increasingly accustomed to paying for any and all information they access, they will begin also to demand payment for information exacted of them. Even now, people are being advised to charge for information they release. As one daily newspaper columnist put it: "If the request [for information] is from anyone who stands to profit from it, demand to be paid. This means anyone: the shopping mall person who meets you at the entrance, the newspaper representative who calls and asks the last time you read their publication, anyone at all" (Randall, 1994). This advice is proffered on the basis that in an Information Economy, information is valuable, and hence should be sold, not given away. The outlook for community is indeed bleak if citizens (like corporations and governments) come to feel they should have a "timer" running while they engage in "communication." But, on the other hand, why should they not demand payment when the very information they impart will be massaged and sold back to them in one form or another? This dilemma illustrates just how insidious the proliferation of information commoditization can become.

Further commoditization of information has as well significant international distributional and environmental implications. Information as commodity means that information rich, First World countries can and do trade information on world markets in return for foreign exchange with which to purchase energy, natural resources, and cheap labor. Third World countries need information/knowledge to emerge from destitution. "Education is the ultimate resource," according to E. F. Schumacher (1974, pp. 64–83). But dependent nations must trade away endowments of resources, often nonrenewable, to attain information/knowledge from core countries. The First World of course benefits disproportionately from this trade since it accesses scarce resources *at virtually zero real incremental cost* by exchanging "mere" information which, although vital, is infinitely reproducible and which the First World retains even after trade. The energy and natural resources thus attained are then often squandered in western consumptionist culture, severely degrading the environment (c.f. WCED, 1987).

The USA, as world leader in producing information, understandably has insisted that GATT (General Agreement on Tariffs and Trade, re-named as of January 1995 the World Trade Organization) incorporate intellectual property into its treaties (Braman 1990), and that copyright provisions be included in the Canada-US Free Trade Agreement (Parker, 1988). In a fit of pique and with heavy-handedness the USA even with-drew from UNESCO when that body recommended that information be treated more as resource and less as commodity (Preston, Herman, and Schiller, 1989). UNESCO, now suitably chastised, is preparing to welcome the U.S.A. back as a member, possibly in 1997.[5]

Canada, not (yet) a Third World country, is nonetheless certainly a net importer of information from the U.S.A. Expanded transmission capacity, coupled with enhanced capabilities to commoditize information—the very *raison d'etre* of an Information Highway—will assuredly magnify Canada's trade imbalance, forcing the country to rely even more heavily in the future on exports of energy and natural resources, such as water, to the U.S.A.

Utter Madness

European scholar and peace activist, Johan Galtung (1971), in a general theory of international relations, contended that the corporate/governing élite in peripheral countries (for example, "Team Canada" in Canada), generally identifies much more closely with élites in core countries than with the mass of its own population. In Canada and the U.S.A alike the 1980's and early 1990's have seen governance by what may be termed a transnational corporate élite. Galtung's mode of analysis, then, illumi-nates and explains, when other explanations fail, why the Canadian gov-ernment entered into "free trade" deals that erode the very sovereignty of the federal government itself, that increase pressure on government to cut back already inadequate environmental legislation, to cut back social pro-grams, to yet further reduce corporate taxes, and to pursue policies that disadvantage much of domestic labor. Galtung's analysis, coupled with the Joint Committee's "Team Canada" metaphor, explains also the federal government's rush to introduce an Information Highway.

We have entered an era of utter global madness. As seen in Chapter 6, "sustainable development" is incompatible with old-style economic growth, yet globalization, whether through free trade deals or Information Highway initiatives, is all about increased global divisions of labor, increased trade, increased production, and greater waste. Meanwhile, as the Joint Committee notes, pressures mount on government to cut back already inadequate environmental programs in the face of heightened production in order to "harmonize" with such "environmentally conscientious" trading partners as Chile, Mexico, and the U.S.A.

The ethic of greed consecrated by Adam Smith and articulated in free trade deals and Information Highway initiatives also pits Canadian labor against low wage Third World labor. The beauty of globalization from the perspective of the federal government's "Team Canada" corporate sponsors is that even as jobs domestically are being lost to Third World countries, thereby creating downward pressure on wages here, government is pressured into decreasing social programs! What better way could one possibly think of than these to create a compliant domestic work force? Furthermore, in an era when governments are looking for ways to reduce deficits, globalization creates pressures to further reduce corporate taxes, as the Joint Committee attested— yet an added bonus!

And these polices and developments, according to the Special Joint Committee, flow from heightened *"democratization"* in decision-making as the government increasingly yields its decision-making authority to *Team Canada!* The words best suited to describe such "thinking", such rhetoric, are "utter madness."

In *For the Common Good,* former World Bank economist and currently University of Maryland professor, Herman Daly and theologian John Cobb declared, "We human beings are being led to a *dead* end—all too literally; we are living by an ideology of death and accordingly we are destroying our own humanity and killing the planet" (Daly and Cobb, 1989, p. 21). Information Highway is part and parcel of this "ideology of death."

Fortunately, things not yet in place can be stopped with minor disruption compared to things on-going. All with a love of life, of democracy, and of community, should now be opposing "Team Canada" and loudly protesting implementation of an Information Highway.

Notes

Revised and reprinted, with permission, from *Point of View Magazine,* No. 24, summer, 1994, pp. 16–19.

1. Among the provisions of this decision, four are most pertinent for present discussion, namely: (1) approval in three stages of increases in local rates to reduce the "subsidy" from long distance; (2) replacement of rate of return regulation by a less stringent methodology known as price caps, effective 1 January 1998; (3) removal of restrictions on the participation of telephone companies in emerging information and transactional telecommunications service markets; and (4) removal of restrictions on local competition, and promotion of "open access and interoperability principles among networks." According to the Commission, "with very limited exceptions ... all barriers to entry in telecommunications should be removed" (CRTC, 1994, p. 32).

As competition penetrates more and more deeply areas previously deemed to be naturally monopolized, venerable regulatory techniques, principles, and goals are being cast aside. As competition in local and long distance services increases, for instance, the practices of cost averaging and cross subsidization to permit service universality will increasingly be enfeebled. Indeed, in permitting increases in local rates over a three year period in order to increase the profitability of long distance (and help fund construction of an Information Highway), the CRTC implicitly aligned itself with transnational enterprises for whom long distance communication is vital, rather than with the interests of rural Canadians, Canada's poor, infrequent users of long distance, local businesses, and so forth. As well, the principle of common carriage is now being undermined as telecommunication companies are being encouraged by government to enter potentially lucrative content creation activities, thereby further converging telecommunications with broadcasting and other content-centered, "pay-per" sectors.

2. Industry Canada states that the cost of a universal fibre optic network may approach $30 billion (Canada, Industry Canada, 1994, p. 21).

3. According to Stentor, a Canadian Information Highway will provide "an economic opportunity by delivering heightened competitiveness, new revenue sources and greatly enhanced market reach to businesses of all sizes and scope of operations, regardless of geographic location; it will herald a new world for the educational and cultural industries by eliminating the restrictions of time and distance; and it holds the potential of helping to ensure our national health care system and other governmental services remain universal and viable" (Stentor, 1993b).

4. Of the numerous "Free Trade Zones" about the globe, the Maquiladoras in Mexico is among the most infamous. The Maquiladoras is a 12.5 mile wide, and 2,000 mile long "free trade" strip running alongside the U.S.-Mexican border, where wages are less than 10% of comparable U.S. wages, and where companies can get away with "ecocide" due to negligible health and environmental standards. According to Susan Meeker-Lowry, rocks tossed into canals of the Rio Grande cause "black globules [to] bubble from the bottom, releasing an eye-stinging chemical stench" (Meeker-Lowry, 1992, p. 27). See also Nelson, 1989.

5. In 1988, UNESCO's new Director General, Frederico Mayor of Spain, announced the organization would abandon its decade's-old demand for a New World Information and Communications Order in favor of U.S. style "free-flow." In 1989, Mayor toured the U.S.A. to drum up support for American re-entry into UNESCO. Noting that Mayor had "cut the payroll and generally returned

UNESCO to its original mission as a promoter of literacy, a protector of cultural monuments and a champion of a freer flow of information," the *New York Times* reported that the U.S. would likely rejoin UNESCO in 1997 (*New York Times,* 23 February 1994 and 19 February 1994, p. A18; as cited in Fredericks, 1994, p. 17). Citing U.S. officials, the *Times* reported that membership in UNESCO would "help American scientists, educators and global networks that promote cooperation in science, education, culture and communication." Evidently "increasingly globalized telecommunications infrastructures, developed within the context of the Information Highway, [can] be better exploited for use in developing countries if the U.S. [is] again in UNESCO" (Fredericks, 1994, p. 18). See also Roach, 1993.

12

"Life is Information": Canadian Communication and the Legacy of Graham Spry

By nature I am compelled to be a reformer. I can always imagine improvements, always scent evils, and very easily hate some wrongly based institution.
—Graham Spry

Graham Spry passed away on November 24, 1983. Always the diplomat, this gentle and witty man nonetheless was impassioned and tenacious in pursuing voluntarist politics, in his view a most effective way of bringing about institutional reform consistent with strongly-held philosophical and moral convictions. A life-long organizer and activist, Graham Spry made contributions to Canadian public affairs, particularly in the fields of journalism, broadcasting, and health care, that continue to touch daily the lives of all Canadians. Consider the following:

In the early 1930's Graham Spry rescued the now venerable *Canadian Forum* from bankruptcy. In the thirties as well he was instrumental in mobilizing support for creation of the Canadian Radio Broadcasting Commission and of its successor, the Canadian Broadcasting Corporation, still the centerpiece of the Canadian broadcasting system. In addition his philosophy concerning *public* broadcasting—broadcasting to serve not merely commercial interests but above all educational, democratic, and community needs and a Canadian national purpose—persists in the mandates of provincial broadcasting undertakings like TV Ontario, in legislation creating the Canadian Radio-television and Telecommunications Commission (CRTC), and in aims of voluntarist groups such as Friends of Canadian Broadcasting. Finally, but not exhaustively,

Graham Spry played a key role in successful implementation of the first public medicare plan in North America. His legacy endures indeed.

In scholarly communication Canada has for years been blessed with contributions of the highest order: the works of Harold Innis, Marshall McLuhan, George Grant, Dallas Smythe, and Northrop Frye particularly spring to mind. Due perhaps to a markedly less voluminous scholarly output, Graham Spry has seldom been included in such august groupings. Yet as well as activist and organizer, Spry was also a communication theorist, an historian, and a political analyst whose interests in communication spanned the centuries. Witness his article on "The Fall of Constantinople—1453," his unfinished book manuscript on Russian history, his assessment of "India and Self-Government," and his several published analyses of francophone-anglophone relations within Canadian Confederation. Graham Spry, in other words, was both atypical and exemplary in combining scholarship, analysis, and theory with organizing skills, activism, and engagement.

As the final chapter of this book, it is not merely appropriate, but also instructive, to recall and reconsider some of Graham Spry's life and thought. In this age of neoconservativism, globalization, heightened commoditization, and polarization between rich and poor, we have much to learn from Spry the activist and from Spry the thinker, and most particularly from Spry the integrated person who blended so effectively qualities seldom found in balanced proportion in even the most highly gifted individuals.

In the decade or so since Graham Spry's death political and commercial conservativism have attacked, seemingly relentlessly, many of the programs, institutions, and ideals for which he fought—public broadcasting, universal medicare, social democracy, a sense of life in community, Canadian cultural independence, equality, and sharing. For Social Democrats in the tradition of Spry these have been dark years indeed. Through it all, the dark and the bright, however, Graham Spry in his writings bids us to take heart, for:

> "Nothing is here for tears, nothing to moan." What the situation now commands is an urgent and renewed sense of the prime and essential purposes, a fresh and wise use of imagination and, above all will, will, will, the determination to achieve these purposes (Spry, 1972).

Spry's Activism

Graham Spry was born at St. Thomas, Ontario on 20 February 1900, to what his wife, Irene Spry, has called a "genteel" family. In England with his parents during the First World War (his father was a military officer), he enlisted shortly after his eighteenth birthday, downcast that he was even then too young for active combat. With the Armistice Spry returned to Canada, enrolled at the University of Manitoba, became editor of the student newspaper, and won the gold medal in history (1922). He attained further journalistic experience as reporter and editorial writer with the *Manitoba Free Press* (1920–1922). A Rhodes Scholar, he earned a second B.A. in history from Oxford in 1924. (Years later, 1938, he fulfilled also Oxford's requirements for the M.A.). His years at Oxford influenced his subsequent life in many ways, but perhaps most importantly it was as a student abroad that his love for Canada deepened and grew strong. Aware that all too frequently fine Canadian minds remained abroad, depriving Canada of their talents, while pursuing personal career aspirations, Spry resolved "to read everything with a view to application in Canada, [aiming] not to be a typical and good Oxonian, but a typical and better Canadian" (quoted in Potvin, 1992, p. 37).

In Canada once more in 1926, Spry became national secretary of the Association of Canadian Clubs, adding significantly to his influential Canadian contacts. The Canadian Clubs were then experimenting with radio through the broadcast of luncheon speeches, "impressed, from a publicity and educational point of view, with the advantages of reaching a much larger audience than could fill a hotel lunch room" (Potvin, 1992, p. 65). Spry at this time also inaugurated and edited *Independence*, the monthly journal of the League of Nations Society in Canada, serving also on the League's executive.

In 1930, with Alan Plaunt, Graham Spry formed, and until 1936 worked vigorously on behalf of, the Canadian Radio League, a voluntarist association dedicated to the establishment of public broadcasting in accordance with recommendations of the 1929 Aird Royal Commission. Spry, Plaunt, and the League maintained that radio broadcasting, while important for certain, albeit limited commercial purposes, should by no means be primarily a business. Rather, it should be treated primarily as an instrument for the cultivation of public opinion, of education, and entertainment, and make the home "not merely a billboard, but a theatre, a concert hall, a club, a public meeting, a school, a university."

For Spry and the League, the public or national interest was not, and never properly could be reduced to merely the summation of private interests. The nation, rather, for Spry and the League was itself an entity with characteristics distinct from those of its components. For national well-being, the parts must act and interact in ways consistent with the welfare of the whole.

No where, in Spry's view, was the dichotomy between unrestrained private, commercial interest and broader public and national interests more marked than in Canadian broadcasting. As Spry wrote in 1931, commercial pressure within an unregulated, advertiser-financed system leads inexorably to "stultified educational uses of broadcasting," to programming "designed for and serving principally companies desiring to advertise themselves or their products," to concentration of control in the hands of a few powerful private interests, to malformed and uninformed public opinion, and to an association of Canadian stations "with the American chains to broadcast American rather than Canadian programmes." In the early 1930's Spry coined his famous and oft-repeated aphorism, "The State or the United States," to underline the fact that in broadcasting (as in other matters), Canada as a nation, as a community, as a social organism, cannot not survive without government actively coordinating, and in some measure directing activities, paralleling to a degree the function of the brain in biological organisms.

Much has been written about the voluntary efforts of the Canadian Radio League and of Graham Spry in bringing about public broadcasting in Canada. Margaret Prang (1965), for instance, concluded: "All the evidence suggests that the League's role was a major one, that it did much to prevent the radio issue from becoming a partisan question, and that it forestalled a postponement of the formation of a policy during the exigencies of the depression, a postponement which might have been fatal to the cause of public control."

In addition to his radio activism, between 1932 and 1934 Spry was also publisher of the *Farmers' Sun*, always a money losing venture, renaming it *New Commonwealth* to reflect its new alignment with the democratic socialist party, the Cooperative Commonwealth Federation (CCF). In 1935 Spry also purchased, for one dollar, the *Canadian Forum*. The early and mid thirties also saw him join and become active in the League for Social Reconstruction (organized in 1931 by Frank Underhill and Frank Scott as a "Canadian Fabian Society") and in this connection become a contributing editor of *Social Planning for Canada*, published in 1935. As well Spry joined the CCF, was a signatory of the *Regina Manifesto* (1933), was twice an unsuccessful political candidate in Toronto, and served as Vice-chairman of the CCF's Ontario Council.

Lacking an income, financial exigencies caused Graham Spry to relinquish some of these connections, eventually securing an executive position in England with a U.S. oil company. Branded a radical, he had unfortunately by 1936 become unemployable in Canada. In England he subsequently became personal assistant to Sir Stafford Cripps of the British War Cabinet, and accompanied Cripps on his mission to India. In 1948, endeavoring to reestablish formal ties with his native country, which had in important respects spurned him, Spry became at Saskatchewan Premier Tommy Douglas's behest, Agent General for Saskatchewan in Britain. Among other accomplishments Spry recruited medical personnel to help neutralize the 1962 doctors' strike against the introduction of provincial medicare.

Whether at home or abroad Graham Spry maintained a keen interest in

Canadian public affairs—particularly broadcasting and francophone-anglophone relations; he secured leaves of absence as needs arose to return home to help influence events in broadcasting. "Retiring" in Canada in 1968, Graham Spry continued to lend his energy, engaging personality, and substantial intellect, both individually and through a revitalized Canadian Broadcasting League, to support his beloved CBC, until his death.

Spry's Thought on Information and Community

Graham Spry, in his later years at least, was fond of remarking, "Life is information." In a 1972 paper, "Culture and Entropy: A Lay View of Broadcasting," prepared for The Royal Society of Canada, he went some distance in unpacking the meaning of this brief, three word sentence.

Culture and entropy, he wrote, are opposing terms, the former being an expression for social organization or integration, the latter for disorganization or disintegration. These terms, he continued, although opposed, are joined through the concepts of information and communication.

Culture, according to Spry, *is* information, or at least is the product of information. "Information is the prime integrating factor creating, nourishing, adjusting and sustaining society." Society he defined as "a people in communication." Citing Norbert Wiener, Spry declared: "Properly speaking the community extends only so far as there extends an effectual transmission of information."

These concepts—information and communication—point to important parallels between the individual organism on the one hand and society (the social organism) on the other. According to Spry,

> A society, a community, a nation, like any other organism, is a function of a network; society is organized, integrated and made responsive by information. In the human being, the central nervous system including the brain is that most powerful, most complex and highest of all networks of life—a network of 12,000 to 20,000 million neurones. [In a marginal note of 1981, Spry revised this estimate upward to 100 billion neurones]. Each of these cells is, so to speak, a two-way electric and chemical re-broadcasting station, creating by means of its axons, dendrites and synapses, an incalculable total of channels or inter-relationships.

For individual organisms, Spry continued, life depends upon and may be defined in terms of the existence and continued use of the neural communication network; death, conversely, entails the disintegration or non-use of this neural network. Likewise, in society, communal vitality requires reciprocal message transmission and reception; social disintegration, the analogue of individual death, results from too much noise, from insufficient feedback (necessary for homeostasis), or from silence (breakdown or non-use of the communication system).

While significant parallels between individual and social organisms can be drawn, there is also, however, an important difference. As Spry explained,

> The wisdom of the community or society, balanced against the wisdom of the body, is elementary, rudimentary, inexperienced and very, very recent. … Whereas the human body as inherited through the genetic code generation after generation has millennia of experience as a single, unified system, sensitive and responsive to changes in the internal and external environment, human societies have only very recently developed rudimentary processes of social adjustment and social response.

What, then, Spry asked, permits societies, comprised of separate individuals, to attain and maintain organization (social homeostasis) rather than disintegrating into chaos or social death? His reply: the means of communication, that is the media. Media, and the individuals or groups controlling media, "condition" and "program" societies. Media as "central nervous system" of the social organism transmit instructions on how members are to respond to environmental change and regulate in a general way society's relationships with its environment. Society's "genetic program"—its traditions, languages, laws, customs, institutions, and so forth—are continuously conditioned and modified (mutated) as new information is diffused through its media of communication. The implication is that media can either contribute to the vitality and growth of a society, or can be entropic, inducing disintegration and death.

Spry's Vision and Canadian Media Today

When Graham Spry set about forming the Canadian Radio League in the early 1930's, the challenge was clear: make room in a crowded and finite radio frequency spectrum, dominated largely by American commercial stations and networks, for a substantial, non-commercial, Canadian presence. To this day the ideal has persisted, but the challenge has grown more severe. Technological trends, commercial pressures, and philosophical/political currents combine to undermine the predominance within Canada of Canadian and of public broadcasting.

In terms of evolving technology, three trends need to be highlighted. First is the exponential expansion in transmission capacity: Cable systems each year diffuse new packages of specialty (non broadcast) television services; thousands of movie titles are now available on demand through video stores for playback on VCRs; imminent is the possibility of receiving, by means of small and relatively inexpensive dishes, hundreds of direct broadcast satellite television channels; and then too, of course, there is also the prospect of an "Information Highway." The spectrum of constraint of the 1930's, in other words, is increasingly a spectrum of abundance.

Second, through satellites particularly, but increasingly also through transoceanic and landline fibre optics, the world shrinks into the proverbial "global village." Information increasingly can be gleaned instantaneously from geographically dispersed locations, while conversely programming/instructions are sent worldwide at lightning speed.

These foregoing technological trends combine with a third, and also with commercial considerations. In the 1930's the medium of communication of most concern to Graham Spry was relatively inexpensive radio broadcasting, which diffused indiscriminately programming to all within the coverage area of a transmitter. Today radio has been largely superseded by much more expensive video, whose cost characteristics bestow tremendous financial advantage to programmers reaching large, often transnational audiences. Through cable and through scrambling/ descrambling technologies (the third technological trend highlighted here), moreover, people are required increasingly to pay directly to access the bulk of the expanded programming fare.

For both technological and financial reasons, therefore, broadcasting inclusive of all citizens, including particularly the financially underprivileged, is becoming increasingly marginalized, raising the prospect of yet further and more pronounced cleavages, domestically and internationally, between the information rich and poor. As well, technological innovations permit people increasingly to receive and send messages in real time according to communities of interest distinct from and independent of location; people-in-communication (Spry's definition of community), therefore, are increasingly less likely to be defined by political boundaries. Moreover, due in part at least to information's inexhaustible economies of scale, the pronounced tendency is toward heightened concentration of control internationally through formation of transnational informational conglomerates, exacerbating unidirectional flows from central, primarily American, production centers. This became particularly evident and ominous during the Persian Gulf War as citizens, political leaders, and news agencies alike relied on essentially a single news source (Cummings, 1992; Mowlana, Gerbner, and Schiller, 1992).

The foregoing describes the so-called "new broadcasting environment," and one may properly ask in this context exactly how much remains relevant for the 1990's and the new millennium of Graham Spry's aspirations and thought. Quite a lot, I believe, but to adequately address this question we should appraise critically philosophical/policy currents that have run alongside and beneath the technological/ commercial trends just noted.

Spry's Thought in an Age of Neoconservativism

Technological and commercial trends in broadcasting and communication correspond to, help reinforce, and are in important respects dependent upon neoclassical and neoconservative movements in North America and elsewhere. Theoretical neoclassicism, particularly as it emerged from long gestation at the University of Chicago, has provided intellectual ground for neoconservative policy—particularly privatization, deregulation, reduction in social programs, user fees, reduced governmental activism, and globalization through freer international markets for commodities, capital, and information.

At the very heart of neoclassical philosophy and of neoconservative policy, it is argued here, has been a conception of information/communication diametrically opposed to the perspective articulated by Graham Spry. One way to appraise the relevance of Spry's position for the present and the future is to compare his depiction of information/communication with its opposite.

Neoclassicists have viewed information as mere commodity (akin to toasters, according to a former Chairman of the U.S. Federal Communications Commission), while communication for them is but a variant of commodity exchange. Neoclassical economists George Stigler, Ronald Coase, and Gary Becker each won Nobel prizes in large part for expounding on this theme. Human relations, they believe, are utilitarian and fleeting: autonomous economic agents come together briefly to trade and then go their separate ways, untouched and untouchable. Society is merely the summation of individuals, not an entity distinct in itself. For neoclassicists like Gary Becker social phenomena seemingly as diverse as marriage, family planning, racial discrimination, crime, divorce, drug addiction, politics, and suicide can be understood adequately only through application of the principles of commodity exchange (that is, price, cost, individual utility maximization, supply, demand). This neoclassical viewpoint is precisely what Harold Innis described and warned of in his classic 1938 essay, "The Penetrative Powers of the Price System."

But, refusal to acknowledge, let alone highlight, society as a social organism, and as an entity comprising groups and individuals in dynamic interaction, transforming one another and the social whole through informational exchange, can result in entropy or social breakdown. American cities have long been experiencing entropy on account of the penetrative powers of the price system. For those lacking the means of communicating—the poor, the unemployed, the homeless, the "unskilled"—monetarized/commoditized communication (which comprises not merely media narrowly construed, but as well all forms of human interaction mediated by money or by monetary motives), precludes meaningful participation, leaving available only destructive-modes for articulating their plight—riots, blockades, theft, vandalism, or as the alternative, silence. For the affluent too, although not likewise deprived of material comforts and delights, the price system can be erosive of hitherto permanent and deep-felt connections, commoditizing one's sense of nation, of community, and perhaps especially of self. Neoconservative politicians, for instance, rhetorically aligned Canada's welfare with "Free Trade" Agreements that may well erode Canadian nationhood. Recall, in contrast, however, how *in an act of freedom and refusal to commoditize the self*, Graham Spry resolved as a student to apply his knowledge for the betterment of the Canadian community, irrespective of career prospects abroad.

From the neoclassical perspective, user-pay and ability-to-pay are the sole principles that should govern the production, distribution and diffusion of knowledge and information, and hence human interaction. This recommendation has had in turn important policy repercussions, or at least has been aligned with important policy manoeuvres. The United States pulled out of UNESCO due to the latter's recalcitrance in accepting a commodity-only status for information/knowledge, while domestically Brian Mulroney's government implemented a series of measures both to diminish and to further commercialize the CBC. Likewise universal medicare, surely a communication issue, has come under increasing stress particularly since the 1988 "Free Trade" Agreement. Heightened commodity treatment of intellectual "property" in the form of drug patent legislation inflicts yet higher costs on public medicare.

The neoclassical viewpoint, of course, contrasts starkly with the vision of Graham Spry. For Spry, human relations are not, and should never be allowed to become, mere commodity exchange relations. For him, rather, people influence and transform one another in unpredictable ways, and are as well components of, and participants in, an evolving social whole. Like John Donne, Graham Spry maintained there are no isolated, self-sufficing individuals, that each is a part of the whole. All knowledge, all production, all value, Spry would say, exist only in and by the help of community; people are products of social/communicatory life—born into community, living in community, dying in community. Language, the very means of communication and of understanding, to cite one most obvious but immeasurably important example, provides inextricable commonalty among those who share it: language is both social artifact and public resource, learned and in turn passed on quite outside the bounds of commodity exchange. Since all our social discourse and interaction take place within the frame of language, all commoditization of information/communication can be seen as being quite partial, fragmentary, and artificial.

Graham Spry feared that in Canada the commercial, commoditized view of information/communication was achieving such ascendancy that his country could wither and be swallowed up in what today we may call the transnationalized, commercialized New World Order. "What is the information upon which the Canadian society takes its decisions; who controls its selection and its distribution; and for whose purposes?" Spry asked. For advocates of information-as-commodity-alone, questions such as these cannot even be raised; they lie quite beyond the pale of thought. And hence, the immense utility of neoclassicism for the agencies of global commercialization and transnationalization.

In this remembrance of the manifold contributions of Graham Spry to Canadian communication, it is appropriate to afford him the last words; his writings and thought after all, constitute an enduring part of his legacy. In 1972 Graham Spry declared:

> What we have today is a large measure of concentrated control over more and more of this great national instrument of stations and cable systems—a one-way node for distributing information and influencing public opinion by business and commercial interests. They are a part of the Canadian community but a conflict of interest is inevitable between using revenues for Canadian programming and using them to increase profits and push up quotations on the stock market. ... In terms of Canadian purposes, strategy and Canadian reception of Canadian entertainment, education and information in the home, the trend seems to be irresistibly towards running down, disorganization, randomness, that is towards entropy.

"Irresistible" this trend may indeed appear to be, and this from the person who persevered to help inaugurate Canadian public broadcasting against truly formidable odds! As we press toward the year 2000, neoclassicism and neoconservativism seem more entrenched than ever. In addition, the commercial and technological trends described above remain, gain strength, and gather momentum. Given such ample reasons for despair, let us therefore recall that it was also Graham Spry who admonished, "'Nothing is here for tears, nothing to moan.' ...What the situation now commands ... above all [is] will, will, will."

Note

This is a revised version of an article, entitled, "Canadian Communication and the Legacy of Graham Spry" that appeared in the winter 1993 issue of *Queen's Quarterly*, pp. 989-1003 . Republished by permission of *Queen's Quarterly*.

Conclusion

In every cry of every Man,
In every Infant's cry of fear,
In every voice, in every ban,
The mind-forged manacles I hear.
—William Blake, *London* (1794)

We live in a world of communicatory interaction. "Life," as Graham Spry averred, "*is* information."

For neoclassical economists, however, information is price and price is commoditizable; for them as well, communicatory interaction comprises mere commodity exchange. Yet even these reductionist conceptions of information and communication, as we have seen, pose formidable challenges for the logical integrity of economic orthodoxy. Simply put, neoclassicism's analytical framework of commodity exchange cannot handle information, a serious short coming for a discipline deeming itself to be "the imperial science," particularly so for an era known as the "information age."

Even more to the point, continued adherence to neoclassicism and its reductionist conceptions of information/communication gives rise to severe, real world crises (Schiller, 1984), for example: escalating environmental degradation, increased break-down of human community, widening gaps between rich and poor; heightening problems both financial and curricular in education, increasing concentration of transnational corporate power, immiserization of millions, and ensuing social strife. Neoclassicism's greed ethic and its hedonistic calculus, furthermore, erode the sense of personal freedom and human dignity, as B. F. Skinner understood only too well. In these circumstances, with Jürgen Habermas, one speculates on "which crisis tendencies [will be] transformed into deviant behavior, and in which social groups?" (Habermas, 1975, p. 40).

Neoclassicism's analytical deficiencies and its concomitant propensity to promote crises arise from its failure to acknowledge that human and ecosystem interactions transcend mere commodity exchanges and relations characterized by competition. Three perspectives that highlight neoclassicism's deficiencies in this regard are: systems theory/ecoscience; information's properties; and religious experience and teaching.

Systems are defined as complexes of elements in interaction (von Bertalanffy, 1981, p. 109). Systems theory posits that parts change through interaction, and hence the whole (i.e., the system) is to be seen as more than just the sum of its parts. The eye, for example, neither acts competitively with the ear, nor does it negotiate a *quid pro quo* of so much vision in exchange for a certain amount of hearing. Eye and ear, rather, complement one another in contributing to the survival of the larger organism. The meaning of any and all visual information is modified by auditory information, past and present. Note in this regard the following from Jacques Lusseyran, physically blinded in youth:

> When I came upon the myth of objectivity in certain modern thinkers, it made me angry. So there was only one world for these people, the same for everyone. All the other worlds were to be counted as illusions left over from the past. Or why not call them by their name—hallucinations? I had learned to my cost how wrong they were.

> From my own experience I knew very well that it was enough to take from a man a memory here, an association there, to deprive him of hearing or sight, for the world to undergo an immediate transformation, and for another world, entirely different but entirely coherent, to be born. Another world? Not really. The same world rather, but seen from another angle, and counted in entirely new measures. When this happened, all the hierarchies they called objective were turned upside down, scattered to the four winds, not even theories but like whims (Lusseyran, *And There Was Light*, quoted in McLuhan, 1972, p. vii).

Analogous to organisms are organizations. The principle characteristics of relations among members (i.e., parts) of healthy organizations are complementarity and co-operation, not competition. In pin-making, for example, Adam Smith noted,

> One man draws out the wire, another straights it, a third cuts it, a fourth points it, a fifth grinds it at the top for receiving the head; to make the head requires two or three distinct operations; to put it on, is a peculiar business, to whiten the pins is another; it is even a trade by itself to put them into the paper; and the important business of making a pin is, in this manner, divided into about eighteen operations, which, in some manufactories, are all performed by distinct hands, though in others the same man will sometimes perform two or three of them (Smith [1776] 1937, pp. 4–5).

In neoclassicism pin-making, like all other production, is comprehended as commoditized exchange; the fabled "entrepreneur" stands at the head of the organization, co-ordinating operations by proffering wages to workers who undertake the various specialized operations (Coase, [1937] 1952). As Berle and Means ([1932] 1967) have shown, however, for modern corporations there is no entrepreneur. Ownership is diffused among stockholders, while a professional board of directors and managers is "employed" by the stockholders to run the company. Furthermore, corporations are *persona ficta* (artificial persons), created in law and existing in their own right. Corporations have their own distinct liabilities and rights that transcend the rights and liabilities of the owners or managers. Corporations are empowered to carry on business under their own name, and can sue and be sued. They have perpetual succession, that is continuity as legal entities, even though the individuals comprising them change and indeed pass into dust. A corporation, as John Davis advised, is "invisible, immortal, and rests only in intendment and consideration of the law" (Davis, [1905] 1961). As with organisms, therefore, so too with organizations: parts do not relate to wholes in the manner of commodity exchange since parts and wholes do not go their separate ways once an exchange has been effected.

The same point can be made with respect to ecology. In ecosystems interdependence among components does not always take the form of commodity exchange; nor can relations between components and their larger systems be reduced to *quid pro quo* or to competition. Plant and animal organisms, for example, do not negotiate agreements prior to breathing. Yet all share the same air, the atmosphere in fact binding together all life, past and present. Our next breaths, Guy Murchie remarked, will include "a million odd atoms of oxygen and nitrogen once breathed by Pythagoras, Socrates, Confucius, Moses, Columbus, Einstein or anyone you can think of" (Murchie, 1978, p. 320). Likewise all life shares both the earth's basic elements and the saltiness of the sea.

By depicting organisms and species as components of a larger whole, ecology, an application of systems theory, calls attention to the errors of methodological individualism as practised by mainstream economics. Since each part, both in systems theory and in ecoscience, relates to the whole and affects the functioning of the whole, and likewise since parts are dependent upon the continuance of the whole for their own continued existence, human acts of destruction, for instance burning rain forests, while perhaps making sense in terms of commodity exchange, can be viewed as but another step toward ecological collapse.

A second view that again points to severe deficiencies in comprehending interactions solely in terms of commodity exchange and competition concerns *inherent properties of information*. Information, as Boulding and others have remarked, is indivisible, immaterial (i.e., epiphenomenal), and is retained by the sender after transmission. Information is not subject to the laws of thermodynamics and can, in principle, increase without limit. Furthermore, information constitutes a *symbolic* as opposed to a material environment, what Barrington Nevitt called the "communications ecology." This symbolic environment is every bit as interactive and evolutionary as is the physical environment, and of course it is dependent upon the physical environment for its existence. As we have indeed seen, transformations in the physical environment can be interpreted as alterations in the informational constitution of matter and energy.

Information's properties point to sharing, to commonality, to community, to radical interdependence, and hence to the existence of non commoditized modes of interaction, and as well, therefore, to the existence of systems that transcend individuals. Recognizing and taking into account the properties of information, then, raises the prospect of giving further vent to economies based on gifts or grants, and to an economics discipline that acknowledges synergies, rather than one fixated on competition and on commodity exchanges.

Many of life's most basic processes are much more akin to gift transmittals than they are to commodity exchanges. Genetic information is passed along as gifts or one-way transfers from parents to offspring. Noogenetic information, similarly, communicated by teaching and every day living, often comprises predominantly one-way transfers as older generations transmit accumulated wisdom, including the knowledge of language, to the young. In discourse, selves develop in unpredictable ways as utterances of discursive partners are retained and transformed, reentering discursive acts, sometimes years later, in conversations with other dialogic communicants.[1]

Gift relations are markedly different from commodity relations and from competition. Gifts establish "a feeling-bond between two people, whereas the sale of a commodity leaves no necessary connection" (Hyde, 1979, p. 56). Indeed gifts can bring people together and make one body out of several (Hyde, 1979, p. 57). Unemployment insurance, medicare, old age assistance, and related social programs are in essence community gifts whereby those never or seldom unemployed, the young, and the healthy help sustain those less fortunate. Social programs, in other words, help build and sustain a sense of community. Commodity exchange, by contrast, in the absence of such gift relations, alienates those marginalized by the market system, and those thus rejected may come to feel, and justifiably so, little obligation or loyalty to a system designed for and benefiting primarily the rich. As Hyde remarks, "because of the bonding power of gifts and the detached nature of commodity exchange, gifts have become associated with community and with being obligated to others, while commodities are associated with alienation and freedom" (Hyde, 1979, pp. 66-7).

Third, *religious experience and teaching* affirms that all exist in the context of a larger, spiritual whole. As William James has noted,

The characteristics of the religious life, as we have found them, include the following beliefs:-

1. That the visible world is part of a more spiritual universe from which it draws its chief significance;

2. That union or harmonious relation with that higher universe is our true end;

3. That prayer or inner communion with the spirit thereof—be that spirit "God" or "law"—is a process wherein work is really done, and spiritual energy flows in and produces effects, psychological or material, within the phenomenal world (James, [1901-2] 1960, p. 464).

The ethics of greed and of rugged individualism promulgated by materialism and by neoclassical economics are quite inconsistent with James's sentiments and more generally with religious convictions, the reverends Malthus and Sumner, and Max Weber's *Protestant Ethic and the Spirit of Capitalism* notwithstanding. John's Gospel, for example, records the following as the essential goal of the religious life: "As thou, Father, art in me, and I in thee, that they also may be one in us. ... I in them, and thou in me, that they may be made perfect in one."

Why then does neoclassicism continue to be taught in the universities? Why is neoclassicism *still* the orthodoxy of the economics profession? Why do governments pursue, single-mindedly it seems, neoclassical policy prescriptions? By neoclassical-style reasoning, the answer is simple: neoclassicism as a mode of thought increases profits, for some. According to neoclassicism, there is no higher criterion of truth than profit, and indeed the higher the profitability, the greater the "truth!"

It follows therefore, continuing to pursue neoclassicism's logic in this regard, that profits made from promulgating neoclassical modes of thought suffice to prove the value (i.e., the "truth") of neoclassicism. As long as neoclassical dogma continues to earn an income for its expositors, its usefulness ("truthfulness") is concretely demonstrated, and in accordance with Say's law neoclassical acolytes will continue to be produced to meet continuing Demand.

From whence cometh this Demand, one might well ask. Why verily from those institutions and concentrations of wealth and power that profit from the propagation of a doctrine "justifying" greed and the amassing of riches in the context of imminent ecosystem collapse, breakdown in human community, and the destitution of millions. Such, unfortunately, *is* the political economy of neoclassical economics.

What then can be done? How can neoclassicism be "put in its place," so to speak, and thereby the destructive policies "legitimated" by neoclassicism and pursued unflinchingly by governments and transnational corporations be exposed for what they are for all who care to see? According to neoclassicism and the market system it "justifies," neoclassicism's "truth" value will decline only as a result of a concomitant decline in the demand for neoclassical economists and for neoclassical modes of analysis; neoclassicism as commodity, after all, attains its value ("truth") from Market Demand.

A decline in the Demand for neoclassicism, however, would seem to imply a prior and considerable restructuring of economic power—*from* those institutions of concentrated wealth that contrive the Demand for neoclassical economics in the first place, *to* those marginalized by neoclassicism and by the market system. In the absence of a power shift, Demand for neoclassicism will continue unabated, and hence neoclassicism, on its own terms, will continue to be "true." How such a power shift is to be accomplished, given hegemonic control over the means of culture, is then highly problematic, recalling indeed the ancient dilemma of the chicken and the egg!

Stated otherwise, criteria of truth other than mere profitability must once again come to the fore and be more widely shared. Only then will neoclassicism be generally recognized as constituting one of this century's biggest lies. But again, given the powerful interests served by continued propagation of neoclassical ideology, and given also the extent to which our culture has descended into commoditized, monetarized, and individualized economic/social relations, revitalization of more ancient standards of truth is not necessarily an easy task. One senses that perhaps real world living conditions for the great majority of humanity, unfortunately, may deteriorate even further—environmentally, socially, economically, politically—before hegemonic indoctrination loses its force.

In this war over even the very *criterion* of truth, critical communication studies, aligned as it is with institutional economics and political economy, has an important role to play. A theme of this book has been that critical communication studies *can* help undermine deadly economic doctrine. Were critical communication studies to become more self-evidently true, particularly for those marginalized by our current, moribund economic order and for those sympathetic to their plight, then critical communication studies, along with the eco-sciences, would go some distance in helping avert looming ecosystem disaster and social catastrophe, notwithstanding the present predominance and enthusiastic diffusion of hegemonic discourses such as neoclassicism by those aligned with concentrations of political and economic power. Critical communication studies, seemingly pessimistic due to its realism, is in fact a hopeful and fruitful way of conceptualizing and pursuing human justice, ecological sanity, and human community. The optimism of critical communication studies stems from the fact that it does not take as unalterable our current unjust and moribund economic order.

As crises mount and as alienation due to heightened commoditization spreads, let it be remembered that the official version of the order of things is never the only version. Let us also hope that from the depths of human despair and out of longings for community, for environmental health, for a renewed sense of human dignity, for justice, and for a vibrant democracy, alternative modes of thinking, analyzing, feeling, and acting will emerge and find expression. In the emergence of such healthier and more vibrant modes of thought and praxis, expansive conceptions of information and communication are sure to play central roles.

Note

1. As Northrop Frye maintained, "The new poem, like the new baby, is born into an already existing order of words, and is typical of the structure of poetry to which it is attached. ... Just as a new scientific discovery manifests something that was already latent in the order of nature, and at the same time is logically related to the total structure of the existing science, so the new poem manifests something that was already latent in the order of words" (Frye, 1957, p. 97).

Bibliography

Adams, Walter 1990. "Public Policy in a Free Enterprise Economy." In Walter Adams (Ed.). *The Structure of American Industry,* 8th edition. New York: Macmillan Publishing Company, pp. 349–376.

Adams, Walter, and Brock, James W. 1986. *The Bigness Complex.* New York: Pantheon.

Adams, Walter, and Brock, James W. 1991. *Antitrust Economics on Trial: A Dialogue on the New Laissez-Faire.* Princeton, New Jersey: Princeton University Press.

Adler, Mortimer J. 1981. *Six Great Ideas.* New York: Macmillan Publishing Co. Inc.

Adorno, Theodor 1991. *The Culture Industry: Selected Essays on Mass Culture.* Edited by J. M. Bernstein. London: Routledge.

Akerlof, George A. 1970. "The Market for 'Lemons': Quality, Uncertainty and the Market Mechanism." *Quarterly Journal of Economics* 84 (3), August. pp. 488-500.

Alchian, Armen 1950. "Uncertainty, Evolution, and Economic Theory." *Journal of Political Economy 58* (3), pp. 211–221.

Allard, T. J. 1976. *The C.A.B. Story 1926–1976: Private Broadcasting in Canada.* Ottawa: Canadian Association of Broadcasters.

Allen, Beth 1990. "Information as an Economic Commodity." *American Economic Review* 80 (2), May, pp. 268–273.

Anderson, Michael H. 1984. *Madison Avenue in Asia: Politics and Transnational Advertising.* London: Associated University Presses.

Appadurai, Arjun, ed. 1986. *The Social Life of Things: Commodities in Cultural Perspective.* Cambridge: Cambridge University Press.

Ardrey, Robert 1966. *The Territorial Imperative: A Personal Inquiry into the Animal Origins of Property and Nations.* New York: Atheneum.

Arrow, Kenneth J. [1962] 1971. "Economic Welfare and the Allocation of Resources for Invention." In *The Rate and Direction of Inventive Activity: Economic and Social Factors.* Princeton, New Jersey: National Bureau of Economic Research, pp. 609-26; reprinted in *Economics of Information and Knowledge,* edited by D. M. Lamberton. Harmondsworth: Penguin, pp. 141–159.

Arrow, Kenneth 1979. "The Economics of Information." In *The Computer-Age: A Twenty-Year View,* edited by Michael Dertouzos and Joel Moses. Cambridge, Massachusetts: MIT Press, pp. 306-317.

Ayres, Clarence E. 1957. "Institutional Economics—Discussion." *American Economic Review, Papers and Proceedings* 47.

Ayres, Clarence E. 1989. "Ideological Responsibility." In *The Methodology of*

Economic Thought (2nd ed.), edited by Mark R. Tool and Warren J. Samuels. New Brunswick, New Jersey: Transaction Publishers.

Ayres, Robert U., and Kneese, Allen V. 1969. "Production, Consumption, and Externalities." *American Economic Review* 59 (3), June, pp. 282–97.

Babe, Robert E. 1979. *Canadian Television Broadcasting Structure, Performance and Regulation*. Ottawa: Supply and Services for the Economic Council of Canada.

Babe, Robert E. 1990. *Telecommunications in Canada: Technology, Industry and Government*. Toronto: University of Toronto Press.

Babe, Robert E., ed. 1994. *Information and Communication in Economics*. Boston/Dordrecht/London: Kluwer Academic Publishers.

Babe, Robert E. 1994a. "Information Theory in Economics." In *The Elgar Companion to Institutional and Evolutionary Economics*, edited by Geoffrey M. Hodgson, Warren J. Samuels, and Marc R. Tool. Aldershot, England: Edward Elgar Publishing Limited, pp. 360–366.

Babe, Robert E., forthcoming. "Convergence and New Technologies." In *Canada's Cultural Industries: Into the Twenty-first Century*, edited by Michael Dorland. Toronto: James Lorimer and Company.

Bacon, Francis [1617] 1952. *New Atlantis*. Reprinted in Francis Bacon, *Advancement of Learning, Novum Organum, New Atlantis*. Chicago: Encyclopaedia Britannica.

Bacon, Francis [1620] 1952. *Novum Organum*. Reprinted in Francis Bacon, *Advancement of Learning, Novum Organum, New Atlantis*. Chicago: Encyclopaedia Britannica

Bagdikian, Ben 1990. *The Media Monopoly*, 3rd edition. Boston, Massachusetts: Beacon Press.

Barbour, Ian 1990. *Religion in an Age of Science*. The Gifford Lectures 1989–1991, Volume 1. New York: Harper Collins.

Barnard, Elaine 1982. *The Long Distance Feeling: A History of the Telecommunications Workers Union*. Vancouver, British Columbia: New Star Books.

Barnet, Richard J., and Cavanaugh, John 1994. *Global Dreams: Imperial Corporations and the New World Order*. New York: Simon and Schuster.

Barnet, Richard J., and Müller, Ronald E. 1974. *Global Reach: The Power of the Multinational Corporations*. New York: Simon and Schuster.

Barnett, Harold, and Morse, Chandler 1963. *Scarcity and Growth: The Economics of Natural Resource Availability*. Baltimore, Maryland: John Hopkins Press.

Barnouw, E. 1978. *The Sponsor: Notes on a Modern Potentate*. New York: Oxford University Press.

Barthes, Roland 1972. *Mythologies*. New York: Hill and Wang.

Barzun, Jacques [1941] 1981. *Darwin, Marx, Wagner: Critique of a Heritage*. 2nd edition. Chicago: University of Chicago Press.

Basalla, George 1988. *The Evolution of Technology*. Cambridge: Cambridge University Press.

Bates, Benjamin 1988. "Information as an Economic Good: Sources of Individual and Social Value." In *The Political Economy of Information*, edited by Vincent Mosco and Janet Wasko. Madison, Wisconsin: University of Wisconsin Press.

Bateson, Gregory 1979. *Mind and Nature: A Necessary Unity*. New York: E. P. Dutton.

Baumol, William J., and Oates, Wallace E. 1971. "The Use of Standards and Prices for Protection of the Environment." In *The Economics of the Environment: Papers From Four Nations,* edited by Peter Bohm and Allen V. Kneese. London: Macmillan, pp. 53–65.

Becker, Gary 1976. *The Economic Approach to Human Behavior.* Chicago: University of Chicago Press.

Bell, Daniel 1973. *The Coming of Post-industrial Society.* New York: Basic Books.

Bell, Daniel 1976. *The Cultural Contradictions of Capitalism.* New York: Basic Books.

Bell, Daniel [1977] 1980. "Teletext and Technology." *Encounter* 68 (6) June, pp. 9-29. Reprinted in Daniel Bell, *The Winding Passage: Essays and Sociological Journeys 1960-1980,* pp. 34–65. New York: Basic Books.

Bell, Daniel 1979. "The Social Framework of the Information Society." In *The Computer Age: A Twenty-Year View,* edited by M. Dertouzos and J. Moses, pp. 34-65. Cambridge, Massachusetts: MIT Press.

Bell Telephone Company of Canada 1923. *Annual Report.*

Bell Telephone Company of Canada 1950. *Annual Report.*

Bell Telephone Company of Canada 1959. *Annual Report.*

Bell Canada 1978. *Argument.* CNCP Interconnection case, 29 May, p. 6 of Part ii, Tab 4.

Beniger, James R. 1986. *The Control Revolution, Technological and Economic Origins of the Information Society.* Cambridge, Massachusetts: Harvard University Press.

Bentham, Jeremy [1830] 1978. *Principles of the Civic Code.* Extracted in *Property: Mainstream and Critical Positions,* edited by C. B. Macpherson. Toronto: University of Toronto Press, pp. 41-58.

Berger, Peter, and Luckman, Thomas 1966. *The Social Construction of Reality.* Harmondsworth, England: Penguin.

Berle, Adolph, and Means, Gardiner C. [1932] 1967. *The Modern Corporation and Private Property.* New York: Harcourt, Brace and World.

Besen, Stanley, Manning, W., and Mitchell, B. 1978. "Copyright Liability for Cable Television." *Journal of Law and Economics* 21 (1), pp. 67-95.

Blaug, Mark 1968. *Economic Theory in Retrospect.* Homewood, Illinois: Irwin.

Bonney, Bill, and Wilson, Helen 1990. "Advertising and the Manufacture of Difference." In *The Media Reader,* edited by Manuel Alvarado and John O. Thompson. London: British Film Institute, pp. 181-198.

Boorstin, Daniel J. [1961] 1978. *The Image: A Guide to Pseudo Events in America.* New York: Atheneum.

Borchardt, K. 1970. *Structure and Performance of the U.S. Communications Industry.* Boston, Massachusetts: Harvard University Press.

Boulding, Kenneth E. 1945. *The Economics of Peace.* New York: Prentice-Hall, Inc.

Boulding, Kenneth E. [1953] 1968. *The Organizational Revolution: A Study in the Ethics of Economic Organization.* Chicago: Quadrangle Books.

Boulding, Kenneth E. [1955] 1974. "Notes on the Information Concept." *Exploration.* Toronto, pp. 103 -112. Reprinted in Kenneth E. Boulding, *Collected Papers,*

Volume 4: Toward A General Social Science, edited by Larry D. Singell. Boulder, Colorado: Colorado Associated University Press, pp. 21–32.

Boulding, Kenneth E. [1956] 1961. *The Image: Knowledge and Life in Society.* Ann Arbor, Michigan: University of Michigan Press.

Boulding, Kenneth E. [1957] 1971. "A New Look at Institutionalism." *American Economic Review* 47 (2), May. Reprinted in Kenneth E. Boulding, *Collected Papers, Vol. 2: Economics*, edited by Fred R. Glahe. Boulder, Colorado: Colorado Associated University Press, pp. 89–100.

Boulding, Kenneth E. 1958. *The Skills of the Economist* Toronto: Clarke, Irwin & Company Limited.

Boulding, Kenneth E. [1959] 1971. "Foreword to T. R. Malthus, *Population, The First Essay.*" Ann Arbor, Michigan: Ann Arbor Paperbacks. Reprinted in Kenneth E. Boulding, *Collected Papers, Volume 2: Economics*, edited by Fred R. Glahe. Boulder, Colorado: Colorado Associated University Press, pp. 135–142.

Boulding, Kenneth E. [1962] 1963. *Conflict and Defense: A General Theory.* New York: Harper & Row, Publishers.

Boulding, Kenneth E. 1963. "The Knowledge Industry." *Challenge*, May, pp. 36-38.

Boulding, Kenneth E. {1964} 1965. *The Meaning of the Twentieth Century: The Great Transition.* New York: Harper and Row, Publishers.

Boulding, Kenneth E. [1966] 1993. "The Economics of the Coming Spaceship Earth." In *Environmental Quality in a Growing Economy*, published for Resources for the Future, Inc. by The John Hopkins Press. Reprinted in *Valuing the Earth: Economics, Ecology, Ethics*, edited by Herman E. Daly and Kenneth N. Townsend. Cambridge, Massachusetts: MIT Press, pp. 297–309.

Boulding, Kenneth E. [1966] 1995. "Expecting the Unexpected: The Uncertain Future of Knowledge and Technology." In *Prospective Changes in Society by 1980 Including Some Implications for Education.* Reprinted in Elise Boulding and Kenneth E. Boulding. *The Future: Images and Processes.* Thousand Oaks, California: Sage Publications, pp. 7–25.

Boulding, Kenneth E. [1969] 1971. "Economics as a Moral Science." *American Economic Review*, 59, March, pp. 1–12. Reprinted in Kenneth E. Boulding *Collected Papers, Vol. 2: Economics.* Boulder, Colorado: Colorado Associated University Press, pp. 449–460.

Boulding, Kenneth E. 1970. *A Primer on Social Dynamics: History as Dialectics and Development.* New York: The Free Press, Collier-Macmillan.

Boulding, Kenneth E. 1973. *The Economy of Love and Fear: A Preface to the Grants Economy.* Belmont, California: Wadsworth Publishing Company.

Boulding, Kenneth E. 1978. *Ecodynamics: A New Theory of Societal Evolution.* Beverly Hills, California: Sage Publications.

Boulding, Kenneth E. [1979] 1995. "The Limits to Societal Growth." In *Social Growth: Processes and Implications*, edited by Amos H. Hawley. Reprinted in Elise Boulding and Kenneth E. Boulding, *The Future: Images and Processes.* Thousand Oaks, California: Sage Publications, pp. 26–38.

Boulding, Kenneth E. 1981. *Evolutionary Economics.* Beverly Hills, California: Sage Publications.

Boulding, Kenneth E. [1983] 1995. "World Society: The Range of Possible

Futures." In *How Humans Adapt: A Biocultural Odyssey*, edited by Donald J. Ortner. Washington, D.C.: Smithsonian Press. Reprinted in Kenneth E. Boulding and Elise Boulding, *The Future: Images and Processes*. Thousand Oaks, California: Sage Publications, pp. 39–56.

Boulding, Kenneth E. 1985. *The World as a Total System*. Newbury Park, California: Sage Publications.

Boulding, Kenneth E. 1992. "From Chemistry to Economics and Beyond." In *Eminent Economists*, edited by Michael Szenberg. Cambridge: Cambridge University Press, pp. 69–83.

Bowles, Samuel, and Gintis, Herbert 1987. *Democracy and Capitalism: Property, Community and the Contradictions of Modern Social Thought*. New York: Basic Books.

Braman, Sandra 1989. "Defining Information: An Approach for Policymakers." *Telecommunications Policy*, September, pp. 233-242.

Braman, Sandra 1990. "Trade and Information Policy." *Media Culture and Society*, 12. London/Newbury Park/New Delhi: Sage, pp. 361–385.

Britnell, G. E. 1934. *Public Ownership of Telephones in the Prairie Provinces*. Master's Thesis, University of Toronto.

Bronfenbrenner, Martin 1966. "A 'Middlebrow' Introduction to Economic Methodology." In *The Structure of Economic Science: Essays on Methodology*, edited by Sherman Roy Krupp. Englewood Cliffs, New Jersey.: Prentice-Hall Inc., pp. 5–24.

Bronowski, Jacob [1956] 1972. *Science and Human Values*. New York: Perennial Library.

Canada, Board of Railway Commissioners 1926. Transcript—Case 955-971. Ottawa, Vol. 455, 19 April.

Canada, Board of Transport Commissioners 1964. *Judgements, Orders, Regulations, and Rulings*. Ottawa, 3 June.

Canada, Board of Transport Commissioners 1966. *Judgement*. Case 9551701, 4 May.

Canada, Canadian Radio-television and Telecommunications Commission 1979. "CNCP Telecommunications: Interconnection With Bell Canada." Telecom Decision CRTC 79-11, 17 May.

Canada, Canadian Radio-television and Telecommunications Commission, Committee on Extension of Service to Northern and Remote Communities 1983. *The 1980's: A Decade of Diversity—Broadcasting, Satellites and Pay-TV*. Ottawa: Supply and Services.

Canada, Canadian Radio-television and Telecommunications Commission 1992. "Competition in the Provision of Public Long Distance Voice Telephone Services and Related Resale and Sharing Issues." Telecom Decision CRTC 92-12, 12 June.

Canada, Canadian Radio-television and Telecommunications Commission 1994. "Review of Regulatory Framework." Telecom Decision CRTC 94–19, 16 September.

Canada, Consultative Committee on the Implications of Telecommunications for Canadian Sovereignty 1979. *Telecommunications and Canada*. Ottawa: Supply and Services.

Canada, Department of Communications 1971. *Instant World: A Report on Telecommunications in Canada.* Ottawa: Information Canada.

Canada, Department of Communications 1983. *Towards A New National Broadcasting Policy.* Ottawa: Supply and Services.

Canada, Hon. Francis Fox, Minister of Communications 1983. *Culture and Communications: Key Elements of Canada's Economic Future.* Ottawa: Supply and Services.

Canada, House of Commons Select Committee on Telephone Systems 1905. *Proceedings.* Ottawa: King's Printer.

Canada, Industry Canada 1994a. *The Canadian Information Highway: Building Canada's Information and Communications Infrastructure.* Ottawa: Supply and Services.

Canada, Industry Canada, 1994b. *Privacy and the Canadian Information Highway: Building Canada's Information and Communications Infrastructure.* Ottawa: Minister of Supply and Services.

Canada, Pelletier, G. (Hon.), Minister of Communications 1973. *Proposals for a Communications Policy for Canada: A Position Paper of the Government of Canada.* Ottawa: Information Canada.

Canada, Privacy Commissioner 1994. *Annual Report 1993–94.* Ottawa: Canada Communications Group.

Canada, Science Council of Canada 1982. *Planning Now for an Information Revolution: Tomorrow is Too Late.* Ottawa: Supply and Services.

Canada, Special Joint Committee of the Senate and the House of Commons Reviewing Canadian Foreign Policy 1994. *Canada's Foreign Policy: Principles and Priorities for the Future.* Ottawa: Publications Service, Parliamentary Publications Directorate.

Canadian National Railway Company and Canadian Pacific Limited 1980. Partnership Agreement, 13 March.

Carey, James W. 1981. "Culture, Geography, and Communications: The Work of Harold Innis in an American Context." In *Culture, Communication, and Dependency: The Tradition of H. A. Innis,* edited by William H. Melody, Liora Salter, and Paul Heyer. Norwood, NJ: Ablex Publishing Corp.

Carey, James W. 1989. *Communications as Culture: Essays on Media and Society.* Boston, Massachusetts: Unwin Hyman.

Chaffee, S. H., and Hochheimer, J. L. 1985. "The Beginnings of Political Communication Research in the United States: Origins of the 'Limited Effects' Model." In *Mass Communication Review Yearbook,* vol. 5, edited by Michael. Gurevitch and Mark Levy. Beverly Hills, California: Sage Publications, pp. 75-104.

Chase, Samuel, ed. 1968. *Problems in Public Expenditure Analysis.* Washington, DC: Brookings.

Chomsky, Noam 1989. *Necessary Illusions: Thought Control in Democratic Societies.* CBC Massey Lectures. Montreal: CBC Enterprises.

Clarke, Arthur C. 1964. *Profiles of the Future.* New York: Bantam Books.

Clement, Wallace and Williams, Glen, eds. 1989. *The New Canadian Political Economy.* Kingston, Ont.: McGill-Queen's University Press.

Coase, R. H. 1960. "The Problem of Social Cost." *Journal of Law and Economics* 3, pp. 1-44.

Coase, R. H. [1937] 1952. "The Nature of the Firm." *Economica* 4, pp. 386-405. Reprinted in *Readings in Price Theory,* edited by George J. Stigler and Kenneth E. Boulding. Homewood, Illinois: Irwin, pp. 331–351.

Coase, R. H. 1959. "The Federal Communications Commission." *Journal of Law and Economics* 2, October, pp. 1–40.

Cole, G. D. H. 1967. *A History of Socialist Thought,* Vol. 1: The Forerunners 1789-1850. New York: St. Martin's Press.

Combs, James E., and Nimmo, Dan 1993. *The New Propaganda: The Dictatorship of Palaver in Contemporary Politics.* New York/London: Longman.

Csikszertmihalyi, Mihaly, and Rochberg-Halton, Eugene 1981. *The Meaning of Things: Domestic Symbols and the Self.* Cambridge: Cambridge University Press.

Cummings, Bruce 1992. *War and Television.* London/New York: Verso.

Czitrom, Daniel 1982. *Media and the American Mind.* Chapel Hill, North Carolina: University of North Carolina Press.

Daly, Herman E. 1979. "Entropy, Growth, and the Political Economy of Scarcity." In *Scarcity and Growth Reconsidered,* edited by V. Kerry Smith. Published for Resources for the Future. Baltimore, Maryland: John Hopkins Press, pp. 67–94.

Daly, Herman E. 1991. *Steady-State Economics,* 2nd edition. Washington, DC: Island Press.

Daly, Herman E. 1993. "Introduction to Essays Toward a Steady-State Economy." In *Valuing the Earth: Economics, Ecology, Ethics,* edited by Herman E. Daly and Kenneth N. Townsend. Cambridge, Massachusetts: MIT Press, pp. 11–47.

Daly, Herman E., and Cobb, John 1989. *For the Common Good: Redirecting the Economy Toward Community, the Environment and a Sustainable Future.* Boston, Massachusetts: Beacon Press.

Danielian, N. R. [1939] 1974. *AT&T: The Story of Industrial Conquest.* New York: Arno Press.

Darnell, Donald K. 1972. "Information Theory: An Approach to Human Communication." In *Approaches to Human Communication,* edited by Richard Budd and Brent Ruben. Rochelle Park, New Jersey: Hayden Book Company, pp. 156-169.

Darwin, Charles [1859] 1959. *On The Origin of the Species By Means of Natural Selection, Or the Preservation of Favoured Races in the Struggle for Life,* edited by Morse Peckham. Philadelphia, Pennsylvania: University of Pennsylvania Press.

Dasah, Bernard Z. 1992. "The Treatment of Information/Communication by Neoclassical Economics." Unpublished paper, University of Ottawa/McGill University.

Davis, John P. [1905] 1961. *Corporations: A Study of the Origin and Development of Great Business Combinations and of their Relation to the Authority of the State.* New York: Capricorn Books.

Debreu, G. [1959] 1989. *Theory of Value.* New York: Wiley. Excerpted in *Uncertainty in Economics: Readings and Exercises,* edited by Peter Diamond and Michael Rothschild, revised. San Diego, California: Academic Press, pp. 163–173.

Delia, J. G. 1987. "Communication Research: A History." In *Handbook of Communication Science,* edited by C. R. Berger & S. H. Chaffee. Beverly Hills, California: Sage Publications, pp. 20–98

Demsetz, Harold 1969. "Information and Efficiency: Another Viewpoint." *Journal of Law and Economics* 12 (1), pp. 1-22.

Dennis, Everette E. 1991. "In Context: Environmentalism in the System of News." In *Media and the Environment,* edited by Craig L. Lamay and Everette E. Dennis. Washington, DC: Island Press for The Freedom Forum Media Center, pp. 55–64.

de Sola Pool, Ithiel 1983. *Technologies of Freedom.* Cambridge, Massachusetts: MIT Press.

de Sola Pool, Ithiel 1990. *Technologies Without Boundaries: On Telecommunications in a Global Age.* Edited by Eli M. Noam. Cambridge, Massachusetts: Harvard University Press.

Dewees, D. N., Everson, C. K., and Sims, W. A. 1975. *Economic Analysis of Environment Policies.* Study prepared for the Ontario Economic Council. Toronto: University of Toronto Press.

Dewey, John. 1915. *Democracy and Education.* New York: Macmillan.

Diamond, P.A. 1978. "Welfare Analysis of Imperfect Information Equilibrium." *Bell Journal of Economics* 9(1), pp. 82–105.

Dietz, Frank J., van der Ploeg, Frederick, and van der Straaten, Jan 1991. "Environmental Policy and the Economy: An Introduction." In *Environmental Policy and the Economy.* Amsterdam: North Holland, pp. 1–16.

Donne, John 1623/1624. *Meditation XVII.*

Dordick, Herbert E., and Wang, Georgette 1993. *The Information Society: A Retrospective View.* Newbury Park, California: Sage Publications.

Dorfman, Joseph 1932. "The 'Satire' of Thorstein Veblen's Theory of the Leisure Class." *Political Science Quarterly* 72, pp. 363–409.

Dorfman, Joseph 1934. *Thorstein Veblen and His America.* New York: Viking Press.

Drucker, Peter 1968. *The Age of Discontinuity.* New York: Harper and Row.

Dyer, Alan W. 1986. "Semiotics, Economic Development, and the Deconstruction of Economic Man." *Journal of Economic Issues* 20 (2), June, pp. 541–549.

Dyer, Alan W. 1989. "Making Semiotic Sense of Money as a Medium of Exchange." *Journal of Economic Issues* 23 (2), June, pp. 503-510.

Dyer, Gillian 1982. *Advertising As Communication.* London: Methuen.

Edgell, Stephen, and Tilman, Rick 1989. "The Intellectual Antecedents of Thorstein Veblen: A Reappraisal." *Journal of Economic Issues* 23 (4), December, pp. 1003–1026.

Editorial Board, Ottawa Citizen 1991. "Bank vs. Suzuki: Everyone is Free to Choose." *Ottawa Citizen,* 12 March, p. A10.

Eff, E. Anton 1989. "History of Thought as Ceremonial Genealogy: The Neglected Influence of Herbert Spencer on Thorstein Veblen." *Journal of Economic Issues* 23 (3), September, pp. 689–716.

Ehrlich, Paul R., Ehrlich, Anne H., and Holdren, John P. [1977] 1993. "Availability, Entropy, and the Laws of Thermodynamics." *Ecoscience.* San Francisco:

Freeman. Extracted in *Valuing the Earth: Economics, Ecology, Ethics,* edited by Herman E. Daly and Kenneth N. Townsend. Cambridge, Massachusetts: MIT Press, pp. 69–73.

Elliott, John E. 1978. "Institutionalism as an Approach to Political Economy." *Journal of Economic Issues* 12(1). March, pp. 91–114.

Ellul, Jacques [1954] 1964. *The Technological Society.* New York: Vintage.

Ellul, Jacques [1965] 1973. *Propaganda: The Formation of Men's Attitudes.* New York: Vintage Books, Random House.

Ellul, Jacques 1980. "The Power of Technique and the Ethics of Non-power." In *The Myths of Information: Technology and Post Industrial Culture,* edited by Kathleen Woodward. Madison, Wisconsin: Coda Press.

Ely, Richard T. and Hess, Ralph H. 1937. *Outlines of Economics,* 6th edition. New York: Macmillan.

Evans, Christopher 1979. *The Mighty Micro: The Impact of the Computer Revolution.* London: Victor Gollancz.

Ferguson, Charles 1972. *Microeconomic Theory.* 3rd ed. Homewood, Illinois: Irwin.

Fetherstonaugh, R. C. 1944. *Charles Fleetford Sise, 1938-1918.* Montreal: Gazette Publishing.

Fisher, Anthony C., and Peterson, Frederick M. 1976. "The Environment in Economics: A Survey." *Journal of Economic Literature* 14 (1), pp. 1–33.

Fiske, John 1982. *Introduction to Communication Studies.* London/New York: Methuen.

Fiske, John 1987. "British Cultural Studies and Television." In *Channels of Discourse,* edited by Robert C. Allen. Chapel Hill, North Carolina: University of North Carolina Press, pp. 254-289.

Fiske, John 1989. *Understanding Popular Culture.* London: Unwin Hyman.

Forsdale, L. 1981. *Perspectives on Communications.* Reading, Massachusetts: Addison Wesley.

Franklin, Ursula 1990. *The Real World of Technology.* CBC Massey Lectures. Montreal: CBC Enterprises.

Fredericks, Kathryn 1994. "United States Information Policy and Dependency in the South." Department of Communication, University of Ottawa.

Friedman, Milton 1953. *Essays in Positive Economics.* Chicago: University of Chicago Press.

Friedman, Milton 1962. *Price Theory: A Provisional Text.* Chicago, Illinois: Aldine.

Friedman, Milton 1962a. *Capitalism and Freedom.* Chicago: University of Chicago Press.

Friedman, Milton [1970] 1985. "The Social Responsibility of Business Is to Increase Its Profits." *New York Times.* Reprinted in *Contemporary Issues in Business Ethics,* edited by Joseph R. Desjardins and John J. McCall. Belmont, California: Wadsworth Publishing Company, pp. 21–25.

Friedman, Rose, and Friedman, Milton 1980. *Free to Choose.* New York and London: Harcourt Brace Jovanovich.

Freiman, Mark J. 1984. "Consumer Sovereignty and National Sovereignty in Domestic and International Broadcasting Regulation." In *Cultures in Collision: The Interaction of Canadian and U.S. Television Broadcast Policies*. New York: Praeger, pp. 104–121.

Frye, Northrop 1957. *Anatomy of Criticism*. Princeton, New Jersey: Princeton University Press.

Frye, Northrop 1957. *Anatomy of Criticism: Four Essays*. Princeton, New Jersey: Prineeton University Press.

Galbraith, John Kenneth 1967. *The New Industrial State*. Boston, Massachusetts: Houghton Mifflin.

Galbraith, John Kenneth 1983. *The Anatomy of Power*. Boston, Massachusetts: Houghton Mifflin.

Galtung, Johan 1971. "A Structural Theory of Imperialism." *Journal of Peace Research* 2, pp. 81–117.

Gandy, Oscar 1993. *The Panoptic Sort: A Political Economy of Personal Information*. Boulder/San Francisco/Oxford: Westview Press.

Garson, Barbara 1988. *The Electronic Sweatshop: How Computers are Transforming the Office of the Future into the Factory of the Past*. New York: Simon and Schuster.

George, Henry [1880] 1930. *Progress and Poverty: An Inquiry Into the Causes of Industrial Depressions and of Increase of Want With Increase of Wealth*. New York: The Modern Library.

Georgescu-Roegen, Nicholas 1971. *The Entropy Law and the Economic Process*. Cambridge: Harvard University Press.

Georgescu-Roegen, Nicholas [1971] 1993. "The Entropy Law and the Economic Problem." University of Alabama Distinguished Lecture Series, no. 1; reprinted in *Valuing the Earth: Economics, Ecology, Ethics*, edited by Herman E. Daly and Kenneth N. Townsend. Cambridge, Massachusetts: MIT Press, pp. 75–88.

Georgescu-Roegen, Nicholas [1975] 1993. "Energy and Economic Myths." *Southern Economic Journal* 41 (3), January; reprinted in *Valuing the Earth: Economics, Ecology, Ethics*, edited by Herman E. Daly and Kenneth N. Townsend. Cambridge, Massachusetts: MIT Press, pp. 89–112.

Ginsberg, Benjamin 1986. *The Captive Public: How Mass Opinion Promotes State Power*. New York: Basic Books.

Globerman, Stephen 1983. *Cultural Regulation in Canada*. Montreal: Institute for Research on Public Policy.

Goodland, Robert 1992. "The Case That the World Has Reached Limits." In *Population, Technology, and Lifestyle: The Transition to Sustainability*, edited by Robert Goodland, Herman E. Daly and Salah El Serafy. Washington, DC: Island Press, pp. 3–22.

Goodland, Robert, Daly, Herman E., and El Serafy, Salah (Eds.) 1992. *Population, Technology and Lifestyle: The Transition to Sustainability*. Washington, D.C.: Island Press.

Gordon, Anita, and Suzuki, David 1990. *It's A Matter of Survival*. Cambridge, Massachusetts.: Harvard University Press.

Gordon, Scott 1991. *The History and Philosophy of Social Science*. London and New York: Routledge.

Gramm, Warren 1989. "The Selective Interpretation of Adam Smith." In The *Methodology of Economic Thought*, edited by Marc R. Tool and Warren J. Samuels. New Brunswick, New Jersey: Transaction Publishers, pp. 277–300.

Grant, George 1969. *Time As History*. Massey Lectures, Ninth Series. Toronto: Canadian Broadcasting Corporation.

Gray, Alexander 1931. *The Development of Economic Doctrine: An Introductory Survey*. London: Longmans.

Gray, Horace M. 1981. "Reflections on Innis and Institutional Economics." In *Culture, Communication, and Dependency: The Tradition of H. A. Innis*, edited by William H. Melody, Liora Salter, and Paul Heyer. Norwood, New Jersey: Ablex Publishing Corp.

Grindlay, Thomas 1975. *A History of the Independent Telephone Industry in Ontario*. Toronto: Ontario Telephone Services Commission.

Grossman, Sanford J., and Stiglitz, Joseph E. 1980. "On the Impossibility of Informationally Efficient Markets." *American Economic Review*. June, pp. 393–402.

Gruchy, Allan, C. 1973. "Law, Politics, and Institutional Economics." *Journal of Economic Issues* 8 (4), pp. 623–643.

Haavelmo, Tryve, and Hansen, Stein 1992. "On the Strategy of Trying to Reduce Economic Inequality by Expanding the Scale of Human Activity." In *Population, Technology, and Lifestyle: The Transition to Sustainability*, edited by Robert Goodland, Herman E. Daly and Salah El Serafy. Washington, DC: Island Press, pp. 38–51.

Habermas, Jürgen 1975. *Legitimation Crisis*. Boston: Beacon Press.

Hackett, Robert A. 1991. *News and Dissent: The Press and the Politics of Peace in Canada*. Norwood, New Jersey: Ablex Publishing Corp.

Hall, Stuart 1982. "The Rediscovery of 'Ideology': Return of the Repressed in Media Studies". In *Culture, Society and the Media*, edited by Michael Gurevitch et al. London/New York: Methuen.

Hamilton, L. Clarke, and Ploman, Edward W. 1980. *Copyright: Intellectual Property in the Information Age*. London: Routledge and Kegan Paul.

Harlow, Alvin [1936] 1971. *Old Wires and New Waves*. New York: Arno Press.

Hayden, F. Gregory 1993. "Ecosystem Valuation: Combining Economics, Philosophy, and Ecology." *Journal of Economic Issues* 27 (2), June, pp. 409–419.

Hayek, F. A. 1945. "The Use of Knowledge in Society." *American Economic Review* 35 (4), September, pp. 519–530.

Hayek, F. A. [1952] 1976. *The Sensory Order: An Inquiry Into the Foundations of Theoretical Psychology*. Chicago: University of Chicago Press.

Heilbroner, Robert L. 1974. *An Inquiry Into The Human Prospect*. New York: W.W. Norton & Company, Inc.

Heilbroner, Robert 1990. "Economics As Ideology." In *Economics As Discourse: An Analysis of the Language of Economists*, edited by Warren J. Samuels. Boston/Dordrecht/London: Kluwer Academic Publishers, pp. 101–116.

Heinricks, Geoff 1989. "Whose News? Business Circles The Globe." *This Magazine* 23, September, pp. 14–21.

Hepworth, Mark 1990. *Geography of the Information Economy.* New York: Guilford Press.

Hepworth, Mark 1994. "The Information Economy in a Spatial Context: City States in a Global Village." In *Information and Communication in Economics,* edited by Robert E. Babe. Boston/Dordrecht/London: Kluwer Academic Publishers, pp. 211–231.

Herman, Edward S. 1989. "U.S. Mass Media Coverage of the U.S. Withdrawal from UNESCO." In William Preston Jr., Edward S. Herman and Herbert I. Schiller. *Hope and Folly: The United States and UNESCO, 1945-1985.* Minneapolis: University of Minnesota Press, pp. 203-284.

Himmelweit, S. 1977, "The Individual as Basic Unit of Analysis." In *Economics An Anti Text,* edited by Francis Green and Peter Nore. London: The Macmillan Press, pp. 21–35.

Hopper, A. B. and Kearney, T. 1962. "Synoptical History of Organization, Capital Stock, Funded Debt and Other General Information as of December 31,1960." Montreal: CNR.

Hubbert, M. King 1993. "Exponential Growth as a Transient Phenomenon in Human History." In *Valuing the Earth: Economics, Ecology, Ethics,* edited by Herman E. Daly and Kenneth N. Townsend. Cambridge, Massachusetts: MIT Press, pp. 113–126.

Hyde, Lewis 1979. *The Gift: Imagination and the Erotic Life of Property.* New York: Vintage Books.

Ingrau, Bruna, and Giorgio Israel 1990. *The Invisible Hand: Economic Equilibrium in the History of Science.* Cambridge, Massachusetts.: MIT Press.

Innis, Harold A. 1923. *A History of the Canadian Pacific Railway.* Toronto: University of Toronto Press.

Innis, Harold A. [1929] 1956. "The Work of Thorstein Veblen." *Southwestern Political and Social Science Quarterly,* 10, pp. 56–68; reprinted in *Essays in Canadian Economic History,* edited by Mary Q. Innis. Toronto: University of Toronto Press, pp. 17–26.

Innis, Harold A. [1938] 1956. "The Penetrative Powers of the Price System." In *Essays in Canadian Economic History,* edited by Mary Q. Innis. Toronto: University of Toronto Press, pp. 252–272.

Innis, Harold A. [1950] 1972. *Empire and Communications.* Toronto: University of Toronto Press.

Innis, Harold A. [1951] 1971. *The Bias of Communication.* Toronto: University of Toronto Press.

Irwin, Manley 1984. *Telecommunications America: Markets Without Boundaries.* Quorum Books: Westport, Connecticut.

Jacob, François 1973. *The Logic of Life: A History of Heredity.* Princeton, New Jersey: Princeton University Press

James, William [1901–2] 1960. *The Varieties of Religious Experience.* Glasgow: William Collins Sons & Co. Ltd.

Jenner, R. A. [1966] 1971. "An Information Version of Pure Competition." *Economic Journal* 76, pp. 786–805. Reprinted in *Economics of Information and Knowledge,* edited by D. M. Lamberton. Harmondsworth: Penguin pp. 83–108.

Jonscher, Charles 1982. "Notes on Communication and Economic Theory." In *Communication and Economic Development*, edited by D. M. Lamberton and M. Jussawalla. Elmsford, New York: Pergamon Press. pp. 60-69.

Kahn, Alfred 1970. *The Economics of Regulation: Principles and Institutions, Vol. 1.* New York: John Wiley and Sons.

Kaplan, Abraham 1964. *The Conduct of Inquiry: Methodology for Behavioral Science.* New York: Harper and Row.

Kapp, K. William 1972. "Environmental Disruption and Social Costs: A Challenge to Economics." In *Political Economy of Environment: Problems of Method*. Paris: École Pratique des Hautes Etudes and Mouton & Co., pp. 91–123.

Katz, Elihu, and Lazarsfeld, Paul 1955. *Personal Influence: The Part Played by People in the Flow of Mass Communications*. New York: The Free Press.

Keenan, Greg, and Pitts, Gordon 1994. *Report on Business, Globe and Mail,* 24 December, pp. B1, B15.

Kern, Stephen 1983. *The Culture of Time and Space, 1880-1918*. Cambridge, Massachusetts: Harvard University Press.

Klamer, Arjo 1990. "The Textbook Presentation of Economic Discourse." In *Economics As Discourse: An Analysis of the Language of Economists*, edited by Warren J. Samuels. Boston/Dordrecht/London: Kluwer Academic Publishers.

Klamer, Arjo, McCloskey, Donald M., and Solow, Robert. M. 1988. *The Consequences of Economic Rhetoric*. Cambridge: Cambridge University Press.

Klapp, Orrin E. 1978. *Opening and Closing: Strategies of Information Adaptation in Society*. Cambridge, England: Cambridge University Press.

Knight, Frank 1946. *Risk, Uncertainty and Profit*. Boston: Houghton Mifflin Company.

Knight, Frank 1953. "Theory of Economic Policy and the History of Doctrine." *Ethics* 63, pp. 279-287.

Koestler, Arthur [1967] 1975. "The Holon." In *The Ghost in the Machine*. London: Pan Books, pp. 45–58.

Koestler, Arthur 1979. *Janus: A Summing Up*. London: Pan Books.

Kroker, Arthur 1984. *Technology and the Canadian Mind: Innis/McLuhan/Grant*. Montreal: New World Perspectives.

Kuhn, Thomas 1970. *The Structure of Scientific Revolutions*. 2nd ed. Chicago, Illinois: University of Chicago Press.

Lamberton, Donald M. 1984. "The Economics of Information and Organization." *Annual Review of Information Science and Technology* 19, pp. 3-30.

Lamberton, Donald M. 1990. "Information Economics: 'Threatened Wreckage' or New Paradigm?" CIRCIT Working Paper 1990/1. Melbourne: Centre for International Research on Communication and Information Technologies.

Lamberton, Donald M. 1994. "The Information Economy Revisited." In *Information and Communication in Economics*, edited by Robert E. Babe. Boston/Dordrecht/London: Kluwer Academic Publishers, pp. 1–33.

Lasswell, Harold [1948] 1971. "The Structure and Function of Communication in Society." In *The Communication of Ideas*, edited by L. Bryson. Reprinted in Wilbur. Schramm & D. Roberts, *The Process and Effects of Mass Communication*.

Urbana, Illinois: University of Illinois Press, pp. 84-99.

Lazarsfeld, Paul F. [1941] 1972. "Administrative and Critical Research." *Studies in Philosophy and Social Sciences* 9(1). Reprinted in Paul F. Lazarsfeld, *Qualitative Analysis: Historical and Critical Essays*. Boston, Massachusetts: Allyn and Bacon, pp. 157-167.

Lears, T. J. Jackson 1983. "From Salvation to Self-Realization: Advertising and the Therapeutic Roots of the Consumer Culture, 1880-1930." In *The Culture of Consumption: Critical Essays in American History 1880-1980*, edited by Richard Wightman and T. J. Jackson Lears. New York: Pantheon, pp. 1–38.

Leiss, William 1990. *Under Technology's Thumb*. Montreal and Kingston: McGill-Queen's Press.

Lerner, Daniel 1958. *The Passing of Traditional Society: Modernizing the Middle East*. New York: Free Press.

Lerner, Max 1950. "Editor's Introduction." *The Portable Veblen*. New York: Viking Press, pp. 1–49.

Leshan, L., and Margenau, H. 1982. *Einstein's Space and Van Gogh's Sky: Physical Realty and Beyond*. New York: Macmillan.

Lewis, C. S. [1943] 1978. *The Abolition of Man*. Glasgow: William Collins Sons & Co. Ltd.

Lippmann, Walter 1922. *Public Opinion*. New York: Free Press.

Lippmann, Walter 1955. *The Public Philosophy*. New York: Mentor.

Litman, Barry R. 1990. "The Motion Picture Entertainment Industry." In *The Structure of American Industry*, 8th edition, edited by Walter Adams. New York: Macmillan, pp. 183–216.

Lowery, Shearon A., and DeFleur, Melvin L. 1988. *Milestones in Mass Communication Research*, 2nd Edition. New York: Longman.

Lukács, Georg 1971. *History and Class Consciousness: Studies in Marxist Dialectics*, translated by Rodney Livingstone. Cambridge, Massachusetts: MIT Press.

Lurie, A. 1985. *The Language of Clothes*. New York: Vintage.

Lutz, Mark A., and Lux, Kenneth 1988. *Humanistic Economics: The New Challenge*. New York: The Bootstrap Press.

Lux, Kenneth 1990. *Adam Smith's Mistake: How A Moral Philosopher Invented Economics and Ended Morality*. Boston: Shambhala Publications.

Macbeth, Norman 1971. *Darwin Retried*. New York: Dell Publishing.

MacGibbon, D. A. 1917. *Railway Rates and the Canadian Railway Commission*. Boston.

Machlup, Fritz 1961. *The Production and Distribution of Knowledge in the United States*. Princeton, New Jersey: Princeton University Press.

Machlup, Fritz 1980. *Knowledge: Its Creation, Distribution and Economic Significance. Volume 1: Knowledge and Knowledge Production*. Princeton, New Jersey: Princeton University Press.

Macpherson, C. B. 1965. *The Real World of Democracy*. Massey Lectures, fourth series. Toronto: CBC.

Magder, Ted 1989. *Taking Culture Seriously: A Political Economy of Communications. In The New Canadian Political Economy*, edited by Wallace Clement and Glenn Williams. Montreal: McGill-Queen's Press.

Malthus, Thomas Robert [1798] 1986. *An Essay on the Principle of Population as it Affects the Future Improvement of Society, With Remarks on the Speculations of Mr. Godwin, M. Condorcet, and Other Writers*. London: J. Johnson. Reprinted in *The Works of Thomas Robert Malthus, Vol. 1, An Essay on the Principle of Population*, edited by E. A. Wrigley and David Souden. London: William Pickering.

Malthus, Thomas Robert [1803] 1992. *An Essay on the Principle of Population; Or, A View of its Past and Present Effects on Human Happiness; With an Inquiry Into Our Prospects Respecting the Future Removal or Mitigation of the Evils Which It Occasions*, edited by Donald Winch. Cambridge: Cambridge University Press.

Marcel, Gabriel 1978. *Man Against Mass Society*. South Bend, Indiana: Gateway Editions, Ltd.

Marshall, Alfred [1890] 1938. *Principles of Economics: An Introductory Volume*. 8th Edition, London: Macmillan.

Mattelart, Armand 1994. *Mapping World Communication*. Translated by Susan Emanuel and James A. Cohen. Minneapolis, Minnesota: University of Minnesota Press.

McCloskey, Donald N. 1990. *If You're So Smart: The Narrative of Economic Expertise*. Chicago: University of Chicago Press.

McCracken, Grant 1988. *Culture and Consumption: New Approaches to the Symbolic Character of Consumer Goods and Activities*. Bloomington/Indianapolis: Indiana University Press.

McLuhan, Marshall 1964. *Understanding Media: The Extensions of Man*. New York: Mentor.

McLuhan, Marshall 1972, "Foreword." In Harold A. Innis, *Empire and Communications*, edited by Mary Q. Innis. Toronto: University of Toronto Press, pp. v–xii.

McManus, John 1973. "Federal Regulation of Telecommunications in Canada." In *Telecommunications for Canada: An Interface of Business and Government*, edited by H. E. English. Toronto: Methuen.

Meadows, Donella H. 1991. "Changing the World Through the Information Sphere." In *Media and the Environment*, edited by Craig L. LaMay and Everette E. Dennis. Washington, DC: Island Press, pp. 67–79.

Meek, Ronald L., ed. 1954. *Marx and Engels on Malthus: Selections From the Writings of Marx and Engels Dealing With the Theories of Thomas Robert Malthus*. United States: International Publishers.

Meeker-Lowry, Susan 1992. "Maquiladoras: A Preview of Free Trade." *Z Magazine*. October, pp. 25–30.

Melody, William 1991. "The Information Society: The Transnational Economic Context and Its Implications." In *Transnational Communications: Wiring the Third World*, edited by Gerald Sussman and John A. Lent. Newbury Park/London/New Delhi: Sage Publications, pp. 27–41.

Miller, Daniel 1987. *Material Culture and Mass Consumption*. Cambridge, Massachusetts: Basil Blackwell.

Mills, C. Wright 1953. "Introduction to the Mentor Edition." In *Thorstein Veblen, The Theory of the Leisure Class*. New York: New American Library, pp. vi–xix.

Milton, John [1674] 1969. "Paradise Lost." In *Milton: Poetical Works*, edited by Douglas Bush. Oxford, England: Oxford University Press.

Mishan, E. J. 1971a. "The Postwar Literature on Externalities: An Interpretative Essay." *Journal of Economic Literature* 9 (1), March, pp. 1–28.

Mishan, E. J. 1971b. "Pangloss on Pollution." In *The Economics of Environment: Papers From Four Nations,* edited by Peter Bohm and Allen V. Kneese. London: Macmillan, pp. 66–73.

Mitchell, Wesley C. 1967, 1969. *Types of Economic Theory: From Mercantilism to Institutionalism* (2 vols.). New York: Augustus M. Kelley Publishers.

Monetary Times. 1891-92 Vol. 25.

Monetary Times 1892-93 Vol. 26

Montreal Daily Star 1881, 26 July.

Montreal Gazette 1879, December.

Mosco, Vincent 1989. *The Pay-per Society: Computers and Communication in the Information Age.* Toronto: Garamond.

Mosco, Vincent, and Wasko, Janet, editors, 1988. T*he Political Economy of Information.* Madison, Wisconsin: University of Wisconsin Press.

Mowlana, Hamid, Gerbner, George, and Schiller, Herbert I. 1992. *Triumph of the Image: The Media's War in the Persian Gulf—A Global Perspective.* Boulder/San Francisco/Oxford: Westview Press.

Mulgan, G. J. 1991. *Communication and Control: Networks and the New Economies of Communication.* New York: Guilford Press.

Mumford, Lewis 1962. *Technics and Civilization.* New York: Harcourt, Brace and World.

Murchie, Guy 1978. *The Seven Mysteries of Life: An Exploration in Science and Philosophy.* Boston: Houghton Mifflin.

Musgrave, Richard 1959. *The Theory of Public Finance: A Study in Political Economy.* New York: McGraw-Hill.

Nelkin, Dorothy 1987. *Selling Science: How The Press Covers Science and Technology.* New York: Freeman.

Nelson, Joyce 1989. *The Sultans of Sleaze: Public Relations and the Media.* Toronto: Between the Lines.

Nelson, Joyce 1994. "Pulp and Propaganda." *Canadian Forum,* July-August, 1994, pp. 14–19.

Nelson, P. 1970. "Information and Consumer Behavior." *Journal of Political Economy* 78 (2). March/April, pp. 311–329.

Nevitt, Barrington 1982. *The Communication Ecology: Re-presentation versus Replica.* Toronto: Butterworths.

Nichols, M. E. 1948. *(CP): The Story of the Canadian Press.* Toronto: Ryerson.

Nora, Simon, and Minc, Alain 1980. *The Computerization of Society: A Report to the President of France.* London: MIT Press.

Northern Electric Company and Bell Canada 1975. *Prospectus,* 7 October.

Olewiler, Nancy 1993. *Pricing and the Environment. Discussion Paper Series,* No. 93-22. Kingston, Ontario: Queen's University School of Policy Studies.

Olson, Scott R. 1989. "Mass Media: A Bricolage of Paradigms. " In *Human Communication as a Field of Study: Selected Contemporary Views,* edited by Sara Sanderson King. Albany, New York: State University of New York Press.

Ong, Walter 1967. *The Presence of the Word*. New Haven: Yale University Press.

Ontario, Rural Telephone Committee of the Hydro-Electric Power Commission of Ontario 1953. *Report Concerning Rural Telephone Service in Ontario*. Toronto: Hydro-Electric Power Commission.

Ontario Telephone Service Commission 1977. Testimony of R. Barnard. Transcript, 3 August.

Oser, Jacob 1963. *The Evolution of Economic Thought*. New York: Harcourt, Brace and World.

Palmer, Margaret 1994. "Anti-Environmentalism in the Mainstream Media: Hegemonic Forces Shaping Consent for Clearcutting in Canada." Unpublished paper, Department of Communication, University of Ottawa.

Parenti, Michael 1993. *Inventing Reality: The Politics of News Media*, 2nd ed. New York: St. Martin's Press.

Parker, Ian C. 1977. "Harold Innis, Karl Marx and Canadian Political Economy." *Queen's Quarterly*, winter, pp. 545-563.

Parker, Ian C. 1980. "Culture as Economics, Economics as Culture." *Culture and Context* 1, pp. 75-111.

Parker, Ian C. 1988. "The Free Trade Challenge." *Canadian Forum*, March. pp. 29–35.

Parsons, Howard L., ed. 1977. *Marx and Engels on Ecology*. Westport, Connecticut: Greenwood Press.

Patten, William 1926. *Pioneering the Telephone in Canada*. Montreal: Privately Printed.

Pelton, Joseph 1983. "Life in the Information Society." In *Telecommunications: Issues and Choices for Society*, edited by Jerry L. Salvaggio. New York: Longman, pp. 51–58.

Perinbanayagam, R. S. 1991. *Discursive Acts*. Hawthorne, New York: Aldine De Gruyter.

Peterson, Theodore 1979. "Magazine Advertising: Its Growth and Effects." In *The Commercial Connection: Advertising and the American Mass Media*, edited by John W. Wright. New York: Delta Books, Dell Publishing Co., Inc., pp. 38–58.

Pigou, A. C. [1920] 1932. *The Economics of Welfare*, 4th edition. London: Macmillan and Co., Limited.

Ploman, Edward, and Hamilton, L. Clark 1980. *Copyright: Intellectual Property in the Information Age*. London: Routledge and Kegan Paul.

Polanyi, Karl [1944] 1957. *The Great Transformation: The Politics and Economic Origins of Our Time*. Boston: Beacon Press.

Polkinghorne, John 1987. *One World: The Interaction of Science and Theology*. Princeton: Princeton University Press.

Popper, Karl 1963. *Conjectures and Refutations: The Growth of Scientific Knowledge*. New York: Harper & Row, Publishers.

Porat, Marc 1976. *The Information Economy*. Stanford, California: Centre for Interdisciplinary Research.

Porat, Marc 1977. *The Information Economy: Definition and Measurement, Special Pub-*

lication 77-12(1). Washington, DC: Office of Telecommunication, U.S. Department of Commerce.

Porat, Marc U. 1978. "Communications Policy in an Information Society." In *Communications for Tomorrow*, edited by Glenn O. Robinson. New York: Praeger.

Potvin, Rose 1992. *Passion and Conviction: The Letters of Graham Spry*. Regina: Canadian Plains Research Centre, University of Regina,.

Prang, Margaret 1965. "The Origins of Public Broadcasting in Canada". *The Canadian Historical Review* 46, March pp. 1–31.

Preston, William Jr., Herman, Edward S. , and Schiller, Herbert I. 1989. *Hope and Folly: The United States and UNESCO 1945-1985*. Minneapolis: University of Minnesota Press.

Quinpool, John 1936. *First Things in Acadia*. Halifax, Nova Scotia: First Things Publishers.

Radner, Roy [1968] 1989. "Competitive Equilibrium Under Uncertainty." *Econometrica* 56, pp. 31-58. Reprinted in *Uncertainty in Economics: Readings and Exercises*, edited by Peter Diamond and Michael Rothschild. San Diego, California: Academic Press, pp. 177–204.

Ramstad, Yngve 1994. "Veblen, Thorstein." In *The Elgar Companion to Institutional and Evolutionary Economics*, edited by Geoffrey Hodgson, Warren J. Samuels and Marc R. Tool. Aldershot, England: Edward Elgar Publishing Limited, pp. 363–368.

Randall, Neil 1994. "Don't Give Your Thoughts Away." *Kitchener Waterloo Record*, 17 October.

Reynolds, Lloyd G. 1989. "Dissent a Century Ago: The Veblen Era." In *Unconventional Wisdom: Essays in Economics in Honor of John Kenneth Galbraith*, edited by Samuel Bowles, Richard Edwards, and William G. Shepherd. Boston: Houghton Mifflin.

Riesman, David [1953] 1960. *Thorstein Veblen: A Critical Interpretation*. New York: Seabury Press.

Rifkin, Jeremy 1987. *Time Wars*. New York: Simon and Schuster.

Righter, Rosemary 1978. *Whose News? Politics, The Press and the Third World*. New York: Times Books.

Ritchie, L. David 1991. *Information*. Newbury Park, California: Sage.

Roach, Colleen 1993. "Dallas Smythe and the New World Information and Communication Order." In *Illuminating the Blindspots: Essays Honoring Dallas W. Smythe*, edited by Janet Wasko, Vincent Mosco, and Munjunath Pendakur. Norwood: New Jersey: Ablex Publishing Corp., pp. 274-301.

Robins, Kevin, and Webster, Frank 1987. "The Communications Revolution: New Media, Old Problems." *Communication* 10, pp. 71-87.

Robinson, Gertrude J. 1984. "Mass Communication in Ferment: Open Questions in the Historiography of the Field." Montreal: McGill Graduate Program in Communication.

Robinson, Gertrude J. 1986. "Here be Dragons: Problems in Charting the History of Communication Studies in the United States." Montreal: McGill Graduate Program in Communication.

Robinson, Joan 1962. *Economic Philosophy*. Chicago, Illinois: Aldine.

Rothschild, Michael 1974. "Searching for the Lowest Price When the Distribution of Prices is Unknown." *Journal of Political Economy* 82 (4), July/August, pp. 589–611.

Rothschild, Michael and Stiglitz, Joseph 1976. "Equilibrium in Competitive Insurance Markets: An Essay on the Economics of Imperfect Information." *Quarterly Journal of Economics* 90, pp. 629–650.

Rotstein, Abraham 1988. "The Use and Misuse of Economics in Cultural Policy." In *Communication Canada*, edited by Rowland Lorimer and Donald Wilson. Toronto: Kagan and Woo, pp. 140-156 .

Roszak, Theodore 1973. *Where The Wasteland Ends*. Garden City, New York: Anchor Books.

Ruben, Brent D. 1972. "General Systems Theory: An Approach to Human Communication." In *Approaches to Human Communication*, edited by Richard W. Budd and Brent D. Ruben. Rochelle Park, New Jersey: Hayden Book Company, Inc., pp. 120–144.

Rubin, Michael Rogers, ed. 1983. *Information Economics and Policy in the United States*. Littleton, Colorado: Libraries Unlimited.

Ruth, Matthias 1993. *Integrating Economics, Ecology and Thermodynamics*. Dordrecht/Boston/London: Kluwer Academic Publishers.

Rutherford, Paul 1982. *A Victorian Authority: The Daily Press in Late Nineteenth Century Canada*. Toronto: University of Toronto Press.

Samuels, Warren J. 1966. *The Classical Theory of Economic Policy*. Cleveland: World Publishing Company.

Samuels, Warren J. 1971. "Interrelations Between Legal and Economic Processes." *Journal of Law and Economics* 14(2), pp. 435-450.

Samuels, Warren J. 1987. "Institutional Economics." *The New Palgrave: A Dictionary of Economics*, edited by John Eatwell, Murray Milgate, and Peter Newman. New York: Stockton Press, pp. 864–866.

Samuels, Warren J. 1990a. "Introduction." In *Thorstein Veblen, The Place of Science in Modern Civilization*. New Brunswick, New Jersey: Transaction Publishers.

Samuels, Warren J., ed. 1990b. *Economics as Discourse: An Analysis of the Language of Economists*. Boston/Dordrecht/London: Kluwer Academic Publishers.

Samuelson, Paul 1964. "Public Goods and Subscription TV: Correction of the Record." *Journal of Law and Economics* 7, pp. 81-83.

Schiller, Herbert I. 1984. *Information and the Crisis Economy*. Norwood, New Jersey: Ablex Publishing Corporation.

Schiller, Herbert I. 1989a. *Culture Inc.: The Corporate Takeover of Cultural Expression*. New York: Oxford University Press.

Schiller, Herbert I. 1989b. "Is There A United States Information Policy?" In William Preston, Jr., Edward S. Herman, and Herbert I. Schiller, *Hope and Folly: The United States and UNESCO, 1945-1985*. Minneapolis: University of Minnesota Press, pp. 285–311.

Schiller, Herbert I. 1994. "Commentary." In *Information and Communication in Economics*, edited by Robert E. Babe. Boston/London/Dordrecht: Kluwer Academic Publishers, pp. 138–145.

Schramm, Wilbur 1989. "Human Communication as a Field of Behavioral Science: Jack Hilgard and his Committee." In Sara Sanderson King, editor. *Human Communication as a Field of Study: Selected Contemporary Views*. Albany, New York: State University of New York Press, pp. 13-26.

Schramm, Wilbur, and Roberts, D., eds. 1971. *The Process and Effects of Mass Communication*. Urbana, Illinois: University of Illinois Press.

Schumacher, E. F. [1973] 1989. *Small Is Beautiful: Economics as if People Mattered*. New York: Perennial Library, Harper & Row, Publishers

Schumpeter, Joseph A. 1954. *History of Economic Analysis*. New York: Oxford University Press.

Schumpeter, Joseph A. 1962. *Capitalism, Socialism and Democracy*, 3rd ed. New York: Harper Torch Books.

Scitovsky, Tibor 1976. *The Joyless Economy: An Inquiry into Human Satisfaction and Consumer Dissatisfaction*. New York: Oxford University Press.

Seligman, Ben B. 1963. *Main Currents in Modern Economics: Economic Thought Since 1870*. New York: The Free Press of Glencoe.

Serafini, Shirley, and Andrieu, Michel 1980. *The Information Revolution and Its Implications for Canada*. Ottawa: Information Canada.

Shannon, Claude E., and Weaver, Warren [1949] 1963. *The Mathematical Theory of Communication*. Urbana, Illinois: University of Illinois Press.

Shepherd, William G. *The Treatment of Market Power: Antitrust, Regulation and Public Enterprise*. New York: Columbia University Press.

Smith, Adam [1759] 1966. *The Theory of Moral Sentiments*. New York: Augustus M. Kelley.

Smith, Adam [1776] 1937. *An Inquiry Into the Nature and Causes of the Wealth of Nations*. New York: The Modern Library.

Smith, Adam [1776] 1952. *The Wealth of Nations*. Chicago: Encyclopaedia Britannica.

Smith, Anthony 1980. *The Geopolitics of Information: How Western Culture Dominates the World*. London: Faber and Faber.

Smythe, Dallas W. 1977. "Communications: Blindspot of Western Marxism." *Canadian Journal of Political and Social Theory* 1(3), pp. 1-27.

Smythe, Dallas W. 1981. "Communications: Blindspot of Economics." In *Culture, Communication, and Dependency: The Tradition of H. A. Innis*, edited by William H. Melody, Liora Salter, Paul Heyer. Norwood, New Jersey: Ablex Publishing Corp., pp. 111-125.

Smythe, Dallas W. 1986. "The 1986 Southam Lecture: Culture, Communication 'Technology' and Canadian Policy." *Canadian Journal of Communication* 12 (2), pp. 1-20.

Smythe, Dallas W., and Dinh, Tran Van 1983. "On Critical and Administrative Research: A New Critical Analysis." *Journal of Communication* 33 (3), pp. 117-127.

Soderbaum, Peter 1990. "Neoclassical and Institutional Approaches to Environmental Economics." *Journal of Economic Issues* 24 (2), June, pp. 481–492.

Solomon, Jack 1988. *The Signs of Our Time: The Secret Meanings of Everyday Life*.

New York: Harper and Row.

Solow, Robert M. 1974. "The Economics of Resources or the Resources of Economics." *American Economic Review,* May, pp. 1–14.

Spence, Michael 1974. "An Economist's View of Information." In *Annual Review of Information Science and Technology 9,* edited by C. Caudra, A. Luke and L. Harris. Washington, DC: American Association for Information Science, pp. 57-78.

Spencer, Herbert [1904] 1966. *A System of Synthetic Philosophy: Vol. 1—First Principles,* 6th edition. Republished in *The Works of Herbert Spencer,* Osnabruck: Otto Zeller.

Spry, Graham 1931. "A Case for Nationalized Broadcasting." *Queen's Quarterly.* Winter, pp. 151–169

Spry, Graham 1953. "The Fall of Constantinople—1453." *Middle Eastern Affairs* 4 (6-7), June-July, pp. 201–208.

Spry, Graham 1961. "The Decline and Fall of Canadian Broadcasting." *Queen's Quarterly* 68 (2). Summer, pp. 213–225.

Spry, Graham 1971. "Public Policy and Private Pressures: The Canadian Radio League 1930-6 and Countervailing Power." In *On Canada: Essays in Honour of Frank Underhill.* Toronto: University of Toronto Press, pp. 24–35.

Spry, Graham 1971. "Canada: Notes on Two Ideas of Nation in Confrontation." *Journal of Contemporary History,* July, pp. 173–196.

Spry, Graham 1972. "Culture and Entropy: A Lay View of Broadcasting." The Royal Society of Canada, Ottawa, Ontario, March.

Staniland, Martin 1985. *What Is Political Economy?: A Study of Social Theory and Underdevelopment.* New York: Yale University Press.

Stentor Telecom Policy Inc. 1993a. *The Beacon Initiative: Backgrounder, Building A Stronger Canada Through The Beacon Initiative.*

Stentor Telecom Policy Inc. 1993b. *The Information Highway, Canada's Road to Economic and Social Renewal.*

Stigler, George J. [1960] 1968. "The Economics of Information." *Journal of Political Economy* 69 (3). Reprinted in George Stigler, *The Organization of Industry.* Homewood, Illinois: Richard D. Irwin, pp. 171-190.

Stigler, George J. [1962] 1968. "Information in the Labor Market." *Journal of Political Economy* 70 (5). Reprinted in *The Organization of Industry.* Homewood, Illinois: Irwin, pp. 191–207.

Stigler, George J. 1966. *The Theory of Price,* 3rd ed. New York: Macmillan.

Stigler, George J. 1983. "Nobel Lecture: The Process and Progress of Economics." *Journal of Political Economy* 91 (4), pp. 529-545.

Stigler, George J. 1988. *Memoirs of an Unregulated Economist.* New York: Basic Books.

Stigler, George J., and Becker, Gary 1977. "De Gustibus Non est Disputandum." *American Economic Review* 67 (2), pp. 75-90.

Stiglitz, Joseph E. 1979. "A Neoclassical Analysis of the Economics of Natural Resources." In *Scarcity and Growth Reconsidered,* edited by V. Kerry Smith and published for *Resources for the Future.* Baltimore, Maryland: John Hopkins

Press, pp. 36–66.

Stiglitz, Joseph E. 1985. "Information and Economic Analysis: A Perspective." *Economic Journal* 95, pp. 21–41.

Sumner, William Graham 1963. *Social Darwinism: Selected Essays of William Graham Sumner,* edited by Stow Persons. Englewood Cliffs, New Jersey: Prentice-Hall.

Surtees, Lawrence 1992. *Pa Bell: A. Jean de Grandpré & The Meteoric Rise of Bell Canada Enterprises.* Toronto: Random House.

Sutherland, J. G. 1978. "Telecommunications in Canada." In CNCP Tele-communications, Statement of Evidence, Application for Interconnection to Bell Canada.

Suzuki, David 1994. *Time To Change: Essays.* Toronto: Stoddart Publishing.

Szenberg, Michael, ed. 1992. *Eminent Economists.* Cambridge: Cambridge University Press.

Tehranian, Majid 1990. *Technologies of Power: Information Machines and Democratic Prospects.* Norwood, New Jersey: Ablex Publishing Corp.

Teilhard de Chardin, Pierre [1955] 1970. *The Phenomenon of Man.* Glasgow: William Collins Sons & Co., Ltd.

Telser, Lester G. 1973. "Searching for the Lowest Price." *American Economic Review* 63(2), May, pp. 40–49.

Thayer, Lee 1970. "On Human Communication and Social Development." Paper presented at the First World Conference on Social Communication for Development, Mexico City.

Thayer, Lee 1987. *On Communication: Essays in Understanding.* Norwood, New Jersey: Ablex.

Thompson, W. L. 1947. *Wiring a Continent: The History of the Telegraph in the United States, 1832-1866.* Princeton, New Jersey: Princeton University Press.

Tinder, Glenn 1989. *The Political Meaning of Christianity: An Interpretation.* Baton Rouge: Louisiana State University Press.

Troyer, W. L. *The Sound and the Fury: An Anecdotal History of Canadian Broadcasting.* Toronto: Personal Publishers.

UNESCO, International Commission for the Study of Communication Problems (MacBride Commission) 1980. *Many Voices, One World: Communication and Society Today and Tomorrow.* New York: UNESCO

United States, Federal Communications Commission [1939] 1974. *Investigation of the Telephone Industry in the United States.* House Document No. 340, 7th Congress, 1st Session. New York: Arno Press.

Weber, Max [1904–5] 1958. *The Protestant Ethic and the Spirit of Capitalism.* New York: Charles Scribner's Sons.

Veblen, Thorstein [1899] 1953. *The Theory of the Leisure Class.* New York: New American Library.

Veblen, Thorstein [1892] 1990. "Some Neglected Points in the Theory of Social-ism." *Annals of American Academy of Political and Social Science* 2. Reprinted in Thorstein Veblen, *The Place of Science in Modern Civilization and Other Essays,* edited by Warren J. Samuels. New Brunswick, New Jersey: Transaction Publishers, pp. 387–408.

Veblen, Thorstein 1896. "Review of Enrico Ferri's Socialisme et Science Positive." *Journal of Political Economy,* December, pp. 98–103.

Veblen, Thorstein [1898] 1990. "Why is Economics Not an Evolutionary Science?" *The Quarterly Journal of Economics* 12, July. Reprinted in Thorstein Veblen, *The Place of Science in Modern Civilization and Other Essays,* edited by Warren J. Samuels. New Brunswick, New Jersey: Transaction Publishers, pp. 56–81.

Veblen, Thorstein [1898] 1964. "The Instinct of Workmanship and the Irksomeness of Labor." *American Journal of Sociology* 4, September. Reprinted in Thorstein Veblen, *Essays on Our Changing Order,* edited by Leon Ardzrooni. New York: Augustus M. Kelley, Bookseller, pp. 78–96.

Veblen, Thorstein [1898] 1964. "The Beginnings of Ownership." *The American Journal of Sociology* 4, November. Reprinted in Thorstein Veblen, *Essays on Our Changing Order,* edited by Leon Ardzrooni. New York: Augustus M. Kelley, Bookseller, pp. 32–49.

Veblen, Thorstein [1899] 1964. "Mr. Cummings's Strictures on 'The Theory of the Leisure Class'." *Journal of Political Economy* 8, December. Reprinted in Thorstein Veblen, *Essays on Our Changing Order.* New York: Augustus M. Kelley, Bookseller, pp. 16–31.

Veblen, Thorstein [1899] 1953. *The Theory of the Leisure Class: An Economic Study of Institutions.* New York: New American Library.

Veblen, Thorstein [1899] 1990. "The Preconceptions of Economic Science: I." *Quarterly Journal of Economics* 13, January. Reprinted in Thorstein Veblen, *The Place of Science in Modern Civilization,* edited by Warren J. Samuels. New Brunswick, New Jersey: Transaction Publishers, pp. 82–113

Veblen, Thorstein [1900] 1990. "The Preconceptions of Economic Science: III." *The Quarterly Journal of Economics* 14, February. Reprinted in Thorstein Veblen, *The Place of Science in Modern Civilization,* edited by Warren J. Samuels. New Brunswick, New Jersey: Transaction Publishers, pp. 149–179.

Veblen, Thorstein [1904] 1950. *The Theory of Business Enterprise.* Extracted in *The Portable Veblen,* edited by Max Lerner. New York: Viking Press, pp. 335–348.

Veblen, Thorstein [1906] 1990. "The Place of Science in Modern Civilization." *American Journal of Sociology* 9, March. Reprinted in Thorstein Veblen, *The Place of Science in Modern Civilization,* edited by Warren J. Samuels. New Brunswick, New Jersey: Transaction Publishers, pp. 1–31.

Veblen, Thorstein [1908a] 1990. "The Evolution of the Scientific Point of View." *University of California Chronicle* 10 (4). Reprinted in Thorstein Veblen, *The Place of Science in Modern Civilization and Other Essays,* edited by Warren J. Samuels. New Brunswick, New Jersey: Transaction Publishers, pp. 32–55.

Veblen, Thorstein [1908b] 1990. "Professor Clark's Economics." *The Quarterly Journal of Economics* 22, February. Reprinted in Thorstein Veblen, *The Place of Science in Modern Civilization,* edited by Warren J. Samuels. New Brunswick, New Jersey: Transaction Publishers, pp. 180–230.

Veblen, Thorstein [1909] 1990. "The Limitations of Marginal Utility." In *The Place of Science in Modern Civilization,* edited by Warren J. Samuels. New Brunswick, New Jersey: Transaction Publishers, pp. 231–251.

Veblen, Thorstein [1910} 1950. "Christian Morals and the Competitive System." *International Journal of Ethics.* Reprinted in *Essays on Our Changing Order* (1934), and in *The Portable Veblen,* edited by Max Lerner. New York: The Viking Press, pp. 480—498.

Veblen, Thorstein [1914] 1964. *The Instinct of Workmanship and the State of the Industrial Arts.* New York: Augustus M. Kelley, Bookseller.

Veblen, Thorstein [1919] 1990. *The Place of Science in Modern Civilization and Other Essays,* edited by Warren J. Samuels. New Brunswick, New Jersey: Transaction Publishers.

Veblen, Thorstein [1925] 1964. "Economic Theory in the Calculable Future." *American Economic Review* 15 (1), Supplement, March. Reprinted in Thorstein Veblen, *Essays on Our Changing Order,* edited by Leon Ardzrooni. New York: Augustus M. Kelley, Bookseller.

Vogel, Harold L. 1990. *Entertainment Industry Economics: A Guide For Financial Analysis.* 2nd Edition. Cambridge: Cambridge University Press.

von Bertalanffy, Ludwig 1981. *A Systems View of Man,* edited by P. A. LaViolette. Boulder, Colorado: Westview Press.

von Weizsäcker, Carl Friedrich 1980. *The Unity of Nature.* New York: Farrar, Straus and Giroux.

Wade, Larry 1983. *Political Economy.* Boston: Kluwer-Nijhoff Publishing.

Wallace, Alfred Russel [1870] 1973. *Contributions to the Theory of Natural Selection: A Series of Essays.* New York: AMS Press Inc.

Wallace, Alfred Russel 1905. *My Life: A Record of Events and Opinions.* London.

Weber, Max 1954. *Max Weber on Law in Economy and Society.* Cambridge, Massachusetts: Harvard University Press.

Webster, Frank 1980. *The New Photography.* London: J. Calder.

Weizenbaum, Joseph 1979. "Once More: The Computer Revolution." In *The Computer Age: A Twenty-Year View,* edited by Michael Dertouzos and Joel Moses. Cambridge, Mass: MIT Press, pp. 439-458.

White, Leslie 1949. *The Science of Culture.* New York: Farrar, Straus and Giroux.

Whitehead, Alfred North 1929. *Process and Reality.* New York: Macmillan.

Wiener, Norbert [1950] 1967. *The Human Use of Human Beings: Cybernetics and Society.* New York: Avon Books.

Williams, Raymond 1974. *Television: Technology and Cultural Form.* Glasgow: Fontana/Collins.

Williams, Raymond 1980. "Advertising: The Magic System." In *Problems in Materialism and Culture.* London: Verso.

Wilson, Kevin 1988. *Technologies of Control: The New Interactive Media for the Home.* Madison, Wisconsin: University of Wisconsin Press.

Winch, Donald 1992. "Introduction." In T. R. Malthus. *An Essay on the Principle of Population or A View of Its Past and Present Effects on Human Happiness,* edited by Donald Winch. Cambridge: Cambridge University Press, pp. vii–xxiii.

Winner, Langdon 1977. *Autonomous Technology.* Cambridge, Mass.: MIT Press.

Winter, James 1992. *Common Cents: Media Portrayal of the Gulf War and Other Events.* Montreal and New York: Black Rose Books.

Wood, N. 1978. *The Trinity in the Universe*. Grand Rapids. Michigan: Kregel Publications.

World Commission on Environment and Development (WCED) 1987. *Our Common Future*. New York: Oxford University Press.

Wrigley, E. A. 1986. "Introduction." In *The Works of Thomas Robert Malthus*, Volume 1; *An Essay on the Principle of Population*, edited by E. A. Wrigley and David Souden. London: William Pickering, pp. 7–39.

Wright, Robert 1988. *Three Scientists and Their Gods: Looking for Meaning in an Age of Information*. New York: Times Books.

Young, R. M. 1969. "Malthus and the Evolutionists: The Common Context of Biological and Social Theory." *Past and Present* 43, pp. 109–145.

About the Book and Author

Many governments are pursuing with relentless vigor a neoconservative/transnational corporate program of globalization, privatization, deregulation, cutbacks to social programs, and down-sizing of the public sector. Countries are forming into giant "free trade" blocs. Increasingly they lack the will and desire to resist encroachments of world "superculture." Furthermore, they encourage heightened commoditization of information and knowledge, for instance through stiffer intellectual property laws, through "Information Highway" initiatives, and through provisions in bilateral and multilateral trade treaties. The analytical underpinning, and ideological justification for this neoconservative/transnational corporate policy agenda is mainstream (neoclassical) economics.

Focusing on the centrality of information/communication to economic and ecological processes, *Communication and the Transformation of Economics* cuts at the philosophical/ideological root of this neoconservative policy agenda. Mainstream economics assumes a commodity status for information, even though information is indivisible, subjective, shared, and intangible. Information, in other words, is quite ill-suited to commodity treatment. Likewise, neoclassicism posits communication as comprising merely acts of commodity exchange, thereby ignoring gift relations, dialogic interactions, the cumulative, transformative properties of all informational interchange, and the social or community context within which communicative action takes place.

Continuing in the tradition of writers such as Russel Wallace, Thorstein Veblen, Karl Polyani, E. F. Schumacher, Kenneth E. Boulding, and Herman Daly, Robert Babe proposes infusing mainstream economics with realistic and expansive conceptions of information/communication in order to better comprehend twenty-first century issues and progress toward a more sustainable, more just, more humane, and more democratic economic/communicatory order.

Robert E. Babe is professor of communication, University of Ottawa.

Index